Women's Work, Men's Work

ꙮꙮꙮ Women's Work,

ꙮꙮꙮꙮꙮ Men's Work

The Informal Slave Economies of

Lowcountry Georgia ꙮ Betty Wood

THE UNIVERSITY OF GEORGIA PRESS | ATHENS AND LONDON

© 1995 by the University of Georgia Press, Athens, Georgia 30602
All rights reserved
Designed by Louise OFarrell. Set in 10/13½ Linotype Walbaum
by Tseng Information Systems, Inc.
Printed and bound by Thomson-Shore, Inc.

The paper in this book meets the guidelines for permanence and
durability of the Committee on Production Guidelines for Book
Longevity of the Council on Library Resources.

Printed in the United States of America

99   98   97   96   95   C   5   4   3   2   1

LIBRARY OF CONGRESS CATALOGING IN PUBLICATION DATA
Wood, Betty.
Women's work, men's work : the informal slave economies of
lowcountry Georgia / Betty Wood.
p. cm.
Includes bibliographical references and index.
ISBN 0-8203-1667-9 (alk. paper)
1. Slavery—Economic aspects—Georgia. 2. Slaves—Georgia—
Economic conditions. 3. Plantation life—Georgia—History—19th
century. 4. Georgia—Economic conditions. 5. Georgia—History—
1775–1865. I. Title.
E445.G3 W665   1995
306.3'62'0975809034—dc20   94-5968

BRITISH LIBRARY CATALOGING IN PUBLICATION DATA AVAILABLE

For Sheila Cooper, Jim Cooper,
Sylvia Frey, and Mary Turner

Contents

Acknowledgments

THERE ARE many people I wish to thank for their assistance as I was researching and writing this book. First and foremost, my warmest thanks go to Malcolm Call for soliciting my manuscript, and to Kim Cretors for working so patiently with me to produce the finished text. I am also grateful to Anne Gibbons for her meticulous copyediting.

Without exception, the staffs of the libraries and archives I visited were immensely helpful and most congenial. I would like to take this opportunity to thank those of the Georgia Historical Society; the South Carolina Historical Society; the Georgia State Archives; the University of Cambridge Library; Duke University Library; the University of Georgia Library; Indiana University Library; the University of Richmond Library; the University of South Carolina Library; and Tulane University Library. I could not have completed my research in the United States had it not been for the sabbaticals and financial support I received from the University of Cambridge and Girton College.

I would like to express my thanks to those scholars who have chaired or commented on the conference and seminar papers I have given as this book took shape. I am particularly indebted to O. Vernon Burton, Catherine Clinton, Jean Friedman, Rosemary Hynes, and Charles Joyner.

Many British and American friends have helped in various ways in my work on this book. I am pleased to be able to formally thank Catherine Atherton, Tony Badger, Charlotte Erickson, Meryl Foster, Steve Hindle, Hardy and Suzanne Jackson, Hazel Mills, Polly O'Hanlon, Alastair Reid, Miri Rubin, Constance and Carl Schulz, Dorothy and John Thompson, Robert Wardy, and Frank Wilkinson for the support I have received from them over the years.

Finally, my deepest thanks go to those who have contributed most, directly and indirectly, to this book. To my friends the late Phinizy Spalding, and Margie Spalding, I owe far more than I can say. I am deeply indebted to four other friends, Sheila Cooper, Jim Cooper, Sylvia Frey, and Mary Turner for their wise counsel, their scholarly guidance, and their unwavering encouragement. This book is for them because without them it could not have been written.

Women's Work, Men's Work

Introduction

DURING THE LAST few years the quasi-independent economic activities of captive West Africans in the plantation societies of the Caribbean and the American South have attracted an ever-increasing amount of scholarly interest.[1] Sidney Mintz and Douglass Hall's pioneering essay on internal marketing in Jamaica was largely responsible for identifying the critical significance of this aspect of slave life. Those who have followed in their footsteps are universally agreed on one key point: these activities had far more than a purely material meaning and relevance for the enslaved populations of the societies in question.

Where scholars disagree, and often seriously so, is in their characterization of the quasi-independent slave economies and in their estimations of precisely what the significance of these economic activities was for bondmen and bondwomen both before and after the ending of chattel slavery.[2] An assessment of the gains and losses accruing to bondpeople as producers and as consumers can produce starkly different conclusions. On the one hand, and in the most positive light, it may be argued that these activities helped to generate an individual, familial, and communal empowerment that severely challenged the authority claimed by the master class at the same time as it prepared bondmen and bondwomen for life in a market economy after the ending of chattel slavery.

An alternative interpretation is that from the owners' perspective this was an essentially limited empowerment that was largely acceptable to them, and one that some thought worth encouraging, simply

1

because it kept bondmen and bondwomen tied to their workplaces and forged an ethos that blunted the impulse for overt physical resistance to the institution of chattel slavery. In such an interpretation, the willing transformation of bondpeople into a protopeasantry that by and large was content to continue operating within the demands and constraints imposed by their owners could be seen as something of a triumph for the master class. One of the main objectives of this study is to assess the merits of these competing claims.

Differing interpretations of the character and significance of the quasi-independent economic activities of bondpeople are clearly reflected in the manner in which scholars have chosen to categorize them: as "internal," "domestic," and "family" economies, or as peasant breaches in the slave mode of production. This study will certainly not dissent from the position that ascribes a paramount importance to the African and African-American family in the definition and modus operandi of the slave economies that evolved in the predominantly rice-growing coastal counties of Georgia, the lowcountry, during the second half of the eighteenth century and the first third of the nineteenth. It will, however, seek to argue that there is also a compelling case for describing them as informal economies. This is a construct that acknowledges the significance of the themes that are fundamental to the concepts of family, domestic, and internal economies and emphasizes the profound importance of the continuous, often immensely complicated, interplay between those economies and the formal slave economy with which they coexisted.

The quasi-independent economic behavior of bondpeople in lowcountry Georgia (as well as in the other plantation societies of the American South and the Caribbean), the bondpeople's continuing struggle to secure and retain recognized rights as producers and consumers, took place within, and was deeply embedded in, the context of what may be termed the formal slave economy. In the lowcountry, as elsewhere, that formal economy, which was profit seeking, market directed, and ostensibly under the control of whites, included the hours worked by bondpeople, the rations and clothes they received from their owners, and the hiring out of their labor. The owners' consensus on these matters was formalized in public laws, slave codes, and local ordinances, which in effect enshrined their understanding of the ideal formal slave economy and the manner in which that economy should and would operate.

In practice, the operation of both the formal and the informal slave economies reflected the outcome of continuing negotiations between bondpeople themselves as well as with their owners and other whites. Nowhere did the owners' ideal of the formal economy elaborated in the public laws of slavery persist entirely intact. The boundaries between the formal slave economy and the informal economies that evolved alongside it were seldom static, seldom completely rigid. They are best viewed as being conceptual rather than structural. Economic structures and institutions, for instance local markets, plantation equipment, and transportation facilities, were common to the formal and the informal slave economies. It was the purposes to which those structures and institutions were put, and the profoundly different motives and ambitions informing their use, that differentiated the formal from the informal. The extent to which those motives and ambitions could be realized constantly shifted and was adjusted according to the demands made by bondpeople and their owners, according to the concessions each granted, or managed to wrest, from the other.

As in all the plantation societies of the New World, the negotiations conducted between the bondmen and bondwomen of lowcountry Georgia, their owners, and other whites concerning the economic rights to be exercised by bondpeople involved remorseless struggles that resulted in some gains and some losses for all concerned. Whether they lived in the countryside, as did the vast majority of the lowcountry's enslaved population, or in Savannah, bondmen and bondwomen could seldom forget, and daily had to contend with, the awesome power claimed by their owners and sanctioned by the public laws of slavery: the power to beat, hang, burn, and mutilate in an attempt to impose their wills, and the power to shatter physically, but not emotionally, that which the enslaved men and women of the lowcountry held most dear—their families.

Against such a formidable physical and psychological arsenal, the weapons available to bondpeople may appear to have been puny in the extreme, but they were weapons that could be and were deployed to significant effect as part of the negotiating process. Running away, feigning illness, and various kinds of economic sabotage, as well as

more violent physical assaults on whites and their property, were strata-
gems employed by the bondpeople of lowcountry Georgia between 1750
and 1830. But bondmen and bondwomen could hope to advance, or
simply protect, their interests in other, often equally potent, ways. Some
bondpeople were able to take advantage of the religious belief systems of their owners to preserve the integrity of their family lives. And
the complicity of some whites, which stemmed from a pragmatic self-
interest rather than from any serious qualms about the continuation
of the formal slave economy, could also be turned by bondmen and
bondwomen to their own advantage.

    With the notable exceptions of Peter H. Wood, Philip D. Morgan,
and John Campbell, most of the scholars who have examined the quasi-
independent economic activities of bondpeople in the American South
have had comparatively little to say about the period before 1830.[3] Intra-
as well as interregional variations, and changes over time, particularly
those associated with the American Revolution and the initial stages
of the Second Great Awakening, simply have not attracted the detailed
attention they so clearly merit. Until quite recently much the same was
also true of the specific, and rather different, contributions made by
bondmen and bondwomen to the forging of the informal slave economies of the American South.[4] This study seeks to remedy some of these
deficiencies.

    Scant regard has been paid by scholars to the precise character of
the multifaceted informal slave economies that evolved in lowcountry
Georgia during the second half of the eighteenth century and that had
matured by 1830, and this neglect is reason enough for the present
work.[5] The quasi-autonomous economic activities explored in this book
were deeply rooted in the heritages, experiences, and hopes of enslaved
West Africans. Initially they reflected the modus operandi that these
men and women had managed to hammer out with their South Carolina owners by the middle years of the eighteenth century. This story,
then, opens in 1750, the year in which chattel slavery was sanctioned in
Georgia. But it really begins much earlier, in South Carolina and West
Africa.

    In 1750 the way was finally cleared for what amounted to the South
Carolinian invasion of Georgia. After waging a spirited fifteen-year
battle, the metropolitan founders of Georgia, the trustees, finally conceded defeat and agreed that as of 1 January 1751 enslaved Africans

could be employed in the colony.[6] From the mid-1730s onward there had been those in Georgia who had clamored incessantly for the right to employ enslaved West Africans. But they were not the only ones who sought to overturn the trustees' ban. Many South Carolinians had long hoped to be able to extend their rice-planting operations into the rich coastal and river swamplands of Georgia, and they did just this as soon as the trustees capitulated on the issue of slavery.[7]

Georgia, which reverted to royal control in 1752, retained its political integrity. But the influx of South Carolinians and their bondpeople was to have profound implications for every aspect of life in lowcountry Georgia's evolving plantation economy and society.[8] By 1755 the political dominance of the free South Carolinian migrants was such that they were able to sweep away the rules and regulations that the trustees had hoped would govern slavery and race relations in Georgia and replace them with a slave code closely modeled on that drafted by the South Carolina government fifteen years earlier.[9]

In the summer of 1750, five months before the trustees' ban on chattel slavery was formally lifted, "an exact List" indicated that there were already "three Hundred and Forty Nine Working Negroes, namely two Hundred and two Men, and one Hundred and Forty Seven Women, besides children too young for Labour," in Georgia. Six years later Gov. John Reynolds reported to the Board of Trade that "according to the best account I can get . . . the Number of Negroes are 1,855." By November 1766 that number had grown to "at least 7,800" and, according to Gov. James Wright, Georgia's enslaved population had increased by approximately 900 over the previous six months alone.[10]

Wright did not say so in his report to the Board of Trade, but the recent additions he alluded to reflected the beginnings of a highly significant change in the origins of Georgia's enslaved population. Between the late 1740s and the mid-1760s most bondmen and bondwomen were brought by their owners or transported to Georgia from elsewhere in the Americas, usually from South Carolina but sometimes from the British sugar islands. The majority of them were African-born men and women who had spent varying lengths of time in British America.[11] This pattern changed dramatically during the mid-1760s when lowcountry planters, with the help of Savannah-based merchants, began to participate in the African slave trade.[12]

The immediate significance of Georgia's entry into a direct slave trade with West Africa is indicated by the fact that between 1766 and 1773 the colony's enslaved population, which was concentrated mainly in the lowcountry parishes, increased from "at least 7,800" to an estimated 15,000.[13] Not surprisingly, the age, sex ratios, and West African origins of this human cargo transported to lowcountry Georgia were identical to those that characterized the slave trade to mid-eighteenth century South Carolina.

Lowcountry planters sought young bondpeople for the heavy physical labor associated with rice culture, and they had decided preferences as to which regions and societies of West Africa provided workers who were best suited to their needs.[14] Most of the men and women shipped to the lowcountry were in their teens or twenties and roughly 75 percent of the twenty-five hundred West Africans landed in Savannah between 1766 and 1771 came from Gambia, Sierra Leone, and Angola. Of the remainder, 6 percent were said to come from "Africa," 14 percent from the "Rice Coast," and 5 percent from the "Grain Coast."[15]

By 1760 it was as if the bitter debate that had preceded the introduction of chattel slavery into Georgia had never taken place. Few, if any, Europeans in lowcountry Georgia disputed the proposition that their growing prosperity was directly linked to the employment of enslaved Africans; none questioned the appalling conditions under which those Africans were being transported to the New World. Within a decade or so of the introduction of chattel slavery at least 5 percent of white Georgians, and probably not less than one-quarter of all white households, held at least one bondperson. An analysis of estate records dating from the 1760s and early 1770s, which list roughly four thousand bondpeople, clearly demonstrates the extent to which "a skewed distribution of access to financial capital" had resulted in the concentration of comparatively large numbers of bondpeople in relatively few hands.[16]

During the late colonial period, 75 percent of the bondpeople listed in these records lived on estates containing more than twenty bondpersons; 11 percent were claimed by owners who held fewer than ten bondpeople. Between 1755 and 1775 bondmen outnumbered bondwomen on almost half of the lowcountry's estates; the reverse was true of less than 20 percent of slave holdings. The overall ratio of men to women was on the order of 146 to 100, but the larger the estate the larger the sexual imbalance. On estates with more than forty bondpeople, for instance, the ratio stood at approximately 152 to 100; on those with fewer than ten bondpersons it dropped to 119:100.[17] These sex ratios are similar to those that characterized the South Carolina lowcountry in the 1720s and 1730s when "rice rose from the status of a competing export to become the colony's central preoccupation."[18]

The vast majority of bondpeople worked as field hands. Nevertheless, from the outset a significant number filled a diverse range of skilled and semiskilled, as well as unskilled, positions not only in the countryside but also in the evolving economies of the lowcountry's three main towns, Savannah, Darien, and Sunbury. By 1771 an estimated 821 bondpeople lived and worked in Savannah.[19] These men and women accounted for only between 5 and 6 percent of Georgia's enslaved population; they accounted for about 41 percent of Savannah's inhabitants. This pattern continued to characterize Savannah, and according to one informal census, by 1800 the city had a black majority.[20] *Pobl. Savanah*

The trustees' opponents had argued vociferously that Georgia's economic growth depended on the introduction of enslaved West African workers, and the course of the colony's economic development after 1750 proved them correct.[21] Georgia's population grew from less than four thousand in 1750 to roughly thirty-three thousand on the eve of the Revolutionary War. Rice shipments, mainly through Savannah, increased tenfold between 1755 and 1775, and the colony's other major exports, indigo, skins, tobacco, and timber, showed a comparable increase.[22] By the mid-1770s, however, Georgia was still the runt of the mainland American colonies or, to borrow Harold E. Davis's phrase, a "Fledgling Province."[23] Yet demographically and economically there had been advances during the years of royal government, advances bought at a truly appalling cost to the thousands of Africans and African-Americans who formed the backbone of lowcountry Georgia's work force.

The American War of Independence and the forging of a new nation were to have mixed consequences for slavery and race relations in Georgia. Regardless of their ultimately irreconcilable political differences, Loyalists and Patriots were united in their unwavering commitment to the maintenance of the institution of chattel slavery. There was no sympathy in any quarter of the lowcountry's white society for the antislavery arguments emanating from further north, and any suggestion

that the outcome of the military struggle to secure control of the lower
South might depend on the arming of bondpeople was greeted with
universal horror.[24]

As the war drew to a close, the question that troubled Georgia's
Patriots was not how chattel slavery might be eradicated, but how they
might most expeditiously rebuild their war-torn plantation economy.
Lowcountry planters agitated for bondpeople, both to replace those
who had been "lost" during the war and to expand their operations, and
this was a demand that Savannah merchants were eager to satisfy. In
the post- as in the prewar period the African and domestic slave trades,
rather than natural increase, supplied the enslaved workers demanded
by white Georgians.[25]

Georgia's enslaved population grew to an estimated 29,264 by 1790.[26]
However, it was no longer so heavily concentrated in the lowcountry as
it had been before the war. Revolutionary War bounties in the shape
of land grants and bondpeople, the latter often confiscated from their
Loyalist owners, ensured the rapid spread of a slave-based agriculture
into the Georgia backcountry. The foundations of the Cotton Kingdom
were firmly established by the mid-1780s.[27]

Despite this significant shift in the geographical distribution of Georgia's enslaved population, the racial balance in the lowcountry and the
size of slave holdings remained much the same as in the prewar years.
In Chatham and Liberty counties, for example, "slaves outnumbered
whites by almost four to one."[28] Estates with twenty or more bondpeople
accounted for approximately 70 percent of the lowcountry's enslaved
population; plantations with more than fifty for roughly 40 percent.
Approximately 14 percent of bondpeople were to be found on estates
with fewer than ten bondpersons.[29]

Rice remained the major staple crop in the lowcountry. The withdrawal of the bounty offered by the British for indigo led to the virtual
disappearance of that item from the region by 1800. Economically, the
introduction of long staple, or Sea Island, cotton during the Revolutionary War era more than compensated for the loss of indigo.[30]

From the white Georgian perspective, chattel slavery was in no way a
declining institution during the 1770s and 1780s. On the contrary, these
years witnessed a strengthening of white Georgians' commitment to
that institution. Nothing happened during or as a result of the Ameri-

can Revolution to dispel the pervasive white belief in the comparative profitability of enslaved labor in the context of plantation agriculture. Moreover, the relish with which the bondmen and bondwomen of the lowcountry had sought to liberate themselves from their servitude during the war served only to reinforce the attraction of slavery as a means of attempting to impose racial control.

The American War of Independence held out a dual prospect of freedom for the enslaved population of lowcountry Georgia: freedom they could seize for themselves and freedom they believed they might be able to achieve with the assistance of the British armed forces. Many bondmen and bondwomen took advantage of the dislocation of war, and the preoccupations of their Loyalist and Patriot owners, to flee in the hope of securing thereby their own independence. For some this meant a continuation of the pattern established during the colonial period: heading to the backcountry or to the lowcountry's virtually impenetrable river and coastal swamps in the hope of avoiding recapture.[31] For others it meant making their way to British headquarters in Savannah in the belief that freedom would be theirs in exchange for their support of the British cause. Military necessity had prompted the British to sanction the formation of Lord Dunmore's Ethiopian Regiment in Virginia and offer freedom to those enslaved soldiers who survived the war.[32] A similar exigency might lead them to do likewise in Georgia, or so those bondmen and bondwomen who headed for the British forces fervently hoped. A British victory, and one to which they had contributed, must surely result in their liberation.[33]

In the event, of course, neither metropolitan politicians nor Georgia Loyalists were forced to confront this overly optimistic interpretation of an essentially pragmatic military policy. Most of the bondmen and bondwomen who remained in the lowcountry ended the Revolutionary War for Independence as they had begun it: as chattel slaves. For the foreseeable future, the British evacuation of Savannah ruled out the possibility of chattel slavery in Georgia being brought to an end with the assistance of an external liberator.[34]

The formal and the informal slave economies of the lowcountry were severely disrupted by the Revolutionary War. In one important respect the rebuilding of both economies in the immediate postwar period was identical to the prewar process of plantation formation. In the 1780s and 1790s, as in the 1760s and early 1770s, Georgia planters looked to the African slave trade to satisfy their labor requirements. If an influx of West African men and women constituted one of the most important themes in the rebuilding of the lowcountry's informal slave economies in the late eighteenth century, just as significant was the growing appeal and influence of evangelical Protestant Christianity.[35] Dashed hopes of liberation in 1783 did not crush the longing of the lowcountry's enslaved population for freedom. Beginning in the mid-1780s, however, it did prompt a profoundly important redefinition and restructuring of their concept of freedom. Evangelical religion, in the shape of the Second Great Awakening, provided the vehicle, the ideas, and the language that informed this transformation. It offered the possibility of a spiritual if not a secular autonomy, held out the albeit deferred promise of liberation and equality after death, and empowered believers, individually and collectively, with a new sense of self-worth and self-esteem.

The religious choices made by bondmen and bondwomen during the early national period generated by far the most serious tensions and divisions within the slave quarters of the lowcountry. The ways in which African and African-American believers, as well as their white coreligionists, interpreted and sought to apply the fundamental tenets of Baptist and Methodist religious morality called into question not so much the bondpeople's traditionally established economic rights as the manner in which they were used. The bondpeople's right to their own time was not an issue; how they elected to use that time most certainly was. Moreover, the leaders of the Baptist and Methodist churches, including the African-American leaders of those churches, were insistent that church members change their patterns of expenditure and consumption.

During the 1810s and 1820s, fueled by a combination of evangelical imperatives and the more familiar pragmatic concerns of many owners, the informal slave economies emerged as the central, and most divisive, issue in Savannah politics. Indeed, the city council elections of 1829 turned on this single issue. By the late 1820s, regardless of the religious preferences that divided them and the differing economic and moral choices they wished to exert, the enslaved population of the lowcountry was effectively determining Savannah's domestic political agenda.

If nothing else, the election of 1829 demonstrated for the first time to white Georgians an important truth: the extent to which the behavior, the ambition, of bondpeople was shaping white Georgians' political and economic lives. For many this was a most uncomfortable truth. But it was one they would be forced to wrestle with for the remainder of the antebellum period.

1 ❧ The Right to Time in the Countryside

LONG BEFORE the introduction of chattel slavery to Georgia, one of the most highly prized and jealously guarded rights of bondmen and bondwomen in the British plantation colonies was that to their own time. By the turn of the seventeenth century, both in the sugar islands and on the southern mainland, what owners had initially regarded as the gift, or privilege, of time to their bondpeople was being claimed by the latter as a right.[1] By the 1760s and 1770s the assertion of that same right was already emerging as a prominent feature of lowcountry Georgia's evolving plantation economy. Continuing negotiations over time—the hours and days that bondpeople would be obliged to spend working for their owners and the time they would have to themselves —were a crucially important point of contact between the formal and the informal slave economies. The manner in which those negotiations were resolved—the time that bondpeople claimed as their own and how far owners were willing to accede to such claims—was of fundamental importance in the definition and organization of the bondpeople's quasi-autonomous economic activities.

As chattel slavery took root in each of Britain's plantation colonies, European custom and pragmatic considerations combined to ensure that at least one day a week, as well as certain hours throughout the week, bondpeople would not normally be required to work for their owners. Christian beliefs dictated that Sunday should be a day of rest, not necessarily for captive African workers but certainly for their European owners and overseers. The white residents of the sugar islands and the southern mainland were not renowned for their religious enthusiasm and, in a strict sense, could not be described as Sabbatarians. Nevertheless, their own claim to the Sabbath generated many practical difficulties in directing the work of bondpeople on that day.[2]

There were two other equally practical, and ultimately interrelated, reasons why most planters did not try to force their bondpeople to work for them on Sundays. The profitability of plantation agriculture everywhere in British America depended on a number of variables, not all of which the planters were in a position to control. But one which they could hope to determine was the financial cost of maintaining their bondpeople. Whether planters produced sugar, tobacco, or rice, they believed it was in their interest to spend as little as possible on housing, feeding, and clothing their bondmen and bondwomen. Significant savings could be made by providing minimal amounts of food and clothing, and obliging bondpeople to make up the shortfall by working for themselves on Sundays. But planters saw a second advantage in forcing their bondpeople to work for their own subsistence on Sundays. The sheer necessity of having to work on the Sabbath in order to physically survive, it was widely assumed by owners, would leave bondpeople neither the time nor the energy to engage in individual or collective acts of violent resistance.

Beginning with the Barbadian slave code of 1661, which was the model for that enacted by South Carolina in 1712, the planter-politicians of British America tacitly acknowledged that bondmen and bondwomen would not be required to work for their owners on Sundays.[3] Georgia's planter-politicians were no exception. The code they drafted in 1755, which closely followed that adopted by South Carolina in the immediate aftermath of the Stono Rebellion, declared that on the Sabbath owners must not demand any "Work or Labour (Works of absolute necessity and the necessary Occasions of the Family only Excepted)" from their bondpeople.[4] Albeit in an essentially negative fashion (and with loopholes for owners) bondmen and bondwomen were being guaranteed the right to Sundays. Needless to say, they had no means of securing legal redress for any infringements of that right by their owners, but it was one which in practice they were often able to force the latter to concede simply by refusing to work for them on that day unless they received adequate compensation.[5]

The time that plantation bondpeople had to themselves during the week depended on the labor system favored by their owners, but in practice that too involved the latter in continuous negotiations with their enslaved workers. The precise origins of the task system that had taken root in the South Carolina lowcountry by the early eighteenth century, and that South Carolina rice planters and their bondpeople introduced to lowcountry Georgia during the 1750s and 1760s, are the subject of no little controversy.[6] In the present context, however, the important point is not the antecedents of the task system. More pertinent are its main attributes and the assumptions, of bondpeople and their owners, that underpinned and defined its operation on the rice plantations of lowcountry Georgia and, by the late eighteenth century, the cotton plantations.

The broad parameters of the task system had been established by 1750, and they did not change significantly thereafter. As Philip D. Morgan has pointed out, "a prominent characteristic" of the task system was "a sharp division between the master's 'time' and the slave's 'time.'" This, he continues, was of critical and continuing significance in the definition of "a distinctive internal economy among the slaves."[7] None would dispute that proposition.

By the 1750s the convention on lowcountry rice plantations was that once the assigned daily task had been completed the owner would make no more claims on the bondperson's time. The only legal constraint on owners, which theoretically defined the minimum time that bondpeople could claim as theirs by right, was that owners could not demand more than sixteen hours of work a day from their bondmen and bondwomen.[8] For masters and bondpeople alike, what each deemed to be their own time came to be regarded as inviolate. In practice, the task system entailed a continuing dialogue, continuing negotiations, between owners and their bondpeople as each sought to maximize the duration, and thereby the value, of their own time; as each strenuously resisted any and all attempts by the other to encroach on their time.

By the mid-eighteenth century the lowcountry's rice planters were in broad agreement about the amount of work, the number and type of tasks, they expected their bondmen and bondwomen to perform on a daily and seasonal basis. By the same token, and contributing to the definition of their owners' expectations of them, bondpeople too had forged their own views as to what constituted appropriate work loads. As Edwin C. Holland explained in 1822:

> The daily task does not vary according to the arbitrary will and caprice of . . . owners, and although [it] is not fixed by law, it is so well settled by long usage, that upon every plantation it is the *same*. Should any owner increase the work beyond what is customary, he subjects himself to the reproach of his neighbors, and to such discontent amongst his slaves as to make them of but little use to him.[9]

At particularly busy times in the plantation year, and especially at harvest time, planters might seek "extra work for several days" from their bondmen and bondwomen. The public laws of slavery also permitted them to ask for Sunday work from their bondpeople, should an urgent need for such work arise. Usually bondpeople vigorously resisted any and all encroachments on what they claimed as their own time. Of course, owners had the option of threatening, and carrying out, a whole range of punishments if their bondpeople refused to comply with their wishes. However, when it came to securing the extra work they needed, most planters seem to have found it far easier to negotiate terms with their bondmen and bondwomen than to try to physically coerce them into sacrificing their own time.

The precise outcomes of the negotiations conducted on lowcountry plantations varied from estate to estate, from day to day, and from week to week, but it was not unusual for bondpeople to demand and receive cash payments for any work they undertook in what they and their owners agreed was their own time. Alternatively, they might be promised a "holiday" in lieu of the extra hours or days they worked.[10] Precedents were established on every plantation and were filed away for future reference. Moreover, owners and bondpeople alike could also try to strengthen their bargaining positions by citing the practices and precedents on neighboring estates.

The most comprehensive account of the annual and daily work routines on the lowcountry's rice plantations during the middle years of the eighteenth century is that penned by Pastor Bolzius, the spiritual leader of the Salzburger settlement at Ebenezer.[11] Two important points emerge from his report. Predictably, the actual tasks performed by field hands varied according to the season of the year and often involved rather more than simply rice culture. As part of the drive for economic self-sufficiency, and to make the most efficient use possible of a bound labor force, most lowcountry planters gave over some of their land to the cultivation of such foodstuffs as corn, potatoes, and beans, and the task system applied to these crops as well as to rice. Second, if Bolzius's report is to be believed, owners expected the same amount of field work to be completed each day by every adult bondperson. They appear to have made no allowances for age or gender.

Whether planting corn or hoeing rice, the bondperson's daily task was defined as the acreage to be completed. For instance, when corn was being planted in late spring or early summer "a good Negro man or woman must plant half an acre a day." Rice planting involved two operations, conducted on consecutive days. The first was making furrows for the rice, when each bondperson "must account for a quarter acre daily." The next day the rice was sown and covered, "and half an acre is the daily task of a Negro." After the rice had been sown it was usually time to weed the corn fields for the first time and, "unless the ground is too full of roots," each hand was expected to clear half an acre per day. After this job had been completed it was back "to cultivate the rice a second time," only now "the quality of the land determines their day's work." When the rice and corn crops were "cultivated for the third and last time" hands were expected to "take care of an acre and more [of corn]" per day and half an acre of rice. Bolzius mentioned that after it had been harvested the rice crop was threshed, ground, and stamped by bondpeople during "mornings and evenings," but otherwise he did not discuss autumn and winter work assignments.[12]

By the mid-1780s, in an effort to prevent disputes over the precise amount of land to be worked on any given day, some owners were measuring and marking out their fields.[13] During the next thirty years this became the standard practice on most plantations. As a northern traveler to the lowcountry noted in 1817, "the fields are generally marked off into squares, divided into spaces of 105 feet each, being a quarter of an acre. Two of these quarter acres are generally assigned as a day's task for a negro to hoe."[14]

The work assignments on rice plantations described by Bolzius did not change dramatically between the 1750s and 1830, and during the late eighteenth century they were modified to meet the requirements of the lowcountry's cotton plantations.[15] By the early 1820s the daily tasks associated with cotton cultivation were a quarter of an acre per hand for listing and bedding and half an acre for hoeing. Picking, sorting, ginning, and motting assignments were reckoned in pounds of cotton: field hands were each expected to pick between ninety and one hundred pounds of cotton a day; to sort between thirty and fifty pounds; to gin between twenty and thirty pounds; and to mot between thirty and fifty pounds.[16]

Pastor Bolzius stated unequivocally that "in the planting and cultivating of fields" the daily task of "a good Negro woman" was exactly the same as that of a man.[17] By the 1820s this was still the case on some plantations. Jeremiah Everts recorded that on one Dawfuskie estate he visited "I counted 25 slaves at work in one field. The females have the same tasks assigned them as the males."[18] Frances Kemble also claimed that despite the fact that tasks "profess to be graduated according to the sex, age and strength of the labourer," it had been the practice on the Butler estates "for many years past" for "the men and women who laboured in the fields [to have] the same task to perform." This, she commented, "was a noble admission of female equality." Possibly at his wife's instigation, Pierce Butler "altered the distribution of the work, diminishing the quantity done by women."[19]

In the mid-eighteenth century Pastor Bolzius remarked that gender was not taken into account by owners when the tasks associated with "planting and cultivating" were being assigned. He went on to explain that in other areas of plantation work there was a sexual division of labor. "Men cut the trees," he wrote, "and the women cut the bushes and carry them together, and they share their work, the men doing the hardest, and the women the easiest."[20] Bolzius's comments, although perhaps not doing full justice to the physical demands made of bondmen and bondwomen alike in these operations, were equally applicable to the 1820s. On most plantations the very heaviest labor, such as ditching and the tree felling mentioned by Bolzius, was assigned to bondmen and resulted in the separation of the sexes during the working day. Yet the available evidence suggests that such separations were temporary and infrequent and that there was far less of a sexual division of labor on lowcountry plantations than there was in Savannah or the other, smaller, towns of the coastal counties.

In Savannah, as in Charleston, a bondwoman usually worked in her owner's home, sometimes but not necessarily in the company of other bondwomen, as a domestic servant.[21] The work routines of urban bondwomen might take them out of the home as they performed various errands for their owners; usually those routines did not involve their working alongside men on any regular basis. The largely unskilled urban bondmen, on the other hand, tended to work outside the home and in contexts, most importantly perhaps Savannah's docks and wharfs, where they worked alongside other bondmen day in and day out. This sexual division of labor in the lowcountry towns contrasted sharply with the situation on the majority of plantations where, on most weekdays of the year, bondmen and bondwomen worked alongside each other doing precisely the same jobs.

Detailed work schedules for lowcountry Georgia plantations before 1830 are rare commodities, but one that has survived from the late 1820s is for Colerain plantation. "One of the largest and most efficient rice plantations in Chatham County," its work schedule confirms the argument that in the countryside the sexual division of unskilled labor occurred only occasionally.[22] Indeed, an examination of the Colerain work schedule for the period between 10 March and 22 December 1828, 247 days in all, reveals that on only seventeen days, in December, were bondmen and bondwomen assigned different tasks on the basis of their gender. On three of those days the reason was simply that the estate's bondmen were required to work "on the Public Road."[23]

During the first six days of December "all hands" were employed at "thrashing Rice" or "ditching & banking." After a day off on the seventh, the estate's bondmen were put to work for two days "ditching"; the bondwomen spent their time "hoeing the grass off the 30 acre Square." Between the tenth and thirteenth "all hands" were said by Potter to be "ditching, hoeing and winnowing." The men spent the next eight working days "making up the dam," "cleaning out the Mill Pond," and "putting down a trunk." The women were employed "cleaning up the 30 Acre Square" and "hoeing in the Wampie and Ebo Jack Square."[24] At Colerain, bondmen and bondwomen spent most of their working lives in close proximity, doing precisely the same kinds of tasks. Certainly those comparatively rare occasions when they were separated helped to foster what Michael P. Johnson has aptly described as "the comradeship of work [between] slaves of the same sex."[25] But the pattern of work on the vast majority of lowcountry plantations was one that through most of the year provided a context for the encouragement of "comradeship" between bondmen and bondwomen. That same "comradeship" flourished, and was to find one of its most explicit expressions, in the organization and functioning of the informal slave economies of the lowcountry.

Neither Bolzius in the mid-1750s nor Everts nearly seventy years later so much as hinted that age, physical condition, or gender might have a bearing on the amount of work demanded of bondmen and bondwomen. Basil Hall, however, pointed out that both were significant factors in determining work assignments on the cotton plantations of the Sea Islands. On these estates "a three quarter, or half, or a quarter hand is required to work only that proportion of a task per day." This, Hall claimed, was the "method of tasking, or defining their work, . . . which the slaves prefer to any other." Their "grades" were age related, with "younger slaves [coming] in as one-quarter hands." Owners also took account of the bondperson's physical condition. According to Hall, the grading process took place once a year and "applications are made every year by the slaves to the overseer, or to their master, to reduce the quantum of labour from the highest to the lowest." Every bondperson, Hall continued, "knows his rate, and lawful task, so well, that if he thinks himself imposed upon by the driver, he appeals at once to the master."[26]

During the first half of the eighteenth century South Carolina planters had generally, if grudgingly, come to accept that once the assigned task had been satisfactorily completed no additional demands would be made of bondmen and bondwomen during the rest of the day. As Philip D. Morgan has argued, compared to the dawn-to-dusk labor associated with the gang system, from the bondpeople's perspective the task system "at least had the virtue of allowing [them] a certain latitude to apportion [their] own day, to work intensively at [their] task and then have the balance of [their] time."[27] But how much time was that? And what did bondmen and bondwomen elect to do with it?

Pastor Bolzius offered no clues as to precisely how long particular tasks were likely to take, but clearly a great deal depended on the age and fitness of the bondperson. Motherhood too could lengthen the time it took to complete the allotted daily task and add to the physical exhaustion of the women concerned. On many plantations older, "superannuated" bondwomen took care of babies and young children while their mothers toiled in the fields or swamps. Sometimes mothers had no one to look after their babies and carried them, West African style, strapped to their backs in "a sort of rude knapsack," as they worked. One woman, "who did not appear to be more than twenty years old," asked Charles Ball how would she ever be able to forgive herself if she left "her child in the weeds amongst the snakes. What would be my feelings if I should leave it there, and a scorpion were to bite it?"[28]

By the early nineteenth century many European and Euro-American reporters were painting a somewhat rosy picture of the task system and implying that it was far less exploitative, far less physically demanding, than the gang system. In 1806, Dr. Daniel Turner, who had recently moved from New England to St. Marys, noted that "a field negro frequently completes his task of a day's work by 12 o'clock A.M." Jeremiah Everts reported that on Sea Island plantations "the Negroes . . . are generally through their tasks by two o'clock." Also speaking of the Sea Islands, Basil Hall claimed that "active hands get through their proportion generally by the middle of the day, others in two-thirds of the day."[29] There was broad agreement that field hands, who began their day's work at dawn or shortly thereafter, usually managed to complete their task by midafternoon, and sometimes earlier than that. Frances Kemble, however, remarked of some bondwomen known to her that "it was *only* just six o'clock and [they] had done all their tasks."[30]

European and American commentators based their claims for the relative benefit to bondpeople of the task system on the fact that whether they finished their work by noon, or in midafternoon, they were then "left to employ the balance [of the day], as it is rather well called . . . in their own fields, in fishing, or in dancing; in short, as they please."[31] As Daniel Turner commented, once the bondperson's task had been satisfactorily completed, owners felt they had "no right to call on [her or him] after."[32] The implication was that this "right" to the "balance" of the day was a gift bestowed by owners. Commentators seldom acknowledged (perhaps in the case of casual visitors to the lowcountry because they were simply unaware) that bondpeople were forced to wage a continuing and uncompromising struggle to maintain that "right."

Depending on the season, the speed with which they were able to complete their assigned task, and how far they had to walk back from work, field hands might have seven or eight hours of daylight when they were not at the beck and call of their owners and overseers.[33] Obviously, in the interest of maximizing their own time, individual bondpeople had every incentive to complete their assigned task as quickly and, given that their work was usually checked by the driver or overseer "before they go away,"[34] as satisfactorily as possible. On the other hand, ties of family, kin, and friendship almost certainly prompted the frequent sacrifice of the individual's own time as young and old, strong and weak, women and men came to each other's assistance when the need arose.

What most white commentators failed to take into account, let alone emphasize, when depicting the supposed advantages to bondmen and bondwomen of the task system, was the gruelling and often dangerous nature of the work on lowcountry plantations. For even the fittest field hand, planting, hoeing, and harvesting entailed backbreaking work, week in and week out, with only the Christmas period offering more than one day's respite at a time.[35] Rice cultivation involved strenuous physical labor, much of it during the lowcountry's hot and humid summers; it was also hazardous and unhealthy.

As Anthony Stokes explained in the early 1780s, during the winter months field hands were "turned out to work in the Rice Swamps, half leg deep in water, which brings on pleurisies and peripneumonies." Conditions scarcely improved in the summer when "the quantity of water let into the Rice-fields make it very sickly."[36] Rheumatism, reported Frances Kemble, "proceeds from exposure" and "is almost universal [attacking] indiscriminately the young and the old." Like their compatriots in the sugar islands, the enslaved population of the lowcountry also had to contend with yaws, "a horrible disease" for which contemporary medicine offered no effective remedy.[37] As if pleurisy, peripneumonia, rheumatism, malarial fevers, "fluxes," and yaws were not heavy enough burdens to have to bear, field hands who labored in the rice swamps faced yet another threat. Alligators and poisonous snakes were constant sources of danger to life and limb.[38]

The health and mortality rates of bondpeople in the plantation

economies of the American South and the Caribbean have attracted
an enormous amount of scholarly attention.[39] Obviously, the incidence
of debilitating illnesses and deaths among the enslaved populations of
these regions had a direct bearing on profit margins, on the performance of the formal slave economy in question. But, a point generally
ignored by scholars, what was true of the formal slave economies was
equally true of the informal slave economies. Good health, or the lack
of it, was an important determinant of both the time and the energy
that bondpeople had to expend working on their own behalf as well as
on behalf of their owners.

Few contemporary commentators or modern scholars would disagree with Basil Hall's observation that in the American South rice
cultivation was "the most unhealthy work in which the slaves were
employed, and in spite of every care . . . they sank under it in great numbers."[40] The Colerain work schedule kept in the late 1820s by James
Potter recorded not only the nature of the work undertaken daily by the
bondpeople on that plantation but also the names of those whom he
considered too "sick" to work. Obviously it would be dangerous to extrapolate a pattern of time worked and time "lost" through sickness for
the lowcountry as a whole from the Potter plantation journal. Nevertheless this source offers illuminating and, for the period here under
consideration, unique insights into this critically important question.

On 1 January 1828 twenty-one children and eighty-eight "grown
persons" were on Colerain plantation.[41] Excluding those who were
"superannuated," that is, considered too old for plantation work, and
young children, the work force consisted of forty-one men and thirty-
six women who were organized into two units. The first, under a
driver named Tommy, was composed of twenty-two men, including
Tommy, and seventeen women. The second, whose driver was Edmund,
consisted of nineteen men, excluding Edmund, and nineteen women.
Three of the men were employed as coopers, two as sawyers, one as a
carter, and one worked "in the mill." Two women, Rachel and Cate,
were described as cooks. Membership of a particular unit might well
have reflected, and reinforced, family and kinship ties on Colerain, but
Potter did not mention the basis on which he, possibly with the advice
of Tony and Edmund, assigned slaves to work under each of his drivers.

Neither did Potter provide another vitally important piece of evidence: the precise character of the maladies that afflicted the bond-people on Colerain. Nonetheless his schedule testifies eloquently to the extent to which, throughout the year, the bondpeople were ravaged by ill health of sufficient gravity to make them incapable of work. During the 247 working days on the plantation between 10 March and 22 December 1828, there was not a single day when every bondperson was considered fit enough by Potter to turn out for work. Nor was there any work day when only one bondperson was sick. On any given work day from two to fourteen people (3 to 18 percent) of the work force were considered unfit to work. Overall, of the 19,019 possible work days (77 bondpeople × 247 days), 1,519 (8 percent) were lost to illness.

Potter listed the names as well as the number of bondpeople who were unable to work on any given day, thus allowing analysis of gender differentiations in patterns of ill health at Colerain. Bearing in mind that the ratio of working bondmen to bondwomen on the plantation was roughly equal—there were five more men than women—these differentiations were marked. Every woman of working age on the estate appeared at least once on Potter's schedule; six men, roughly 15 percent of the male work force, did not ever appear on the sick list. The remaining men apparently spent fewer days off work than did women. At least one-half the women, compared with just under one-third of the men, were deemed unfit for work on twelve or more days: the equivalent of two work weeks. Twelve women, one-third of those on the plantation, were "sick" for the equivalent of a month or more; the same was true of barely 15 percent of the men.

Bondwomen faced the same epidemiological environment in the lowcountry and the same health hazards in their working conditions as did bondmen. And there is no firm evidence of gender-based variations in patterns of resistance to the "agues," "fluxes," "fevers," pleurisy, and rheumatism that struck with such regularity in this most sickly of environments. The likeliest explanation for the pronounced gender differences in the record of "sick" slaves on Colerain is to be sought in pregnancy and childbirth or, more specifically, in the complications that could arise during pregnancy and childbirth. An uncomplicated pregnancy might result in a woman's being "relieved of a certain portion of her work in the field, which lightening of labour continues . . . as long as she is so burthened," but work of some kind would still be demanded of her until she gave birth.[42] She would be required to return to the fields within a few days of giving birth. As Frances Kemble commented, enslaved mothers were "driven afield as soon as they recover from child labour."[43]

Complications associated with pregnancy and childbirth certainly appear to have been the reason why at least four of the women on Potter's list spent as much time off work as they did.[44] Five women, Tella, Betty, Balinda, Sue, and Jenny, gave birth during the year and the names of four of them figure prominently on Potter's schedule. Tella, who gave birth on 9 February, was not on Potter's list on 10 March, but she and her baby were reported as being "sick" on the thirteenth and fourteenth of that month. Potter was not specific on this point, but it may have been that it was Tella's baby who was ill, rather than Tella herself, and that she had been given time off work to attend to her sick child.[45]

Betty's case was more clear-cut. She was "sick" for at least ten days before she gave birth on 19 March and remained so until 8 May, a minimum of fifty-seven working days. Her name reappeared on the list on 19 May and she remained off work for another nine days. Balinda's baby girl, Elizabeth, was born on 7 July. Balinda was reported as being "sick" between 2 and 30 June and again between 3 July and 6 August, just over two months in all. Later in the year Sue, who gave birth on 20 November, was "sick" for seventy working days: between 30 September and 22 December. Only Jenny, whose baby was born on 27 June, does not appear on Potter's list either immediately before or after her baby was born. However, she was recorded as having been off work for four days at the very beginning of June, barely three weeks before her confinement.

From the 1750s and 1760s onward, Georgia planters, for simple economic expediency, did what they could to get their ailing bondpeople back to work as quickly as possible. Some brought in medical supplies, often of dubious value, which either they or their overseers dispensed. A typical plantation medicine chest contained emetics, of which the most favored was ipecacuanha; sweating agents, such as saline julep; and cathartics, including calomel and glauber salts. Tinctures and ointments would be kept on hand to deal with minor injuries.[46] In particularly serious cases local doctors might be called in, but this could prove costly.

In the spring of 1765, for instance, William Gibbons paid Dr. Bourquin £1.15.4 for treating his bondman Peter. Six months later two other doctors charged him fifteen shillings for "sundry dressings . . . of a negro fellows finger."[47]

Some planters were reluctant to summon doctors not, they claimed, because of the expense involved, but because they had so little faith in their abilities. In the mid-1790s, for example, Maj. Pierce Butler insisted that his overseer, William Page, give *"every possible* attention . . . to sick Negroes, save and except that of calling in a Doctor, which I never admit of unless for a fracture or venereal complaint." Butler explained to Page that he had "never . . . employed Doctors to my Negroes, because country Doctors have not my confidence because they seldom feel for Negroes as they ought to, and therefore are light on their prescriptions." Butler, and in all probability his bondpeople also, had rather more faith in the nostrums of Nanny and Tenah. "The moment any Negroe complains," Butler wrote to Page, they were "to be attended" by these two bondwomen.[48]

By the early nineteenth century, hospitals, or infirmaries, had been set up on some of the larger lowcountry plantations specifically to attend to the medical needs of bondpeople. But if Frances Kemble's report of the infirmary on her husband's estate is anything to go by, standards of hygiene, as well as the quality of the medical care, in these establishments left a great deal to be desired. The infirmary in question was "a large two-storey building . . . of white washed wood, and contains four large-sized rooms." From the outside it looked most impressive, but the interior was another matter. The windows were "obscured with dirt" and most of the patients "lay prostrate on the floor, without bed, mattress, or pillow, buried in tattered and filthy blankets." And this, Frances Kemble angrily pointed out, was "the hospital of an estate, where the owners are supposed to be humane, the overseer efficient and kind, and the negroes remarkably well cared for and comfortable."[49]

As the Colerain plantation data suggest, contemporary medicine and, if Frances Kemble is to be believed, often squalid plantation infirmaries were of limited value in dealing effectively with the maladies suffered throughout this period by the enslaved population of lowcountry Georgia. As far as the operation of the formal slave economy was concerned, good health, or the lack of it, was one of the prime determinants of daily, weekly, and annual work regimes. But precisely the same was true of the informal slave economies. Bondpeople who were declared by their owner or overseer to be too sick to perform their assigned daily task were scarcely likely to be in a fit condition to take on comparably heavy work, or even any work at all, in their own time. Debilitating illnesses of one kind or another, even without complications of pregnancy and childbirth, were important determinants of bondpeople's time and of the uses to which they were able to put that time. The Colerain material points in quite dramatic fashion, although not in the detail one would wish, to the relationship between health and the internal dynamics of the lowcountry's informal slave economies.

That the task system enabled field hands to have a significant input into the organization of their time, and more importantly into the definition of that time, is indisputable. But all the evidence leads to the same conclusion: tasking involved work that was no less physically demanding than that associated with the gang system. Indeed, it is little wonder that, as a bondwoman on one of the Butler plantations explained to Frances Kemble, after they had completed their daily task many field hands felt "too tired and worn out to do anything but throw themselves down and sleep."[50] Even the healthiest bondmen and bondwomen must have been profoundly fatigued after finishing their assigned task, but the last thing that most of them did was to "throw themselves down and sleep." Their own time was far too necessary, and far too precious, for that.

From the outset the enslaved population of lowcountry Georgia waged an energetic battle to secure and preserve the right to their own time, to impress upon their owners and other whites that their own time was sacrosanct. They forged their own opinions as to how that time, especially their Sundays, might best be used. And so did their owners. But before the end of the eighteenth century there was one pressure most bondpeople in lowcountry Georgia were not exposed to: their owners' insistence that they devote at least a part of their precious Sundays to the practice of Christianity.

Planters and churchmen had rather different views as to how bondmen and bondwomen should spend the one day of the week that they could claim as theirs: the Sabbath. From the late seventeenth century, the Anglican clergy insisted that bondpeople ought, by compulsion if necessary, to spend at least a part of Sunday being instructed in Christianity and attending divine worship.[51] These activities were as unpalatable to most bondmen and bondwomen as they were to most Anglican planters, albeit for different reasons. Neither learning nor practicing the religious beliefs of their owners had a high priority on the Sunday agendas southern bondmen and bondwomen set for themselves during the colonial period. The bondpeople of lowcountry Georgia were to prove no exception to this general rule.

In 1750 the trustees drew up regulations that they hoped would regulate slavery and race relations in Georgia. These included what for the plantation colonies was the novel demand that owners send their bondmen and bondwomen for religious instruction at some time on the Sabbath.[52] They tried to ensure that such instruction would be available by negotiating with the Society for the Propagation of the Gospel in Foreign Parts and the associates of Dr. Bray for the appointment of a catechist who would be mainly responsible for catering to the assumed spiritual needs of Georgia's enslaved population.[53]

In 1751 Joseph Ottolenghe moved to Savannah, where he took up his post as catechist to a population that numbered fewer than three thousand whites and six hundred Africans and African-Americans.[54] He soon began to complain about two main difficulties. Georgia's "penurious Masters," he claimed, believed that "a Slave is ten times worse when a Christian, than in his State of Paganism." Moreover, the colony's predominantly African-born bondmen and bondwomen remained strongly attached to "the old Superstitions of a false Religion."[55]

With one notable, but scarcely surprising, exception reflecting the South Carolina influence, little changed during the eight years that Ottolenghe worked as a paid catechist in Savannah. The trustees' regulation concerning the religious instruction of bondmen and bondwomen, which arguably never had the force of a legal requirement, was ignored by the South Carolina planters and their bondpeople who flooded into Georgia once the ban on chattel slavery had been formally lifted.[56] The South Carolina influence ensured that the slave code of 1755, which tacitly acknowledged the right of bondmen and bondwomen to Sunday, remained silent on the question of the religious lives of Georgia's enslaved population.[57]

As Ottolenghe lamented in his periodic reports to London before he was dismissed from his post in 1759, Georgia Anglicans, like their counterparts elsewhere in British America, simply refused to allow their bondpeople time off work on weekdays for religious purposes. Otto-lenghe's solution was to offer evening classes on Sundays, Tuesdays, and Thursdays, and he claimed that the "large Room" in Savannah he used for his meetings got "as full as it could hold." What this meant in terms of actual numbers is indicated by his comment that sometimes he would have a class of "fifty & more." Bondpeople's attendance at Ottolenghe's classes was most irregular, either by their own choice or by their owners'. Some meetings attracted fewer than ten people and "some will attend for 6 Months and then disappear for 6 Months or [a] Year, & some two, before I see them again."[58]

During what proved to be the last two decades of the colonial period, a few Anglican planters, including James Habersham and William Knox, arranged for the religious instruction of their bondmen and bondwomen on a fairly regular basis.[59] Clearly, these bondpeople re-mained free to accept or reject the dogma presented to them, but they had little choice other than to attend the meetings organized by their owners for their edification.

Very few Anglican planters followed the example set by Habersham and Knox, and the most sustained attempts to convert bondpeople in the years prior to the Revolutionary War were made by the Salzburgers at Ebenezer and by the South Carolina Congregationalists who, begin-ning in the mid 1750s, settled in the district of Midway. But even in these two centers comparatively few bondmen and bondwomen could be persuaded to accept, and to spend their own time practicing, the religious beliefs of their owners.[60] By the mid-1770s only a minuscule proportion of the lowcountry's predominantly African-born population, which numbered around eighteen thousand, opted for Christianity in any form.[61]

The combination of planter and bondpeople's hostility, which so limited the proselytizing activities of Anglican churchmen and a few individual owners, did not mean that the enslaved population of the lowcountry was unfamiliar with the fundamental tenets of Christianity. On the contrary, when an opportunity presented itself, or could be manufactured, they were quick to try to turn the Christianity of their owners to their own advantage. Christian benevolence, or a Christian conscience, could well be exploited by men and women who had little interest, and saw even less virtue, in internalizing the role of dutiful Christian servants as an integral part of the ongoing negotiations they conducted with their owners over all facets of life in the quarters.

One of the most obvious implications of the abysmal failure of Christianity, and more specifically Anglicanism, to make any more than the faintest impression on the hearts and minds of colonial Georgia's enslaved population, is also one of the most significant. The meanings that the bondmen and bondwomen of the lowcountry themselves attached to Sunday, their assertion of their right to that day, and the ways in which they elected to employ it were informed by secular rather than by spiritual, or at least Christian, imperatives.

This is not to suggest that bondmen and bondwomen had no time, or did not wish to find the time, for religious pursuits. They most certainly did. But this time was for religious practices of their own devising, not for those observances that the likes of Ottolenghe, Pastor Bolzius, Habersham, and Knox tried to foist on them. The religious beliefs and rituals that evolved in the quarters of lowcountry Georgia plantations during the second half of the eighteenth century were deeply rooted in what Walter Rodney so aptly described as the "essential oneness" of the religious cultures of West Africa, and not in those of their western European owners.[62] Two of these rituals, those associated with marriage and death, involved occasional rather than regular gatherings, and all the available evidence indicates that they were usually held at night. This may have been because planters were reluctant to allow their bondpeople time off work to marry each other and bury their dead. But given the practice in parts of West Africa, it is just as likely that nighttime burials and second funerals reflected the preference of their organizers.[63]

Sundays, then, held no special religious significance for the vast majority of bondmen and bondwomen in the lowcountry in the years prior to the American Revolution. But in every other respect it was the most important day of the week to them: it was their day. How they used it depended on various considerations and often involved difficult choices. If they had been forcibly separated from loved ones who still lived within reach this was the one day of the week when visits could be made without incurring the wrath of their owners. Some men and women might

have regarded Sunday primarily as a day of rest and relaxation, as a day
when they could recover from the physical exhaustion of the previous
week's work. Yet few bondpeople could completely escape the fact that
the way in which they opted to spend their Sundays, as well as their
own time on weekdays, was inextricably bound up with their standard
of living. Sheer necessity dictated that if they were to raise their living
standards above bare subsistence they would have to find ways of augmenting the minimal amounts of food and clothing distributed by their
owners. Inevitably this would mean having to spend some of their own
time working to support themselves.

By the mid-eighteenth century the enslaved population of the South
Carolina lowcountry, many of whom were taken to Georgia by their
owners during the 1750s and 1760s, had already etched out the essential framework of informal economies that would also characterize the
coastal parishes of Georgia.[64] The bondpeople of lowcountry Georgia
were to prove just as adept in enhancing their living standards, just
as "skilful and industrious," as their compatriots across the Savannah River. Indeed, they proved "skilful and industrious" in ways and
on a scale that surprised and, by the 1760s and 1770s, alarmed their
owners.[65] Following the long-established South Carolina model, much
of the skill and industry of plantation bondpeople in lowcountry Georgia went into the cultivation of crops in their own time. Bondmen and
bondwomen were to find various ways of raising their living standards
above bare subsistence. But, as in the other plantation colonies of the
southern mainland and the Caribbean, more than anything else their
"gardens," or "patches," would form the backbone of their informal
economies.

2 ❧ Patterns of Production and Income Generation in the Countryside

BY THE LATE seventeenth century gardens and provision grounds were well-established features of the informal slave economies of the British sugar islands.[1] Obviously, bondpeople who were expected to work in their own time to feed themselves needed land to cultivate, but whether they claimed this for themselves or had it allocated to them by their owners is far from clear. Precisely the same need for land existed in the Carolina lowcountry and, in all probability, gardens and patches were introduced into that region by the West Indian planters and their bond-people who moved there in such numbers during the 1670s and 1680s.[2]

Comparatively little evidence has survived from either colonial South Carolina or Georgia concerning the precise size and location of their "gardens and patches" or the ways in which bondpeople initially obtained them. (The two words were used interchangeably in the lowcountry.) The most comprehensive account, penned by Pastor Bolzius in the mid-1750s, mentions only that they were "given as much land as they can handle" and that they planted "something for themselves after the days work [and] also on Sundays."[3]

It is most unlikely that owners would have permitted their bondmen and bondwomen to work prime land on their own behalf, although Henry Laurens appears to have been one who did. During the decade before the American Revolution some of his bondpeople had access to land on which they were able to, and chose to, cultivate rice.[4] There is some suggestion that during the eighteenth century the location of gardens, or patches, closely resembled that of Jamaican provision grounds. As Charles Ball recalled, usually the land that bondpeople worked for themselves was "in some remote and unprofitable part of the estate, generally in the woods." They might have to walk upward of a mile and a half to reach their gardens. Frances Kemble reported that on one of her husband's plantations the bondpeople's "task ground" was three miles from their quarters.[5]

In the eighteenth and early nineteenth century, the manner in which the gardens were subdivided, and work on them subsequently organized, reflected and reinforced the crucial significance the predominantly West African-born population of the lowcountry attached to family and kinship networks.[6] In most West African societies "the kinship unit" formed "the basis of community life," and everywhere in the Americas, "wherever possible, the slaves strove to reestablish African patterns of marriage and retain traditional attitudes to family, children and kin."[7] As Jacqueline Jones has recently commented, although always vulnerable to enforced separation, bondpeople's ties of family and kin "provided all slaves with love and affection, a world of their own within a nation controlled by whites."[8] The family and kinship networks that evolved in the quarters of lowcountry Georgia during the second half of the eighteenth century assumed the paramount role in the construction and transmission, both within and between generations, of a vibrant and viable African-American culture.[9]

Whether referred to as "gardens," "private fields," or "task grounds," the lands made available to, or claimed by, bondpeople for their own use performed a pivotal, and dual, function in the ongoing struggle to preserve the well-being, dignity, and integrity of the enslaved African and African-American family. Directly through consumption, and more indirectly through barter and sale, garden produce contributed significantly to the material comfort and health of enslaved families. Just as important was the extent to which gardens provided family members with a profoundly significant degree of autonomy in the organization of at least one area of their lives.[10] W. W. Hazzard spoke for most lowcountry planters when he commented that his bondpeople "manage [their ground] their own way, and the entire produce is appropriated to their own purposes not subject to my control." [11]

As in the sugar islands, the lands initially allocated by lowcountry planters to their bondpeople for gardens were not worked on a communal basis, but were subdivided, almost certainly by the bondpeople themselves, into family or household units. On larger plantations this might mean as many as thirty separate plots.[12] One contemporary report suggests that the "private fields" tilled by an enslaved family or household could run to "5 or 6 acres." [13] Writing in 1831, W. W. Hazzard commented that he allocated "everyone, a task of ground, and a half task for each child capable of working." [14]

Charles Ball's account suggests that these "private fields," "patches," or "gardens" were often demarcated with fences made of "rails" or "brush." [15] Such fences did not preclude the possibility of communal labor, and in times of need bondpeople rallied to one another's assistance. But the fences provided a visible and explicit assertion of possession, of ownership, by the family or household whose members worked the land in question. What many owners had initially regarded as the gift of land was being claimed by those who worked it, by the families and households concerned, as theirs by right to work as they pleased.[16] Masters seldom intervened in the decision making associated with the cultivation of "gardens": bondpeople decided for themselves which crops they would grow and how the work upon what they regarded as their own land would be organized.[17] As James Hamilton Couper discovered, any attempts on the part of owners to trespass on what bondpeople regarded as their customary rights were liable to be vigorously opposed.

Couper, the owner of Hopeton, one of the lowcountry's premier rice plantations, initiated a scheme that involved setting aside a fifty-acre field "for the benefit of twenty-five picked men" who were "some of the most active among his people." He was "in hope of elevating the character of [these men] and giving them more self-dependence." Within three years Couper was forced to abandon an "experiment" that entailed "giving" the bondmen in question "half their Saturday's labor" to cultivate the field. During the first year the men were given no choice but forced to comply with Couper's wishes: "they were compelled to work." At the end of the year "the product amounting to 1500 dollars was divided equally among them," and Couper "took care to give them Silver, hoping that would excite their industry." The following year the element of compulsion was removed. But when the bondmen "were left to their own management, the crop lessened one half." During "the third season they let the land run to waste, so that it was useless to permit them to retain it."

The failure of Couper's "experiment" may have confirmed his opinion of the "character" of his bondmen, but Charles Lyell, who visited Hopeton in the mid-1840s, provided a rather more convincing explanation of why it was these men had "let the land run to waste": the strong preference, the determination, of bondpeople to organize their garden work on a familial, rather than on a communal, basis. Moreover, they had a strong distaste for the explicit element of compulsion in Couper's scheme. As Lyell explained, "there appears to me to be nothing disheartening in this failure, which may have been chiefly owing to their holding the property in common, a scheme which was found not to answer even with the Pilgrim Fathers when they first colonized Plymouth." [18]

By the 1820s and 1830s, gardens were usually depicted by white commentators as being contiguous to the home rather than at some remove from it. At the end of the 1830s, for example, Frances Kemble commented that on her husband's plantations every cabin had "attached" to it "a small scrap of ground for a garden." According to Emily Burke, "each slave had his small patch of ground adjacent to his dwelling," and on Cumberland Island "each [cabin had] sufficient grounds for a garden." [19] These gardens might run to "a half-acre to each family" and, like the more distant patches, were usually "inclosed with palings." [20] Bondpeople's gardens had always been identified, or so it would appear, with particular families and households; now they were quite literally centered on the home. This close proximity of home and garden certainly made for the saving and more flexible use of the bondpeople's own time.

It is not clear whether this apparent shift in the location of gardens was at the behest of owners, who perhaps hoped to be able to more closely supervise the activities of their bondmen and bondwomen. It may have reflected the wishes of bondpeople who were prepared to sacrifice a degree of privacy for the convenience of having immediately accessible plots. Neither is it evident from these later reports whether bondpeople still had access to the more distant gardens alluded to by Ball. That some of them did during the 1820s and 1830s is suggested by the remarks of Frances Kemble and W. W. Hazzard. Jared Sparks, who visited Georgia in 1826, commented that one Sunday he had passed by a "large plantation" where he had seen some bondpeople "at work *by the roadside,* cultivating each his small patch."[21]

Physically there appears to have been a closer identification of gardens with individual families and households after the turn of the eighteenth century. In every other respect, however, gardens retained the dual importance they had always held in the domestic economy of the quarters: the contribution they made to the diet, and thereby to the health, of plantation bondpeople and the possibility they presented of producing surpluses that could be bartered or sold.

Predictably, the balance between production for domestic consumption and production for sale or exchange varied from plantation to plantation, household to household, and from year to year. The quantity and variety of the provisions supplied by owners and the number of mouths to be fed in the household played a crucial role in determining the production targets set for themselves by bondpeople. The achievement of those targets did not depend solely on the time and energy that bondmen and bondwomen were able and willing to spend cultivating their gardens. The amount and fertility of the land at their disposal, together with the weather at particular points in the growing season, could also make a crucial difference. Crop failures, or shortages of particular foodstuffs, could have potentially serious implications for the standard of living and the standard of health enjoyed in the quarters.[22]

Throughout this entire period the overriding objective, and often desperate need, of plantation bondpeople was to add variety and nourishment to the usually sparse rations provided by their owners. The type, amount, and nutritional value of the provisions supplied by owners, who were enjoined by the slave code of 1755 to provide their bondpeople with "sufficient" food, varied somewhat from plantation to plantation.[23] But the intent of most planters was to feed their bondmen and bondwomen as cheaply as they could. As Pastor Bolzius put it, "The upkeep of the Negroes is cut very sparse." He estimated that it cost owners no more than about eight-pence per week to feed each of their bondpeople.[24]

The main components of the rations supplied by owners did not change appreciably between the mid-1750s and 1830. Pastor Bolzius recorded that "year in and year out" most planters provided their bond-people with "nothing but Indian . . . corn." Depending on the season, they might receive "Indian beans . . . instead of corn . . . and at certain times . . . potatoes." Between September and March owners provided "potatoes and small unsaleable rice, [and] also at times Indian corn." During the summer they switched to "corn and beans which grow on the plantation." According to Bolzius, meat was seldom included in the rations issued by owners.[25]

Later accounts paint a broadly similar picture. In 1783, for example, Anthony Stokes recorded that "in the Rice Colonies . . . the Negroes in General have Rice, Indian-corn, potatoes or black-eyed pease sufficient to subsist them." [26] Writing from St. Marys in 1806, the Rhode Islander Dr. Daniel Turner was more specific about the quantity of the provisions supplied by local planters. He declared that it was the usual practice for them to furnish each of their bondpeople "with a peck of corn a week, sometimes potatoes and sometimes meat." [27] Jeremiah Everts, another northerner who traveled in the lowcountry during the early 1820s, was appalled by the provisions distributed on one Sea Island plantation he visited. On this estate, which he failed to identify, "a large portion of [the] slaves rarely tasted flesh. At Christmas, indeed, all are feasted, but generally [their] fare is coarse and scanty." [28]

Charles Ball's account of the rations he received from one of his owners around the turn of the eighteenth century bears out the reports of these two northerners. As Ball wrote in his autobiography, a weekly allocation of "corn was all the provision that our master, or his overseer, usually made for us. I say usually, for whatever was given to us beyond the corn . . . was considered in the light of a bounty bestowed upon us, over and beyond what we were entitled to, or had a right to ex-pect to receive." Every bondperson over the age of six months received a weekly allowance of "half a bushel of ears of corn." Meat featured scarcely at all in their rations: Ball estimated that in any given year they received only enough for "about six or seven meals." It is not clear whether those meals included the "dinner of meat," usually pork, that this owner provided for his bondpeople "on Christmas-day." [29]

Not a great deal changed during the next quarter of a century. Around 1830 on the Telfair estates "the allowance for every grown

Negro however old and good for nothing, and every young one that works in the field is a peck of corn each week, and a pint of salt, and a piece of meat, not exceeding fourteen pounds, per month." Alexander Telfair instructed his overseer that "the sucking children, and all other small ones who do not work in the field, draw a half allowance of Corn and Salt." Three times a year, in July, August, and September, the overseer was to slaughter "A Beef . . . for the Negroes" and "every three years . . . A Turnip Patch to be planted . . . for the use of the Plantation."[30]

In the late 1820s, in what was one of the most detailed contemporary accounts of rations issued by lowcountry owners, the British traveler Basil Hall recorded that "the stated allowance of food to every slave, over fourteen years of age, is nine quarts of Indian corn per week, and for children from five to eight quarts." These amounts, he continued, were said by owners "to be more than they can eat, and the surplus is either sold, or is given to the hogs and poultry which they are always allowed to rear on their own account." Each bondperson was also given "a quart of salt monthly" as well as an unrecorded amount of "salt fish." "Salt beef" was distributed "occasionally, but only as a favour, and can never be claimed as a right." Sometimes sweet potatoes or rice might be provided instead of corn. The rule of thumb was that "a heaped up bushel of sweet potatoes" or "two pecks of rough, that is unhusked, rice" was "considered equal" to the usual corn allowance. Sweet potatoes and rough rice, though, were "not thought so substantial a food as the Indian corn."[31]

R. Q. Mallard's memory of the rations distributed to the bondpeople on the Liberty County plantation where he grew up confirmed much of Hall's contemporary account. According to Mallard, the bondpeople's "food was mainly maize [and] sweet potatoes." Each "full worker" received a "weekly allowance" of "a peck of corn, and four quarts additional for every child; and a half bushel of sweet potatoes to each adult, and to each child in the same proportion." At those times of the year when "the work was usually heavy" these basic rations were supplemented with "molasses, or bacon, or salt fish; and an occasional beef." Like Hall, Mallard claimed that "so abundant were the rations of corn, that at the end of each week the careful householder sent quite a bag of it to the store to be exchanged for calico or tobacco."[32]

The crops grown by enslaved families in their own time remained much the same throughout this eighty-year period. Pastor Bolzius noted that "corn, potatoes, tobacco, peanuts, water and sugar melons, pumpkins, [and] bottle pumpkins" were the items most commonly cultivated by bondpeople in their gardens.[33] By the late 1760s and early 1770s some bondmen and bondwomen were also cultivating rice in their own time.[34] Other crops added to the pastor's list by later commentators were "garden vegetables," which probably included peas, beans, onions, cabbages, and turnips, and the "little patches of sugar cane" that, according to one account, were being cultivated on Cumberland Island by 1840, and possibly even earlier.[35]

It is also evident that benne was introduced into the lowcountry by African-born men and women. In the 1930s Rosanna Williams, who lived in Tatemville, southwest of Savannah, recalled that her African-born father used to "plant mosly benne an rice. . . . He use tuh beat benne seed in mawtuh an pestle, sometime wid a lill shugah an sometimes wid a lill salt an make a pase. He eat it on bread aw he eat it jis so."[36] As Emma Hunter explained, a superstition attached to the cultivation of benne. Her African-born grandmother Betty used to "plant benne seed. Once you staht plantin benne, yuh got tuh plant em ebry yeah aw yuh die."[37]

All the crops grown by bondpeople in their gardens and patches had a potential market value, but some more than others were cultivated specifically with an eye to barter or sale. Henry Laurens's bondpeople, for example, might have consumed some of the rice they cultivated in their own time, but the bulk of it was destined for the market.[38] As is suggested by William Grimes's account of his experiences as a rice grower, this market orientation continued to be the case. Around the turn of the eighteenth century Grimes, at that point in his life owned by Dr. Kollock, worked on a plantation just outside Savannah. By his own admission, Grimes was entirely ignorant of the intricacies of rice cultivation but even so he "undertook to raise" for himself "a small crop . . . of perhaps twenty rods of ground." By watching and learning from local bondmen and bondwomen, "who raise here and there a small piece for themselves," Grimes was able to produce some rice that he sold in Savannah "for $1.25 per hundred, amounting in the whole to about $5 or $6."[39]

By the early nineteenth century occasional references were being made by white commentators to the fact that bondpeople sometimes cultivated "a little cotton" in their "gardens."[40] Unlike rice and cotton, both of which seem to have been grown mainly in the hope and expectation of securing a disposable cash income or its equivalent in goods, tobacco was cultivated mainly for domestic consumption. So great was the bondpeople's demand for tobacco that of all the crops they produced in their own time it was probably among the most highly prized.

The smoking of tobacco, usually in clay pipes, was a pervasive habit among bondmen and bondwomen alike in the lowcountry and had been carried over from West Africa. Many European travelers remarked on the West Africans' fondness for tobacco. The Mandingo people, for example, were said to be "always smoking [*sic*] Tobacco, which serves to amuse them. . . . This Tobacco they raise themselves. Their Pipes are made of Clay, very neat, and of a reddish Colour." Thomas Winterbottom claimed that "[West] Africans are universally enslaved by the charms of tobacco." According to Winterbottom, in parts of Sierra Leone tobacco was "chiefly used in the form of snuff" but "those who live upon the coast frequently smoke this herb, a custom which they have probably copied from Europeans."[41]

If Charles Ball's comments are to be believed, and there is no reason to doubt them, the bondpeople's craving for tobacco, to chew as well as to smoke, was insatiable.[42] Many "misguided" bondmen and bondwomen, he wrote, considered that tobacco was "so indispensable to comfort, nay to existence, that hunger and nakedness are patiently endured, to enable [them] to indulge in this highest of enjoyments."[43] Some owners partially satisfied this craving by distributing tobacco to their bondpeople as reward or as a gift, for example at Christmastime, but such supplies were not regular, nor could they be depended on.[44] Bondmen and bondwomen who smoked regularly had to either grow their own tobacco or find some other means of acquiring it.[45]

Little from the bondpeople's garden was allowed to go to waste. Corn husks, for instance, might be used for the bases of beds or to make "horse or mule collars . . . to sell among the planters."[46] Sometimes, as Pastor Bolzius observed, bondpeople grew crops not to eat, but because they could be made into utensils of various kinds. For instance, such was the ingenuity of bondmen and bondwomen that "stinking pumpkins" could be made into bowls and dishes, probably for domestic use rather than for sale off the plantation.[47] As R. Q. Mallard commented, the "long-necked gourd dipper" was "never absent" from bondpeople's cabins.[48]

The widely reported practice of making utensils from gourds was highly reminiscent of, and almost certainly a continuation of, that carried on in parts of West Africa. As William Smith wrote of Guinea in the mid-1740s, callabash "grow of very different Sizes, so as to contain from Half a Pint to Eight or Ten Gallons." These were "saw'd down the Middle" to make "very good Platters, Bowls, or Drinking Cups, according to their Size; and those with very long Necks make good Ladles; and . . . when whole they are as good a[s] Bottles to keep Liquor in."[49]

Gourds had a cultural as well as a purely utilitarian function and significance. The central role of music making in both the secular and the spiritual lives of the enslaved communities of the southern mainland and the Caribbean is well documented.[50] The drums, rattles, banjoes, and guitars that comprised the bondpeople's main musical instruments were usually homemade. Dry gourds from their gardens, as well as wood, were used as they were in West Africa in the manufacture of all these instruments.[51]

Whatever crops they grew and whatever their intended uses, bondpeople's financial costs in the cultivation of their gardens were virtually nonexistent. Seeds could be saved and stored for planting the following year, cuttings could be taken and rooted. Money did not have to be spent on the purchase of tools; the axes, hoes, spades, hooks, and baskets that planters regularly issued to field hands did not have to be returned at the end of the day's work and were available for use in the bondpeople's own time.[52] Cultivating gardens involved an investment of time and energy rather than an outlay of cash.

Rather more is known about the crops grown by bondpeople and the uses to which they were put than about the precise ways in which families organized the work on their gardens. As far as outlying plots were concerned, the initial process of land clearance might well have involved communal labor, and it is evident that in times of need bondpeople pitched in to help one another.[53] However, the often formal demarcation of gardens, whether they were at some distance or contiguous to the house, by fences is indicative of the extent to which work on them was conducted on a family or household basis. Various, and often changing, circumstances came into play in the precise organization of garden work by enslaved families and households. The most obvious, and important, of these were the number, age, gender, and health of family and household members.

Writing in the first decade of the twentieth century, Charles Spalding Wylly insisted that on the Spalding plantation on Sapelo "the women worked their own plots and gardens; the men fished, wove baskets for sale, and hunted."[54] No extant record from the years before 1830 suggests that garden work was an exclusively female activity. The vast majority of bondwomen in the lowcountry were employed as field hands and clearly possessed all the requisite skills for cultivating gardens. Many of them would have been used to assuming a similar domestic responsibility in West Africa.[55] This does not necessarily mean that they were obliged, chose, or were able to devote the bulk of their own time to such an activity with only the "casual assistance of their husbands and children."[56]

Whether by tradition, choice, or necessity, bondwomen performed a number of functions within the family or household that could cut deeply into the time theoretically available for tending gardens.[57] Child care, especially if the woman had been separated from her sexual partner, could take up much of her time, as could washing, making and mending clothes, and preparing meals. The latter often involved the additional chore of grinding the corn supplied by the owner as well as preparing the other ingredients of the evening meal.

As with crops cultivated for owners, those grown by bondpeople in their own time sometimes required intensive, even daily, attention. At such times, and when the land was being prepared for planting, no doubt all members of the family or household contributed as and when they could. The evidence is slender, but it may be safely assumed that the division of labor on gardens reflected the outcome of negotiations between husband and wife, parents and children. More often than not it was shared work, rather than the exclusive responsibility of any one family member. Mary Turner's argument that in Jamaica "the focus for family life was the provision grounds, which the families worked in common," would seem applicable to lowcountry Georgia.[58]

The precise contribution, in terms of time and assignments, made by each family member to the cultivation of their garden varied, and there

were occasions when some had little choice but to bear a heavier burden than others. It may be posited that under certain circumstances, for
example illness, pregnancy, and childbirth, this additional burden was
willingly shouldered by those family members who were able to work.
Of course, an unwillingness on the part of one family member to co-
operate, or even to negotiate, could result in the others being forced to
assume the entire responsibility not only for cultivating the garden but
also for every aspect of the household economy. The immensely heavy
load that this might entail, and the degree to which around the turn
of the eighteenth century West African concepts of gender roles in the
world of work still played a critically important part in the definition
of the informal slave economies, is evident from an episode related by
Charles Ball.

    Ball encountered a country-born bondwoman named Lydia, who
told him that she had been "compelled" to marry an African-born man
whom she "did not like" and by whom she had a child. Her husband
claimed to have "been a priest in his own nation, and had never been
taught to do any kind of labor." The overseer forced him to work in the
fields with the other hands, but he "refused to give his wife the least
assistance in doing any thing." The result was that Lydia was "obliged
to do the little work that it was necessary to perform in the cabin; and
also to bear all the labor of weeding and cultivating the family patch or
garden."[59] In Ball's experience, the demands made by this husband of
his wife were exceptional.

    Other bondwomen in the lowcountry found themselves forced to as-
sume a similar role to that of Lydia, not because their husbands refused
to contribute to the material well-being of their families but because
they were unable to do so. Just over one-fourth of the women listed on
colonial inventories of estates that recorded marital and family relationships were said to be living with their husbands. Fifty-seven percent of
these couples had at least one child who lived with them. The remaining couples either had no children or had been separated from them—
it is impossible to tell which. Fractionally under 60 percent of all the
women known to have given birth to at least one child appear not to
have had a husband, or the father of their children, living with them at
the time the inventory was taken. There is no way of knowing whether
the men in question were dead, living on a neighboring estate, or had

been sold away. Less than 1 percent of the men on the estates surveyed lived "alone" with their child or children.

A very similar pattern characterized Chatham County during the 1780s and 1790s. Almost exactly one-third of the bondwomen on those estates where marital and family relationships were recorded were married. Two-thirds of the couples listed had at least one child living with them. Just under 42 percent of women are known to have had at least one child, and 47 percent of these mothers (a decrease of 12 percent on the prewar figure) lived "alone" with their offspring. The same was true of 2 percent of men.[60]

The records suggest that during the late eighteenth century approximately half the bondwomen known to have been mothers were living apart from their husbands. With or without their owners' permission, husbands and fathers who lived on neighboring plantations visited their wives and children as often as possible and provided them with whatever material assistance they could.[61] Many women, however, whose partners did not live close at hand, were forced to confront the problem of how they could best provide for their own needs and for those of their children.

The amount and the kind of work done by men and women, young and old, family and nonfamily members of the household to the cultivation of gardens during this eighty-year period varied as individual and group needs and circumstances dictated. What did not vary, however, was the dual, and critically significant, purpose of those contributions. The various crops cultivated by bondpeople in their gardens and private fields supplemented immediate dietary needs. These crops also offered the prospect of surpluses that could be bartered or sold as part of the ongoing endeavor to raise living standards above bare subsistence. Exactly the same was true of the poultry, the pigs, and less frequently the cattle, almost universally kept by plantation bondpeople as an integral part of their domestic economy.[62]

Poultry, usually chickens, sometimes geese, ducks, pigeons, and turkeys, were raised in the quarters of most lowcountry plantations, and provided bondmen and bondwomen with an important "source of both protein and income."[63] As a general rule, bondpeople not only reared "as much poultry as they please" but "as many as they can."[64] On the Butler estates the "abundance" of poultry was said by Frances

Kemble to be "literally a nuisance."[65] Chickens might be allowed to range freely around the quarters, but efficient egg production necessitated the manufacture of coops.[66] By the 1820s and 1830s these were frequently remarked on by white commentators.[67] Other sources indicate that egg production was already a well-established feature of the informal slave economies by the turn of the eighteenth century.[68] Apart from the daily collection of eggs, said by Frances Kemble to be the bondpeople's "only wealth," poultry required comparatively little attention and their upkeep involved no significant expenditure.[69]

As with poultry, the rabbits and pigs bred by many bondpeople took up virtually none of their own time and cost nothing to feed.[70] Pigs might be reared in homemade pens or simply "marked on the ear and allowed to roam freely."[71] Those that were raised in pens had to be fed, and this was done by giving them "surplus corn and vegetables." As John Otto has pointed out, hogs "were ideal domestic stock" because they "converted one-fifth of what they ate into meat, and . . . had large, frequent litters."[72] By no means all planters were keen to allow their bondpeople to keep hogs anywhere in the vicinity of their own residence. As Frances Kemble explained, the bondpeople on her husband's estate "once were, but no longer are, permitted to keep pigs. The increase of filth and foul smells, consequent upon their being raised is, of course, very great." Her husband tried to justify the ban on hogs by suggesting that his bondmen and bondwomen did not have the wherewithal to feed them, but as Kemble unsuccessfully tried to persuade him, "their little 'Kailyard' . . . would suffice to it, and the pork and bacon would prove a most welcome addition to their farinaceous diet."[73]

In the mid-1750s Pastor Bolzius had reported that there were "few goats" but "enough sheep in Carolina, and a good number already in Georgia," but neither sheep nor goats figured to any great extent among the livestock kept by lowcountry planters or their bondpeople. This was simply because they "did not survive well in the coastal zone."[74] Cattle are also notable by their virtual absence from contemporary accounts of the animals raised by bondmen and bondwomen on their own behalf.[75]

Hunting, trapping, and fishing were another important way plantation bondpeople supplemented their diets and secured goods with which to trade. The land and the waterways of lowcountry Georgia offered an abundant and varied array of foodstuffs: game birds, rabbits, opossum, raccoons, squirrels, deer, salt- and freshwater fish, oysters, crabs, and turtles were all there for the taking.[76]

Plantation bondpeople displayed great ingenuity in exploiting these natural resources, and they did not feel in any way constrained to limit their activities to their owner's estate. Formal plantation boundaries were of little or no relevance to them. Much to the annoyance of the planters concerned, the bondpeople's hunting, trapping, fishing, and foraging expeditions, which often took place at night, might involve trips to neighboring plantations. Lachlan M'Gillivray was not alone in his complaint that "for some years past" bondpeople had been "cutting timber and marsh grass, and killing game, on my land, highly prejudicial to my interest."[77] For planters such as M'Gillivray the "trespasses" of which he complained proved as difficult to prevent as the nighttime excursions of bondmen and bondwomen to country stores and the gatherings they organized to celebrate the rituals of marriage and burial.

On most lowcountry plantations bondpeople had ready access to two of the main prerequisites for fishing and hunting: boats or canoes, often of their own manufacture, and firearms. From the mid-1750s they were not denied the right to be in possession of guns with which "to hunt and kill game Cattle Mischievious [sic] Birds or Beasts of Prey." In theory, guns could be carried only in the presence of a white person and had to be returned to the owner or overseer after their use, which could not be on the weekend. In practice, not all owners strictly enforced these requirements.[78] Archaeological evidence strongly supports the proposition that many plantation bondpeople had ready and regular access to guns. Indeed, Charles Ball commented that he had actually been given one as a present by his owner.[79] Hunting expeditions involving the use of firearms were usually made in the company, and thereby under the direct supervision, of the bondperson's owner or a male member of the owner's family. However, particularly trusted bondpeople might be allowed to hunt alone.

Other than the requirement that bondpeople not leave their owner's property without permission, there were no legal restrictions on trapping, as opposed to hunting with a gun. Trapping, whether of land or aquatic species, appears, like hunting, to have been a predominantly male activity, and it was one that demanded skill and resourcefulness.

No doubt some bondmen had acquired their knowledge in West Africa and subsequently passed it on to the young men in the quarters. Many plantation bondpeople proved adept at manufacturing an array of traps, snares, lines, and nets, skills that their owners sometimes sought to exploit.[80]

Plantation bondpeople also proved adept at adopting techniques that maximized their precious time. As William Hampton Adams has observed, trapping was "labor efficient for once the trap is set and baited, it can be left [and checked] periodically at one's convenience."[81] Charles Ball's "principal trapping ground was three miles from home" and he went there "three times a week, always after night, to bring home [his] game, and keep [his] traps in good order."[82] The practice of "garden hunting or trapping" was also cost- and time-effective because "garden predators [could] be trapped or shot during their nocturnal or twilight raids." This would not only safeguard crops "but also furnish extra food for the table."[83]

The flesh of the animals, birds, fish, and shellfish hunted, trapped, and collected by plantation bondpeople comprised an important element in their diets, but it could also be sold or bartered.[84] The hunting and trapping of wild species was important for another reason. Depending on the species, furs and skins could be sold or made up into hats, and sometimes into coats and shoes, to be worn by those whose owners did not provide them with these items of dress.[85]

Another important use for some animal skins was drum making. In the 1930s Robert Pinckney, an eighty-one-year-old African-American who lived on Wilmington Island, recollected that the "ole drums wut duh Africans make wuz make out ub a skin uh some kine uh animal stretch obuh a holluh lawg. Dey didn eben take duh haiah off duh skin. Jis put it on datta way."[86] Contemporaries of Pinckney mentioned that coon skins were particularly favored in drum making.[87] As in South Carolina, pelts that were inappropriate for drum making, or not needed for shoes, coats, and hats, probably found their way into the hands of white furriers or were sold to whites involved in the fur trade.[88]

In addition to hunting, trapping, and fishing, bondpeople exploited local environments in other ways that enhanced standards of living in the quarters. Wild plants, fruits, and berries could be picked for domestic consumption, barter, or sale. Other natural resources, which were widely and freely accessible, formed the basis of the handicraft industries that evolved in the quarters of many lowcountry plantations. Timber was one of the most abundant and versatile of the materials available to plantation bondpeople.

One of the most important and widespread uses of timber was in the construction of boats and canoes, which might be used by bondpeople for their fishing and marketing expeditions or sold to owners and neighboring whites.[89] Local timber was also used by bondpeople to manufacture items of furniture for their cabins. Contemporary white accounts, and recent archaeological research, suggest that "the furnishing of [cabins] was primitive."[90] On the Butler plantations, for example, bondpeople were reported as being without "chairs, tables, plates, knives [and] forks. . . . They sat . . . on the earth or doorsteps, and ate out of their little cedar tubs, or an iron pot, some few with broken iron spoons, more with pieces of wood, and all the children with their fingers."[91]

Most of the fixtures and fittings that were found in cabins were "of home manufacture." Enslaved carpenters and coopers, the men in the household, made "benches," chairs, and shelving from "alternate strips of redolent white cypress and fragrant red cedar." They also produced "boxes" and chests in which family members could store their clothing and other personal possessions.[92] As John Blassingame has pointed out, these items had a significance over and above the degree of material comfort they afforded. The bondman who provided for his family in this way, as well as by hunting, trapping, and fishing, "gained not only the approbation of his wife, but he also gained status in the quarters."[93]

Some of the workmanship of enslaved carpenters was of such a high quality that they were able to sell pieces of the furniture they had made in their own time to their owners. Frances Kemble, for example, recorded that the "cedar tubs" made by her husband's carpenter were of such "exceeding neat workmanship" that she and Pierce Butler used them "for our own household purposes." These same carpenters also made "the wash-stand, clothes presses, sofas, tables etc, with which our house is furnished."[94]

Wood was a universally and freely available natural resource and one used by bondpeople for purposes other than making furniture. For example, plantation bondpeople who lived within striking distance of

Savannah were able to take advantage of the urban demand for timber as a building material and as a fuel. William Grimes, who eventually managed to escape to the North, related that when he worked just outside Savannah for an owner who limited his rations to "a peck of corn per week" he had "often carried on my head a bundle of wood, perhaps three miles, weighing more than one hundred pounds, which I would sell for twelve cents in order to get a supply of necessary food."[95]

Another abundant natural resource available to plantation bond-people was moss. It could be collected and used as an insulating material for "their ill-protected dwellings" or for filling mattresses. Or it could be sold to local storekeepers as a stuffing for furniture. Some indication of the contribution reputedly made by moss to the informal slave economy is suggested by Frances Kemble's comment that one shopkeeper in Darien told her that over the years "he had paid the Negroes of [the Butler estate] several thousand dollars" for this particular commodity.[96] Rushes too were there to be gathered by plantation bond-people and made into mats and "not very durable" collars for horses and mules; "beautiful as well as serviceable baskets" for domestic use or for sale could be woven from wire grass or "wooden splits."[97] And brooms were manufactured from "young white oak or hickory trees."[98] With sufficient know-how reeds could be turned into fifes and flutes.[99]

Until the turn of the eighteenth century, local clays were used by bondpeople in lowcountry Georgia to make Colonoware, "the most common artifact associated with slavery on 18th-century sites."[100] Little is known about the techniques employed by enslaved potters, but clearly they were based on those described by some European visitors to West Africa.[101] In view of the cultural pretensions of most planters, it is unlikely that they would have been interested in purchasing Colonoware vessels from their bondpeople. But bondpeople might well have sold or bartered their pottery to poorer whites. By 1800 or thereabouts Colono-ware had been virtually displaced in lowcountry Georgia by cheaper, mass-produced British ceramics that bondpeople either purchased for themselves or were given by their owners.[102]

Like hunting and trapping, the handicraft industries that developed on lowcountry plantations, especially those that involved woodworking skills, tended to be predominantly male activities. Artisanal skills that bondmen practiced during the working day on behalf of their owners were an invaluable asset in the forging of the informal slave economies. Many of those crafts, however, including pottery and boat building, were not learned from Europeans but were firmly rooted in the West African backgrounds of the practitioners.

From the beginning of slavery in Georgia, bondmen and bondwomen emulated their counterparts in the other British plantation colonies. From an often desperate need and a strong desire to enhance their living standards they gardened, raised livestock, hunted, trapped, fished, and tapped their local environments for the natural resources that would form the basis of their handicraft industries.

Plantation bondpeople in the Georgia lowcountry were able to supplement the meager food rations issued by their owners. But with the exception of a few items, notably shoes and hats, they were unable to exploit the natural resources to augment the equally minimal clothing they received. Additional clothing, or the fabric to make it, might be obtained by the barter or sale of commodities produced in their own time. But clothing as well as other items could be acquired by the sale of something else. By the mid-1770s, if not earlier, one of the most explicit ways in which bondmen and bondwomen in lowcountry Georgia were asserting their right to their own time, and in the process enhancing their living standards, was by negotiating terms for the sale of their labor on Sundays and after their weekday's work. This not only shaped the way in which plantation bondpeople divided their own time between their various productive and recreational activities but also demonstrated the extent to which their owners and other whites were forced to acknowledge their right to that time.

The earliest evidence, from 1773, of lowcountry Georgia bondpeople negotiating terms for Sunday work involved twenty bondmen and bondwomen owned by Gov. James Wright. Wright was away in England and had left the management of his rice plantations in the hands of his friend James Habersham. In the summer of 1773 Habersham reported to Wright the difficulties he had encountered when trying to move twenty "good Hands" from one of the governor's plantations to another "for a complete week." Habersham was taken aback when the bondpeople concerned simply refused to comply with his wishes. He quickly realized that it would behoove him to negotiate terms with them. These bondmen and bondwomen adamantly refused to travel or to work on the two Sundays that would have been involved in their transfer without first ensuring that they would be recompensed. Habersham found himself agreeing to pay them "half a Crown a Piece for the two Sundays" and a "Dram Each" upon their arrival at their temporary workplace. Habersham assured Wright that his money had been "prudently bestowed, as it will make the People happy, and save [you] a great many barrels of Rice." [103]

By the late eighteenth century, plantation bondpeople in lowcountry Georgia had established the customary right to sell their labor during their own time. It was a right many of them exercised on a regular basis, usually, but not exclusively, on Sundays. As Charles Ball commented, "The practice of working on Sunday" was "universal." [104] Sometimes, as was the case with Wright's bondpeople, negotiations would be conducted with the owner or the owner's representative. On other occasions bondmen and bondwomen negotiated for the sale of their labor with overseers who owned land but not the hands to work it. They might also work for a neighboring planter who wished to hire their labor, and they did not necessarily rely on their owners to act as go-betweens. The terms of employment negotiated by bondpeople and the payments they demanded, usually as cash in hand, varied. Plantation bondpeople were sometimes able to drive a hard bargain. At harvest time, for example, their prospective employers had the choice of trying to physically coerce them into performing the extra work required, haggling over demands for payment, or watching at least some of the crop spoil in the fields. James Habersham was not alone among lowcountry planters in finding negotiation the easiest course to follow.

By the mid-1760s plantation bondpeople in lowcountry Georgia were producing not only enough foodstuffs to satisfy their own basic dietary requirements, as well as many of the utensils they required, but also surpluses. Moreover, through the sale of their labor they were beginning to secure variable cash incomes. From one standpoint the spending power represented by these incomes might be considered so minute as to be inconsequential. The $1,500.00 James Hamilton Couper bragged about being able to distribute among the twenty-five bondmen he forced to participate in his "experiment" at Hopeton amounted to $60.00 each, or $1.15 per man per week. The "$5 or $6" made by William Grimes when he sold his rice in Savannah, the "twelve cents" he received for the "more than one hundred pounds" of wood that he carried on his head to the town represented a minuscule rate of financial return on the time he had spent growing, collecting, and delivering these items.

That plantation bondpeople did not derive fortunes from the sale of their produce and their labor is indisputable. But given the physical demands of the work they were coerced into performing for their owners, the remarkable thing is not that they generated such modest incomes in their own time but that they had the strength, the endurance, and the commitment to produce and earn as much as they did. Whether by the sale of their produce, their labor, or both, the sums made by Grimes and by the bondmen on Hopeton and other lowcountry estates were profoundly meaningful to them and to their families. This money enabled them to raise their standard of living above the bare, crude subsistence deemed appropriate for them by their owners. This money enabled them to acquire what were, in the context of the minimal rations and shabby clothing, the uniforms of slavery, provided by their owners, comforts and luxuries. The money also afforded them a degree of autonomy, with options and choices in their lives. Not least of all, this money could be used by bondpeople in ways that provided a tangible expression of their love and respect for one another. But like so much else in the bondpeople's lives, achieving these objectives— and the enjoyment, the satisfaction, and the dignity gained by their realization—was a continuous struggle.

By the mid-eighteenth century lowcountry planters acknowledged that bondpeople had a right to the commodities they produced and the cash income they earned in their own time. They conceded, in effect had been forced to concede, that the crops bondpeople cultivated in their gardens, the poultry and livestock they raised, and the artifacts they manufactured in their own time were their "property" and that "their Little Estates" were not there simply for the taking.[105] But they sought to severely curtail the use bondpeople sought to make of that right.

Plantation owners were virtually unanimous in disputing not the right of ownership, or even the right of bondpeople to compensation for their goods and for the labor they performed in their own time, but the right of bondpeople to dispose of their property and spend their cash income as they saw fit. In the continuing battle to secure their rights as autonomous consumers as well as producers, a battle fought mainly but

not solely against their owners, bondpeople found that they were not entirely alone. They were not without white allies. By the late eighteenth
century bondpeople's insistence that they be allowed to enjoy rights as
producers and consumers was bitterly dividing the lowcountry's white
society. The endeavor and enterprise of bondpeople themselves were in
large measure responsible for the appearance of divisions that, through
the remainder of the antebellum period, they sought to turn to their
own advantage.

3 🌿 *Economic Transactions in the Countryside*

BY THE EARLY 1760s Georgia owners were discovering that which had long been known to their counterparts in the other plantation colonies. They might trim their costs by forcing bondpeople to spend part of their own time working to support themselves, but this entailed costs of another kind, not only to themselves but also to the broader interests of white society. One of these costs, as bondpeople successfully resisted attempts to make them work for nothing in their own time, was the erosion of the absolute authority claimed by owners. Increasingly, however, other costs came to be identified. These stemmed from an industry that manifested itself in the production of surpluses for barter or sale.

The exchange of surpluses within the quarters, and the negotiations these transactions entailed, aroused little or no interest on the part of owners. But when bondmen and bondwomen sought to extend their trading networks beyond the plantation, intervention rapidly became the order of the day. Most owners felt compelled to try to enforce those sections of the slave code that denied bondwomen and bondmen the right to trade on their own behalf, to freely choose their trading partners, and to negotiate the best possible terms for the disposal of their surpluses and the purchase of the goods and services they sought in return. This involved another, equally unsuccessful, endeavor: trying to deter those whites drawn from every stratum of society who were prepared to contravene the law and do business with bondpeople. Black initiatives and white complicity ensured that the ideal, enshrined in successive slave codes, of confining trading activities to the plantation or sanctioning them elsewhere only with the express consent of owners could never be fully realized.

Before the Revolutionary War self-interest, rather than any broader moral, religious, or social purpose, informed both public and private attempts to closely regulate the trading activities of lowcountry Georgia's bondpeople. Moreover, those activities were not the subject of debate, but were universally denounced by local commentators as being detrimental to white interests. No voices were to be heard, as they were by the early years of the nineteenth century, suggesting that the encouragement of black economic initiative might well redound to the benefit not only of owners but also to white society as a whole.[1]

During the 1760s and early 1770s owners and other concerned whites offered two reasons why it was imperative that the trading activities of bondmen and bondwomen be restricted to the estates on which they lived. The first emphasized the physical, rather than the economic, well-being of white society. Slave patrols and urban watches, with their extensive powers of search and seizure, offered some reassurance to whites but did not assuage the fear that racial disorder, possibly even organized rebellion on a scale that would topple white society, might be one of the consequences of a completely unfettered right to trade off the plantation.[2] The other reason often given for cracking down on the trading activities of bondpeople was that to condone any independent marketing was tantamount to encouraging theft. Bondpeople, it was widely held, would not hesitate to steal from their owners or from other whites in order to acquire goods with which to trade.[3]

Not until the turn of the eighteenth century, when bondwomen and bondmen had come to virtually monopolize the supply of certain commodities to the lowcountry's urban markets, did some white critics begin to cite another specifically economic reason for quashing the independent marketing of goods by bondpeople. These commentators said little about the desirability of protecting the interests of white producers. Their argument hinged instead on what they depicted as the exploitation of urban consumers who, they alleged, were being charged excessively high prices by bondpeople who essentially controlled the supply of fresh foodstuffs to the lowcountry towns. Indeed, these commentators claimed, urban consumers were being held to ransom by bondpeople in a totally unacceptable manner.[4]

Before the American War of Independence, patterns of consumption were seldom cited as a reason for severely restricting the trading activities of bondpeople. Only one of the items they reputedly sought on a regular and widespread basis, hard liquor, caused any significant degree of white consternation. As with white assumptions regarding the propensity of bondmen and bondwomen to steal, the anxiety expressed by whites about the drinking habits of bondpeople was essentially pragmatic in character. Planters such as James Houstoun, who issued a public warning to the effect that he would not hesitate to prosecute "all persons" who gave or sold liquor to his bondpeople, were far more concerned with trying to prevent the uninhibited and possibly threatening behavior that drunken bondpeople might exhibit than they were in instilling a Christian morality that attached significance to sobriety.[5]

From the mid-1750s, when Pastor Bolzius wrote that bondmen and bondwomen worked on Sundays and after their weekday's work to obtain the wherewithal to buy "trifles" and "some necessary things," planters and other white commentators often remarked on the trading activities of bondpeople both on and off the plantation.[6] Usually these white critics contented themselves with generalities about the precise character of the trade conducted between plantation bondpeople and their owners. However, they often emphasized the desirability of trying to restrict the trading activities of bondmen and bondwomen to the plantations upon which they lived. For instance, one unnamed overseer declared that "Negroes should in no instance be permitted to trade, except with their masters" for the simple reason that if they were allowed "to leave the plantation with the view of selling and buying" they might be tempted "to roguery," by which he meant theft and drunkenness. It was far more sensible, he concluded, for "each planter [to] have upon his place, a store of such articles as his slaves usually purchase elsewhere."[7]

Other white commentators echoed the words of James Houstoun and averred that if left entirely to their own devices bondmen and bondwomen would expend the bulk of their income "on tobacco and whiskey."[8] By their own admission plantation bondpeople were keen to obtain tobacco. The persistent allegation that they would sell "everything" they produced and, if necessary, appropriate goods that could be traded "for liquor" is more a reflection of white anxieties and expectations than of the actual spending habits of bondmen and bondwomen.[9] The enslaved population of lowcountry Georgia did consume alcohol, but not to the excess claimed by many whites.

From the mid-1750s onward many owners waged a generally unsuccessful struggle to enforce the letter of the law: restricting the trading activities of bondpeople to the confines of the plantation and ensuring that any transactions conducted elsewhere took place only with their blessing. Subtlety was not always the order of the day. In 1765, for instance, John Stevens, of Josephtown, complained in the *Georgia Gazette* that "it has been a common practice for trading boats and others to land their people, and remain whole nights and days on the plantation, to the great prejudice of the subscriber." Stevens warned "all trading boats and others" that any "negro or negroes" found on his plantation "not having a proper note from their owners, shall be whipped according to law, if in the day time." He added that "for the better securing my property by night" he intended to install "two spring-man-traps near my landing and dwelling house, and keep fire arms ready in case of the least attempt." Two years earlier another planter, Patrick Mackay, had adopted a similar approach by announcing that he was "determined to treat all negroes . . . found within my fence after sun-set, and before sun-rise, as thieves, robbers and invaders of his property, by shooting them." Mackay declared that he had "hired a white man properly armed for that purpose."[10]

Stevens and Mackay were seeking to prevent what they depicted as the regular theft of their produce and livestock, not by their own bondmen and bondwomen but by those belonging to other owners. They remained silent, at least in print, as to whether the former colluded with these "invaders." Nevertheless the "spring-man-traps" and armed guards designed to deter unauthorized visitors to their estates must have made it more difficult, but not totally impossible, for their own bondmen and bondwomen to trade off the plantation during the hours of darkness.

The measures favored by Stevens and Mackay never gained widespread currency in the Georgia lowcountry. Most owners were security conscious, but rather than trying to turn their plantations into armed fortresses many sought to remove the incentive for their bondpeople to forge trading links with outsiders, free or enslaved, by offering what amounted to a guaranteed market for their surpluses and a supply of the goods they sought to acquire. The belief that it might prove possible to monopolize the trading activities of plantation bondpeople was already finding favor among the planters of the lowcountry during the decade before the Revolutionary War. Although never implemented with total success, it was an approach that retained its advocates, and attracted no significant criticism, for the remainder of the antebellum period.

The surplus produce the bondmen and bondwomen of the lowcountry might choose to sell to their owners or overseers included the crops they cultivated in their gardens, the fish and game they caught, the wild fruits and honey they collected, the poultry and hogs they reared, eggs, and certain of the handicraft they made in their own time.[11] The commodities plantation bondpeople sought from their owners and others in exchange for their surpluses were those they could not produce for themselves in their own time and, other than tobacco and liquor, they fell into three main categories: food, fabric and ready-made clothing, and utensils. On most plantations, through their own enterprise and industry, bondmen and bondwomen had sufficient fruit, vegetables, eggs, meat, and fish for their immediate needs. They were unable to produce dry goods; and items such as "tea, coffee, sugar, flour and all such articles of diet as are not provided by their masters" figured prominently among the commodities they sought from sources including their owners and overseers.[12]

Bondpeople also needed utensils in which to cook their food. Gourds of various kinds could be used for storing liquids, or as drinking vessels; plates and containers could be made from local clays or wood. Heat-resistant pots and pans, however, items mentioned in many contemporary white accounts of the contents of bondpeople's cabins, could not easily be made from the resources plantation bondpeople had at their disposal.[13]

Bondmen and bondwomen displayed remarkable skill in exploiting their local environments in an attempt to enhance their living standards, but they were severely limited in the use they could make of those environments when it came to meeting one of their most pressing needs: clothing. Plantation owners in the lowcountry sought to minimize their production costs by severely limiting the rations they issued to their bondpeople. Precisely the same rationale operated when it came to clothing them. The assumption of owners, and the reality facing their bondmen and bondwomen, was that the latter must work in their own time not only to feed themselves but also "to earn their few clothes." [14]

Throughout this period most plantation owners provided their bond-people—particularly their field hands, female as well as male—with an absolute minimum of clothing. Pastor Bolzius reported that in the summer some owners issued their bondmen with "a pair of pants of coarse linen and a cap or bad hat for the head" but that many others permitted them "to go naked, except [they] cover their shame with a cloth rag." Bondwomen generally received "a short skirt of coarse linen" or "a petticoat," which left their "upper body . . . bare." They, too, might be given "a handkerchief to cover the head." Bondpeople generally received warmer clothes for the winter when they "must be kept warm": possibly a surtout, or greatcoat, and "a blue or white camisole, a pair of long pants of cloth down to the shoes, no shirt, and a woollen cap." Bolzius estimated that the total cost of clothing each bondperson "comes to about 10s." per bondperson per year. [15]

Some variations existed in the quality and amount of clothing issued to plantation bondpeople, but the standard practice on most estates was for bondmen to be given a jacket and a pair of trousers annually. Published advertisements for fugitives, arguably one of the most informative sources for any analysis of bondpeople's clothing, reveals that smaller proportions of bondmen wore shirts and an even smaller percentage waistcoats, or undervests. Bondwomen were usually issued a dress and, sometimes, a petticoat once a year. All these garments might be bought in ready-made or, on larger plantations, run up by the overseer's wife or by the bondpeople themselves from fabric provided by the owner.

Jackets and trousers were most commonly made of negro cloth, "the coarsest thickest cloth," [16] and oznabrig, less often of homespun. In addition to these three fabrics at least sixteen other types of material, including bearskins and deerskins, were made up into jackets, and seventeen other materials, including wool, corduroy, and nankeen, into trousers or, as they were sometimes referred to, breeches, pantaloons, or overalls.

Oznabrig seems to have been the favored material for shirts, although only a small proportion of bondmen were reported as wearing them. A few shirts were described as being made from various forms of linen and wool; only one was said specifically to have been made from cotton. Waistcoats, or undervests, were made from various fabrics: negro cloth, flannel, shag, nankeen, and swansdown were mentioned by owners. Some planters issued their bondpeople boots or shoes made of leather or cotton, but many did not. Hats and caps of various styles appear in the list of items worn by male fugitives; these might be made of fabric, furs, or from palmetto. It was the common practice for newly imported West African men to be given hats or caps, as well as jackets and trousers.

Bondwomen generally received "a wrapper and petticoat" each year from their owner and periodically a jacket or coat.[17] The published advertisements for female runaways are somewhat less informative than they are for men, but they do suggest rather less variation in the fabrics used in the manufacture of women's clothing. Bondwomen might wear a hat, but apparently not as often as did men, and many more of them seem to have favored handkerchiefs. Only one female fugitive was reported to have been wearing shoes at the time she took flight.

The published advertisements for fugitive bondpeople suggest that there was something of a monotonous uniformity about the amount, the design, and the fabrics of their clothing throughout this period. But advertisements also indicate that there were important variations in the style and color of bondpeople's clothing as well as in the materials from which that clothing was made. A few examples drawn at random from the pages of the lowcountry newspapers will suffice to make the point.

In 1767, for instance, an unnamed bondman who ran away from David Murray was said by his owner to have "carried with him a green coatee, a snuff coloured broad cloth coat broke under the arm, black knit stocking breeches, duck breeches with negro cloth boots, and an old beaver hat with a black satin or silver lace hat-band with a silver buckle." Brutus, a twenty-year-old country-born bondman who absconded in 1783, "had on an old much worn negro cloth jacket, oznabrig overalls broken in the knees, and tied above the ankle with red garters, and a black hat with a tinsel band." In 1805 Thomas Smith noted that his "Negro fellow, Peter, had on when he went away a drab top coat, blue jacket, with yellow cape and cuffs, and blue overalls."[18]

The attire of bondwomen could be just as diverse. Binah, who ran away from Katherine Troup in 1793, "had on a blue negro cloth coat, brown wrapper, grey cloak, shoes and a red striped handkerchief around her head." In 1809 Lucy took flight wearing "a grey bath coating wrapper and striped homespun petticoat." When Sally, a sixteen-year-old country-born woman, absconded in 1816, she was said by her owner to be wearing "a check homespun frock, no shoes or bonnet." The following year Betsey was clad in "a blue homespun frock" and, like Binah, had a "red checkered handkerchief round her head and neck." [19]

Possibly because they did not possess them, the vast majority of bondmen and bondwomen carried with them no more clothes than those they wore on their backs at the time they took flight. In those comparatively rare cases where fugitives were said to have taken extra clothing with them, owners were far more likely to itemize the garments taken by men than they were to list those taken by women. There is no obvious explanation for this different pattern of reporting, but one possibility is that owners were less familiar with the amount and type of clothing acquired by their bondwomen than they were with that in the possession of their bondmen.

The clothing taken by fugitives could range from a single item— a jacket, a pair of trousers, or a wrapper—to comparatively extensive wardrobes. According to his owner, Aleck, who ran away in 1789, "took with him . . . a white negro cloth jacket with a black cape to it, one pair black breeches, one pair nankeen ditto, one white shirt, [and] two felt hats." Nancy, who absconded in 1810, "took away with her one blue calico gown with white sleeves, two homespun ones, one blue and the other white; three shifts and some mock madras handkerchiefs." Eight years later Smart, who was wearing "a negro cloth jacket and pantaloons of white" when he ran away, "carried with him two round jackets, one of dark woollen, and the other of blue homespun, two checked shirts, oznabrig trousers, and a pair of negro shoes." [20] Arguably the main significance of these garments was, as one owner explained in 1800, that they were "dress clothes" and not working clothes. [21] Dress clothes, or the fabrics with which to make them, featured among the top purchasing priorities of bondpeople.

Some owners suggested that their bondmen and bondwomen took considerable pride in their appearance. Martha, for instance, who ran away from Robert Montfort in 1793, was said to be "fond of dress," and

Binah, who fled in 1817, was "neat in her dress." Willis, a twenty-five-year-old mulatto, was described by his master as being "very dressy and genteel in person."[22] Clothing, jewelry—rings, earrings, and beads—and distinctive hairstyles were ways in which bondmen and bond-women could assert themselves and their individuality not only to each other but also to their owners and other whites.[23] A preference for vibrant colors, particularly red, served essentially the same purpose. As Eugene Genovese has pointed out, the reasons for this partiality for red are not entirely clear, but it may well have been deeply rooted in the bondpeople's West African heritages.[24]

Bondmen and bondwomen attached great significance to their clothing and their appearance. In the majority of cases, it may be posited, self-adornment, and the financial outlay it entailed, was not frivolous expenditure or merely conspicuous consumption. Rather, it was an integral aspect, a visible expression, of a continuing struggle to assert individuality, dignity, pride, and self-worth.

Generally speaking, plantation bondpeople secured their clothing and footwear from four main sources. First, there was that issued by their owners, which might include castoffs as well as the jackets, trousers, wrappers, and petticoats that they bought or had made up on the plantation. Second, they might obtain their dress clothes, or the fabric to make them, from a country storekeeper or, if they lived in the vicinity of Savannah, Sunbury, or Darien, from an urban retailer. Third, it seems evident from the surviving transcripts of trials that bondpeople sometimes appropriated items of clothing. Fourth, and for many plantation bondmen and bondwomen a convenient option, clothes might be obtained from their owners and paid for with the proceeds of the sale of surplus produce or Sunday work, or both. It is likely that at times plantation bondpeople resorted to some combination of these options.

The economic transactions conducted between plantation bond-people and their owners involved three often interlocking components: the sale of bondpeople's surplus goods, their labor-for-hire, and the owners' provision of commodities, notably clothing, fabric, and utensils. Contrary to the stipulations of the public slavery laws owners were, in fact, forced to concede bondpeople's right to the goods they produced and any income they earned in their own time.

Plantation bondpeople negotiated two kinds of agreement with their owners. The first, which was entered into between Henry Laurens, Henry Ravenel, and their bondmen and bondwomen in the mid-1760s, and on many other plantations during the next three-quarters of a century, involved owners agreeing to purchase some or all of the surpluses produced by their bondpeople and providing them in return with most of the commodities they wished to acquire. On larger plantations this might entail the setting up of a store where transactions were conducted.

Other owners paid cash for their bondpeople's produce or services but did not supply the goods they sought on a regular basis, possibly because proximity to an urban market such as Savannah, Darien, or Sunbury made this a pointless exercise. This appears to have been the case on a plantation visited by Basil and Margaret Hall in the late 1820s. The owner and his family were "supplied entirely with poultry and eggs" they purchased from their bondmen and bondwomen. On this unidentified estate bondpeople were "regularly paid at the following rates: Eggs 12.5 cents (6d) a dozen; chickens 12.5 cents (6d), fowls 20 to 25 cents, or about a shilling a pair; ducks twice as much." According to Hall, though, they were "left at liberty to carry their poultry to a better market if they can find one."[25]

The comparative popularity of these two types of agreement, and how the balance between them might have changed over time, is difficult to ascertain. However, from the mid-1750s onward the disposal of the surpluses produced by bondpeople, and the acquisition of the goods they needed and wanted, was a matter for negotiation on every lowcountry plantation. The majority of planters were simply unwilling to leave their bondpeople entirely to their own devices. For their part, bondmen and bondwomen recognized that conducting at least some of their business with their owners might be to their own advantage.

Who among Henry Laurens's plantation bondpeople acted as spokespersons, and whether they approached their owner or vice versa, is not recorded. By 1765, however, an agreement had been reached whereby Laurens, who lived in Charleston and seems seldom to have visited his plantations in either South Carolina or Georgia, promised to pay his bondmen and bondwomen the current market price for the rice they produced in their gardens and to secure on their behalf in Charleston the goods they wished to buy. Should the need arise, and provided the overseers were absolutely certain that it was not stolen property but "lawfully belongs to themselves," Laurens's overseers were also authorized to bargain with his bondpeople not only for their rice but also for their "provision . . . at the lowest price that they will sell it for." [26]

Typically, or so it appears, there was no written contract between Laurens and his bondpeople. But in order to avoid any misunderstanding all concerned had a vested interest in ensuring that a formal and regular record was kept of their transactions. Later reports from the lowcountry suggest that bondmen and bondwomen "kept their own accounts," but if any of these were in written form, none seem to have survived. [27] The only extant records kept by lowcountry planters before the 1830s that comprise anything more than the occasional jotting down of an item of produce received and the price paid for it are those kept by Henry Laurens during the mid-1760s and the rather more elaborate reports of the transactions (1763–66 and 1828–33) on Hanover Plantation, a South Carolina estate owned by the Ravenel family. [28]

The bookkeeping procedure employed by Laurens and the Ravenels, and probably by other owners whose dealings with their bondwomen and bondmen were not conducted on an entirely ad hoc basis, was simple. The quantity and value of the commodities purchased from individual bondpeople was listed "on the credit side" and "opposite to that" the amount and cost of "such goods as they take." [29] How often money actually changed hands and how the accounts were balanced is less clear from the records.

Sometimes owners "settled with [their bondpeople] annually, as [they] would with strangers and paid in cash for all [they] had purchased of them during the year." [30] On other estates bondmen and bondwomen demanded and received cash in hand from their owner or overseer for goods and services as and when they supplied them. James Gunnell, for instance, employed as an overseer by "the misses Telfair," reported to his employers that "Andrew sends 5 chickens [and] Jonus sends 8 chickens" and both bondmen "wants the money for them." [31]

The 1829–33 records that have survived for Hanover Plantation show bondmen and bondwomen periodically paying off all or part of an outstanding debt to their owner but do not specify whether payments were made in cash or kind. Similarly, Ravenel recorded his indebtedness to his bondpeople for their produce, but did not indicate whether those debts were settled by cash payments or remained as credits against which purchases could be set.[32] One thing that is clear from the Ravenel records, however, is the absence of interest charges on outstanding debts, whoever owed them. No owner or other white commentator referred to the collection of interest on any lowcountry plantation. Obviously it would be inadvisable to extrapolate overall trading patterns for the lowcountry for this eighty-year period wholly from the records kept by Laurens and the Ravenels. However, these materials do offer valuable, if limited, insights into the character and frequency of what was clearly a profoundly important area of negotiation between the enslaved population of lowcountry Georgia and their owners.

The accounts kept by Laurens and the Ravenels, and the more infrequent descriptions of practices on other estates, confirm that the surpluses that bondpeople most often disposed of to their owners consisted of garden produce, poultry, eggs, meat, and fish. On Hanover Plantation in the mid-1760s fowls, hogs, and corn together comprised 63 percent of all the recorded transactions involving the supply of goods and services to Henry Ravenel by his bondpeople. Poultry accounted for 37 percent of all transactions, hogs for just under 15 percent, and corn for fractionally more than 11 percent. The supply of skills "or a product of skills," including a tub and a basket, and commodities that "reflected the slaves' ability to exploit the environment for fish, honey, or wood" each accounted for 18.5 percent of known transactions.[33]

The Laurens and Ravenel records also indicate that, as white commentators reported throughout this period, the goods most frequently sought by plantation bondpeople in return for their surpluses were molasses or sugar, fabrics, and ready-made clothing. Tobacco does not appear among the items sold by either Laurens or the Ravenels to their bondmen and bondwomen. Rather more predictably, neither does alcohol.

In 1765 and 1766 the wares Henry Laurens ordered for his plantation bondpeople, which presumably they had requested and he expected them to buy, included "15 very gay Wascoat[s] [sic]," "10 Gross short pipes," "Yellow Porringers & Muggs," "Blue Stroud," a dozen hats, seven "home Stove[s]," and assorted "Iron Pots."[34] Laurens suggested a price for each item, but allowed his overseers a certain degree of flexibility in their negotiations with his bondpeople. In 1765, for instance, when rice was fetching 7s. 6d. per bushel in Charleston, Laurens proposed to charge ten bushels of rice for each of the "Wastcoat[s] [*sic*]," which he thought some of his bondmen "may want," unless his overseer thought "them worth more or less." In order to strengthen the latter's negotiating position, Laurens added the comment that the price he was asking represented real value for money because "Wastcoat[s] [*sic*]" of a similar quality that had "to be made up . . . would cost about £4 or £4.10s." [35] To buy a waistcoat from him would mean a savings of between five and fifteen shillings. The asking price for hats, presumably depending on their style or quality, was either 12s.6d. or 15s.; the various "Iron Pots" were to be sold by the overseer "for what they are worth." [36] Bearing in mind that this is an isolated, and not necessarily typical, list of the goods supplied by Laurens and presumably sought by his bondpeople, it is of note that it included no foodstuffs nor any items of ready-made clothing for bondwomen.

The later Ravenel records provide a richly detailed account of the commodities purchased by bondpeople from their owner on Hanover Plantation between November 1829 and 1833. During this time goods to the value of fractionally more than $55.00 were purchased by twenty-one bondmen and twenty-two bondwomen whose average expenditure was just under $1.28. [37] How these bondpeople earned at least part of the money they spent with Ravenel is suggested by the separate list he kept of the fowls and meat he bought from them. For some reason Ravenel kept the account of his payments in shillings and pence and that itemizing the goods purchased by his bondpeople in dollars and cents. [38]

Bondmen accounted for slightly under 55 percent of the total known to have been spent on goods supplied by Ravenel. Their per capita expenditure averaged $1.43, compared to that of $1.13 for bondwomen. The three leading purchasers were men. They included Senty, a carpenter, the only bondperson whose occupation Ravenel noted. Between them, these three men spent $9.90, close to one-third of all known male expenditures and 18 percent of the total male and female expenditures combined. Only one woman, Mary, spent as much as $3.00. The top three women spenders bought goods totaling $8.06 in value. This represented fractionally under 32 percent of all female expenditures and just over 14 percent of all expenditures. Together, these three men

and three women accounted for one-third of the money handed over to
Ravenel. At the other end of the spectrum, the outlay of the five men
who spent least totaled $1.68, or 5.5 percent of male expenditure and
10 percent of all expenditure. The five women who spent least parted
with $1.07, roughly 4 percent of female expenditure and 1.9 percent of
all expenditure. At neither end of the scale were there dramatic gender
differentiations in the amounts of money spent.

Ravenel's records reinforce the contention that bondpeople considered their attire important. For bondmen and bondwomen alike, fabric
and to a lesser extent, based on cash outlay, ready-made clothes were
a top spending priority. Together, these items accounted for almost
exactly 80 percent of total expenditure. Presumably because of the comparative costs involved (and bondpeople's ability to sew) the purchase
of fabric was far and away the favored option of those who, it may be
safely assumed, were in search of dress clothes. The fabrics bought from
Ravenel were mainly homespun, which he offered at $.20 per yard, or
$.25 if it were twilled, and calico, a much cheaper choice at $.13 per
yard. In all, at least 106 yards of homespun and 90 yards of calico were
purchased by Ravenel's bondpeople. The prices they paid indicate they
bought considerably less "pavilion gauze" and "check" than they did
homespun and calico.

Ready-made clothes, which predictably were comparatively more
expensive to buy than the fabric needed to make them, featured far less
prominently on the record of purchases than did fabrics. When they
did appear on Ravenel's list they tended to be for men rather than for
women. But relatively few men could afford, or chose, to buy ready-
made clothing from their owner. Senty, the carpenter, spent $1.00 on
"a Coat" and Hector, who spent the most of any bondperson in this
category, bought two waistcoats for $.63 and two handkerchiefs valued
at $.75. He also spent $1.50 on fabric. August bought two handkerchiefs, as did Morris. Joe and Isaac paid the asking price of $1.50 for
two "Dutch covers." Bondwomen spent comparatively less on ready-
made clothing than did bondmen, and apparently the few items they
did purchase were not for themselves but for men, although Nancy
and Beck did buy themselves "aprons." Maria's purchases included a
waistcoat as well as fabric, and Saby spent $.50 on "pantaloons" and a
waistcoat. Whether these were gifts, which the women paid for out of

their own income, or whether they reflected purchases paid for out of joint earnings is impossible to discern.

No foodstuffs other than molasses were purchased from Ravenel by his bondpeople during this time. Neither did they buy any pots, pans, or other utensils from him. Tobacco and the pipes to smoke it in were also absent from the list of commodities purchased from Ravenel. Either they had supplies of these items already to hand, possibly growing their own tobacco, or they secured them from sources other than their owner.

From Ravenel's perspective, although not necessarily from those of his bondmen and bondwomen, the sums of money he dutifully recorded were modest in the extreme. The important point, however, is that he kept written accounts, principally to avoid misunderstandings with his bondpeople, who may or may not have kept written records of their own but who almost certainly kept a mental tally of what they had spent. Ravenel's written records and his bondpeople's tally, whatever form that tally took, were essential because of the credit arrangements that had been negotiated on Hanover plantation.

If they had the money, which in the case of larger sums might have involved some form of saving or borrowing from one another, bondpeople paid the full amount for their goods in cash at the time they obtained them. But they could also buy goods from Ravenel on credit. In 1830, for instance, a bondman named Jeffrey made a down payment of $.94, either in cash or kind, toward the purchase of "twilled homespun" priced by Ravenel at $1.04. In the same year Nancy bought "Calico and an apron" valued at $1.37 with a down payment of $.87. A list compiled by Ravenel, probably in 1833, shows the outstanding balances between himself and twenty-nine of his bondpeople, sixteen men and thirteen women. Thirteen bondmen and nine bondwomen were in debt to Ravenel to the tune of fractionally under $24.00, getting on for 44 percent of the total spent by his bondpeople between late 1829 and 1833. The average male indebtedness hovered close to $1.36; the average female indebtedness was roughly half that, about $.70 per woman. The largest individual debt was $3.50, owed by a man named Philip, who may have paid off some or all of his arrears when Ravenel bought four "Fowls" from him. The most owed by a woman was Hannah's $1.44. Like Philip, Hannah may have cleared at least some of her debt by selling six "Fowls" to her owner.

There is no readily available explanation as to why, at least on Ravenel's plantation, bondmen ran up larger debts to their owner than did bondwomen. Men without family responsibilities may have been less reluctant to run up debts. Perhaps they were more confident than unattached women that in due course the debt could be paid off through the sale of their skills or surplus produce or both. In some cases the debts incurred by men may have represented a family, rather than an individual, liability. The same may have been true of women like Hannah, whose purchases of cloth and molasses could have been for family, rather than simply personal, consumption. No evidence suggests that bondwomen sought more credit but were denied it by Ravenel. On the other side of the ledger, Ravenel was indebted to seven of his bondpeople, three men and four women, for the sum of $5.50. It is not clear whether he settled these debts with periodic cash payments or, with their agreement, set them against the anticipated future purchases of the men and women concerned.

The bondwomen on Hanover Plantation did not assume the sole responsibility for the purchase of goods from their owner; neither do they appear to have been solely responsible for the purchase of specific goods. The total number of transactions known to have been conducted by women (forty) was not significantly larger than that of those made by men (thirty-six). Moreover, bondmen and bondwomen bought similar commodities and spent roughly the same proportion of their total expenditure on them.

Henry Laurens in the 1760s was one of the first lowcountry planters, but certainly not the last, to appreciate that he could never be entirely certain of monopolizing the trading activities of the bondpeople on his estates. Every owner who operated a plantation store or its equivalent faced the same problem: his bondpeople would do business there only as and when it suited them to do so. Owners could try to convince their bondmen and bondwomen of the advantages of trading with them and threaten them with various punishments if they did not, but they could not actually restrict their transactions to the plantation. From first to last, rural bondpeople dealt with their owners from choice and convenience, not because of coercion or a lack of alternative trading partners.

For plantation bondpeople there could be distinct advantages in conducting at least some of their trading activities with their owners. Provided that acceptable prices could be negotiated, the sheer convenience of having an assured and readily accessible outlet for their surpluses must have been an attractive proposition. By the same token, if owners were willing to supply the goods sought by their bondwomen and bondmen at competitive prices there was little reason for them to look elsewhere. To secure and retain the business of their bondpeople, owners had little choice but to deal fairly with them with regard to the prices they charged and the quality of the commodities they offered. Bondpeople were as aware of the market value of the commodities they grew, raised, hunted, and produced as they were of the retail prices of the items they sought in exchange for their surpluses. They expected their owners to pay "at the market price" for those surpluses and not to overcharge them for their purchases.[39]

From the beginning, owners were the weaker partners in the negotiations that took place on every lowcountry plantation over the trading activities of their bondpeople. And they knew it. Whether buying or selling, bondwomen and bondmen who were dissatisfied with the terms being offered by their owners almost always had the option of taking all or part of their business elsewhere. In 1765, for instance, Henry Laurens agreed to pay his bondpeople the "full value" of every bushel of rice he sold on their behalf in Charleston. But he was not entirely certain that the prices he proposed to charge them for the "sundry articles" they sought in exchange for their rice would be acceptable. He allowed his overseers some flexibility in the negotiation of prices, but threatened his bondmen and bondwomen that if they made "too much fuss & trouble" he might be "discouraged from being their Factor for another Year."[40] Yet as Laurens was the first to appreciate, this was a hollow threat. The withdrawal of his services, and there is no evidence that he did withdraw them, might have inconvenienced his plantation bondpeople. But, as Laurens knew full well, it would only encourage them to take their business elsewhere.

Some of the trading links that Laurens feared might be forged by his bondpeople did not even require them to leave their plantations. With the development of the lowcountry's economic infrastructure it became increasingly possible for plantation bondpeople, more especially those who lived some distance from the region's towns, to find trading partners within relatively close proximity to their estates. Trading boats and country stores, as well as neighboring plantations, competed with owners for the business of rural bondmen and bondwomen.

The commercial success of farms and plantations in the lowcountry depended on various considerations, but high on the list of priorities was easy access to water transportation. Roads and trails existed, but from the first settlement of Georgia an intricate system of navigable waterways provided the all-important arteries through which most of the lowcountry's trade flowed. As Pastor Bolzius explained, "the rivers are their roads, on which they travel very comfortably and cheaply in boats, and on which one or two people can transport several hundred weight at a time."[41] The Savannah River was particularly significant, providing as it did the quickest and cheapest route between what from the 1730s were Georgia's two premier towns, Savannah and Augusta.[42] The rapid spread of rice cultivation in the lowcountry during the quarter of a century before the American Revolution, and of cotton into the backcountry after it, and the expansion of waterborne commerce that this entailed, provided ever-increasing opportunities for plantation bondpeople and the crews of trading vessels to do business together. Moreover, the country stores and taverns that sprang up to cater to the commercial and recreational needs of Georgia's rapidly growing rural population provided plantation bondpeople with a choice of prospective trading partners often within comparatively easy reach of their estates. Increasingly, they had the choice of dealing with the proprietors and patrons of country stores and inns, or the captains and crews of passing river boats, as well as with their owners and overseers.

By the mid-1760s the Georgia government had granted thirty-seven licenses to retail liquor, of which twenty-two were for establishments in Savannah. Those outside Savannah tended to be located "along most of the colony's principal roads."[43] Owners and successive grand juries were convinced that these inns and taverns were simply "haunts for lewd idle and disorderly people, runaway Sailors servants and slaves." Plantation bondpeople, it was asserted, made their way, usually during the hours of darkness, to establishments run by the likes of Luke Dean and Peter Johnson for one purpose and one purpose only: to obtain liquor from white landlords who were by no means reluctant to supply it to them.[44] The liquor might be paid for by the sale of surplus produce, but more probably, so owners believed, by the sale or barter of goods that had been appropriated. Plantation bondpeople, whites believed, would stop at nothing in order to obtain hard liquor.

No doubt some plantation bondpeople lived up to their owner's expectations and made their way to country stores and taverns in search of alcohol. However, these establishments held another, and arguably more important, attraction for the bondmen and bondwomen who patronized them. They provided an alternative outlet for their surplus produce and what in all likelihood was a much wider, if not necessarily significantly cheaper, selection of the goods they sought in exchange for those surpluses. But inns and taverns also offered something else: they were meeting places for bondpeople from different estates. They provided forums for the exchange of news, forums where ties of family and friendship could be affirmed and reaffirmed.

Owners found it virtually impossible to prevent what were usually the nocturnal expeditions of their bondmen and bondwomen to country stores and taverns. As Charles Ball explained, bondpeople were "no less vigilant than their masters" and if necessary they simply waited until their owner or overseer had "retired to his bed" before leaving the plantation.[45] He also pointed to two reasons why so many country storekeepers were willing to "rise at any time of the night" to do business with bondpeople. The first reason had to do with how bondmen and bondwomen paid for their purchases. According to Ball, this sometimes involved barter, but unlike many whites who asked for credit, bondpeople usually paid in cash. Clearly, storekeepers were not likely to extend credit to men and women who might be sold or given away before they could settle their outstanding debts.[46]

Ball's second explanation of why so many country storekeepers were willing to break the law and deal with bondpeople had to do with the prices the merchants could demand for goods not always of the highest quality. Ball implied that plantation bondpeople were often the weaker partners in negotiations with storekeepers, for the latter knew full well they could ask "whatever price [they] please for [their] goods, without danger of being charged with extortion."[47]

Several years later Frances Kemble made precisely the same point. She related the story of a bondman named Dandy who had traded "a quantity of moss and eggs" with a Darien shopkeeper, "who refused

him payment in any other shape," for some material to be made up into
a dress for his wife, Edie. The material was of such an inferior quality
that the dress had torn "all to pieces the first time she had put it on."
This, claimed Kemble, was a perfect illustration of the way in which
"the rascally shopkeepers can cheat these poor creatures to any extent
they please with perfect impunity."[48] No doubt many owners were at
pains to emphasize this point to their bondpeople, if only to encourage
them to restrict their trading activities to the limits of the plantation, to
persuade them to secure whatever items they sought through the good
offices of their masters, mistresses, and overseers.

On one level, of course, Ball and Kemble were perfectly correct:
bondpeople had no formal means of securing redress if they felt they
had been underpaid for their produce, overcharged for their purchases,
or sold shoddy goods. Moreover, depending on where they lived, plantation bondpeople were not always in a position to threaten to take
their business elsewhere, although this option was available to urban
bondpeople and those who lived within fairly easy reach of Savannah.
Bondpeople who were dependent on doing business with retailers in
the other, smaller towns of the lowcountry had a more restricted choice.
As Reuben King commented in 1801, there were only "three stores" in
Darien. King himself was to add to that number five years later.[49] The
fact remains that the growth of Georgia's economic infrastructure did
offer many plantation bondpeople an alternative to trading with their
owners or local storekeepers, although not necessarily on a regular or
predictable basis.

Whether they sought alcohol, or the utensils, cloth, and ready-made
clothing that characterized their purchases from their owners, and
probably from country storekeepers as well, plantation bondpeople
were not always obliged to leave their estates in order to obtain these
commodities or the money with which to buy them. Some of these
transactions, which involved local whites openly visiting the plantation
in search of a commodity or skill they believed could be best provided
by a particular bondperson or persons, were known to owners and were
not altogether frowned on. In February 1803, for instance, Reuben King
made the short voyage from Darien to St. Simons, where his brother
worked as an overseer on the Butler estates, specifically to purchase

from "Mjr. Butlers Negroes 26lb. of Iron in proper Shape for our use at 22 Cents per lb."[50]

Sometimes a mixture of hope and despair, rather than price considerations, prompted whites to seek out bondpersons thought to be possessed of a particular skill. John Newton was a case in point. He had consulted various white doctors in search of a cure for his son's epilepsy, but to no avail. In October 1782 he paid a visit "to George Mires and got a medicine of his negro Primus." Newton did not record how much he gave for his "medicine" or whether he had tried to bargain with Primus. The strong probability is that he was so concerned for his son's health that he willingly paid what Primus asked. Newton, though, was a greatly disappointed client because a month later he noted in his journal that "James had a bad fit—the negro cure not good."[51]

How many other whites followed Newton's example, and how efficacious they found the medicines they purchased from bondpeople, is not recorded. But obviously Primus had secured for himself a reputation as a healer that extended well beyond the boundaries of his plantation. In all probability, however, the business that Primus and other enslaved practitioners of herbal medicine, as well as those familiar with the intricacies of conjure or obeah, conducted with the bondpeople in their localities was a more regular source of income than that derived from the visits of whites in search of a cure. Almost certainly bondpeople such as "Doctor Harry," who ran away in 1790 and whose owner thought him likely to try to "pass for a free Negro Doctor," and "Long Harry," who was known "from his remarkable conjurations of pigs feet [and] rattlesnakes teeth" and was believed by "many . . . to have performed miracles," charged something for their services.[52]

Infinitely more worrisome to owners than the visits paid by the likes of King and Newton to their bondpeople were the essentially clandestine trading links forged with the captains and crews of the vessels that plied the rivers and coastal waterways of the lowcountry. From the standpoint of owners these links proved just as problematical and as difficult to eradicate as the visits paid by their bondmen and bondwomen to country stores and taverns. For many plantation bondpeople they offered alternative, if often unpredictable, sources for some of the commodities they sought to acquire. Rather more indirectly, it was via these connections that many of the bondpeople's surplus products reached their ultimate markets: Savannah, Sunbury, and Darien. The lowcountry's waterways formed a crucially important link between the informal as well as the formal slave economies of countryside and town. Beginning in the mid-1750s the rural and urban worlds of lowcountry Georgia impinged on one another in an increasingly complex fashion.

Planters and merchants alike wanted to minimize the costs entailed in the conveyance of such bulky commodities as rice, corn, and timber, and this they did by employing bondmen not only to construct piraguas, droghers, and flatboats but also to crew them.[53] But as many planters came to appreciate by the early 1760s, cheaper transportation costs often involved another cost: the highly undesirable transactions conducted between their bondpeople and these enslaved rivermen and sailors. These transactions, which might be occasional and by chance or occur on a more regular basis, sometimes involved white complicity, but they were firmly grounded in the initiative of plantation bondpeople. From the outset, dealings between plantation bondpeople and boat hands were assisted by a significant degree of mobility, which was sanctioned by planters as reluctant to dispense with cheaper African-American crews as they were to dispense with their field hands. Moreover, like country storekeepers and taverners, many white captains and crews proved perfectly willing to trade with rural bondpeople. But whether African, African-American, white, or racially mixed, the captains and crews of river and coastal trading vessels were always men. Bondwomen might be employed to load and unload boats, both in the lowcountry's port towns and in the countryside, but there is no firm evidence that during this eighty-year period they were used to crew boats. Transactions between rural bondpeople, boat hands, and sailors might involve bondwomen but they seldom if ever involved negotiations between bondwomen.

Although weakening what owners regarded as a form of dependence on them, in a purely financial sense it was of no real consequence to them when their bondpeople negotiated terms with the captains and crews of trading boats. Why, then, did transactions that might not require bondpeople to leave their plantations so disconcert owners and generate an increasing amount of legislative action designed to prevent such transactions? The two main reasons for this heightened private and public concern were identical to those that prompted many owners to try to prevent their bondpeople from visiting country stores and inns: alcohol and appropriated goods. It was widely held that, whether white or black, free or enslaved, most rivermen had no compunction in accepting stolen property in exchange for the one commodity that bondmen and bondwomen reputedly sought above all else: hard liquor.

Planters who used their own trading vessels crewed by their own bondmen appreciated that such an arrangement provided every opportunity for regular trading links to be established between these crews, who had access to the urban economies of Savannah and the smaller port towns of the lowcountry, and their plantation bondpeople. Many owners themselves organized the collection and delivery of cargoes, which did not necessarily prevent such transactions, but at least made them more difficult to conduct.

During the mid-1760s, for instance, Henry Laurens alerted his overseers to the impending arrival of a vessel from Charleston and reminded them of the need "to take care to prevent an intercourse between Boat and Plantation Negroes."[54] When one of his overseers complained that the bondpeople on the plantation were "stealing [his] Potatoes & Corn," Laurens believed he knew how they would try to dispose of the produce in question. He advised the overseer to "be more careful of the Boat Negroes than usual" and suggested that "every now and then" he make "a Search when the Boat was loaded." If he discovered any contraband he must not "fail to chastise" those concerned, including Abraham, the vessel's captain, who would be held responsible not only for his own transgressions but also for those of his crew members.

Perhaps with good reason, Laurens was deeply suspicious of certain of his bondpeople and instructed his overseers to keep a particularly careful eye on them. For example, he was keen to hear from one overseer "how Adam the Patroon of the Boat behaves" and reminded another that "Amos has a great inclination to turn Rum Merchant which I have strictly forbidden." Laurens believed that Amos "has or may send up some [rum] by flat Boat to Mr. Mayrant's Landing" and ordered his overseer "to search narrowly & if he has more than one Bottle to seize it."[55] Whether Laurens's approach, which included directing his overseers to whip those of his bondpeople found trading illicitly, proved any more successful than the spring-traps and armed guards employed by John Stevens and Patrick Mackay is a moot point.

Trying to prevent commercial liaisons being forged between their plantation bondpeople and the crews of trading vessels they themselves owned and operated proved difficult for planters. Unanticipated overnight moorings of other vessels in the rivers and creeks that cut through their properties, and the opportunities to trade this offered to their bondpeople, posed a far more intractable problem.[56] Sometimes plantation bondpeople entered into regular arrangements with the captains and crews of trading boats. In other cases, as Charles Ball explained, crews and plantation bondpeople who were previously unknown to one another met and did business together almost by chance. One episode he recounted took place at night when, with his master's permission, he was out fishing for shad. He could not help but notice "a large keel-boat . . . on the opposite side of the river, directly against our landing." This was the first time in Ball's experience that such a thing had happened. But even though "hitherto . . . we had not met with an opportunity of entering into a traffic with any of the boat masters," Ball knew full well that one of the commodities often carried by the craft that "frequently passed up the river" was something he wanted desperately to taste: bacon.

The ensuing negotiations with the white captain were initiated by Ball and resulted in "a hundred pounds of bacon" being traded "for three hundred shad." The captain emphasized to Ball that he ran the risk of prosecution for "dealing with a slave," and that "I must expect to pay him more than the usual price." The three hundred shad he demanded "was at least twice as much as the bacon was worth," but this was a price Ball was willing and able to pay. He suspected that the captain might be less than "scrupulous" in weighing out the bacon, but "I was mistaken; for he weighed the flitches with great exactness."[57]

Clearly, and not surprisingly given the terms he had just managed to strike with Ball, the captain was as pleased as Ball with their transaction, and he expressed the hope that they might be able to establish a regular arrangement. He told Ball, "in a low voice," that he would be passing that way again in two weeks' time "when he should be very glad to buy any produce that I had for sale." The terms he stipulated to Ball, rather than negotiated with him, were that he would give him "half as much for cotton as it is worth in Charleston, and pay you either in money or groceries, as you may choose." Partly because of the "iniquity" of stealing cotton from his owner, and partly because "of the danger which attended it," Ball declined the offer.[58]

The clandestine nature on which their success depended makes it impossible to say precisely how many similar offers were made by rivermen and sailors to pay plantation bondpeople in cash or kind for commodities either appropriated from whites or produced by themselves, or how many of those offers were accepted. If the comments of owners and other white commentators are taken at face value, such transactions were extensive. But no firm evidence supports the contention that they necessarily, let alone predominantly, involved commodities appropriated from bondpeople's owners or other whites.

During the colonial period, the Georgia assembly made no specific provision for the public policing of the colony's waterways, an indication, perhaps, of the scale of the lowcountry's internal trade and dealings with the backcountry. The hope might have been that transactions between plantation bondpeople and trading boat crews could be minimized by a combination of private policing and the often unpredictable routes taken by slave patrols. The rapid expansion of plantation agriculture into the backcountry after the American War of Independence, and the concomitant growth of waterborne traffic, particularly between Augusta and Savannah, prompted government action. In 1806 the assembly declared that it had been "found from experience to be highly improper and inexpedient" to allow the trading vessels that plied the Savannah River to be captained by bondmen or free African-Americans. Thereafter, any planter or merchant who permitted a bondperson "to have command, or act as patroon of any boat carrying goods, wares, and merchandise, or produce" between Augusta and Savannah would be liable to a fine of two hundred dollars.[59]

The legislation of 1806 said nothing about crews composed of Africans or African-Americans. It was unthinkable that planters and merchants be denied, let alone through their dominant voice in government deny themselves, this cheaper form of manpower. Moreover, by limiting their attention to the Savannah River they also retained the right to put bondmen in charge of vessels that operated on Georgia's

other waterways. Significantly, in 1806 the assembly ignored the trading connections that might be established between white captains and
crews and plantation bondpeople. This omission was to be remedied a
decade later.

In 1815, in response to the many complaints made by "the inhabitants of this State, residing on or near [the] Savannah river" of "serious
injuries inflicted on their rights and properties by boat's crews," the
assembly again turned its attention to the connections forged between
plantation bondpeople and rivermen. The act of 1806 was not repealed,
but now the responsibility for the conduct of the captains and crews
in their employ was placed on the proprietors of trading boats. They
were legally obliged to draw up "a certificate or bill of lading" itemizing the cargo, the destination, the consignee, and the captain of each
of their vessels before its departure. Failure to produce this document
upon demand could result in a fifty-dollar fine. Moreover, boat owners
were financially liable for "all the pillages and thefts committed by their
respective crews."[60]

A year later the assembly concluded that many of the "thefts" complained of by whites whose farms and plantations fronted the Savannah
River occurred not just because bondmen were used as crew members
but also because they were allowed by their owners "to carry corn,
cotton, or other products to market, as their own property." This practice, the assembly declared, "has been found, by fatal experience, to
be an encouragement to theft." Georgia's planter-politicians sought to
remedy the situation with a two-pronged approach, which again depended on boat owners and captains policing their crews. First, it was
stipulated that henceforth it would be illegal for any enslaved crew
members "to put on board their boat . . . corn, cotton, peas, or other
articles of produce . . . for the purpose of carrying the same to Savannah
or elsewhere to market." Second, they must not be allowed "to barter
or trade, the one with the other, in any article of produce as before
enumerated, under any pretext whatsoever." Any evasions of this legislation would be punishable by a fine, imprisonment, or both "at the
discretion of the Superior Court" of the county in which the offense
was committed. The following year the act was amended to incorporate
"all the rivers that now are, or hereafter may be, made navigable in
this state."[61]

The initiative of plantation bondpeople and rivermen ensured that the legislation of 1816 and 1817 would never secure the objectives of its framers. In practice, as planters and government alike came to appreciate, it was virtually impossible to effectively police Georgia's waterways. As some white commentators were pointing out by the first decade of the nineteenth century, trading links between plantation bondpeople and rivermen were greatly encouraged by the latter's awareness that they could find ready markets for produce in Georgia's towns, particularly in Savannah. Urban consumers, by their willingness to evade the public laws of slavery and purchase commodities from enslaved producers and vendors, had in effect made themselves dependent on bondpeople.

As they had done since the 1760s, plantation bondpeople and rivermen exploited that dependence with considerable success through the first three decades of the nineteenth century. Indeed, in 1836 the Georgia government was forced to concede defeat and amend the act of 1817 in such a way as to permit rivermen "to take with them . . . stock, poultry, or other articles . . . to traffic in" provided that the same were "specified in a bill of lading."[62] De jure recognition was being given to de facto trading links between plantation bondpeople and rivermen, and thereby to an urban dependence that had existed since the late eighteenth century.

4 ❧ Marketing in Savannah

DURING THE trustee period the buying and selling of perishable food-stuffs in Savannah proceeded in an essentially ad hoc fashion. Simply because they did not perceive it to be a particularly pressing need, given the town's modest population growth during the first two decades of settlement, neither the trustees nor their officials in Georgia had seen fit to establish a formal, regular, and closely regulated public market in Savannah. In 1752 Georgia's population, excluding indigenous Americans, totaled only "between 2 and 3,000" Europeans and "about 600 Negroes."[1] The colony's population doubled during the first half of the 1750s,[2] and in 1755 the Commons House of Assembly declared that Savannah's white consumers were in urgent need of protection against the "great Extortions Impositions and Irregularities [being] Committed by Forestallers Ingrossers and other evil disposed persons," and held that such protection could best be guaranteed by the establishment of a public market.[3]

The legislation enacted by the assembly in 1755 provided for a public market in Savannah that would be open "from Sun rise" on weekdays and, except for the sale of fish, be closed on Sundays. Two steps were taken to try to prevent forestalling. Those who intended to buy goods, either in the market or from those who supplied stall-holders, then re-sell them later at a profit would not be allowed to do so before nine o'clock in the morning. This, it was anticipated, would give ordinary customers a chance to obtain what they needed at a reasonable price. Second, those "bringing provisions of any kind to Town for Sale" were required, upon the pain of a ten shilling fine, to "Contract or agree for the same before they be Exposed to Sale in the Market." The act also provided for a clerk of the market, established the rates he would be paid, and named five commissioners who would be responsible for overseeing the market's day-to-day operations.[4]

During the next three-quarters of a century the government of Georgia and, after the American Revolution, the Savannah City Council enacted a steady stream of legislation designed to regulate all facets of the market's activities. Much of that legislation was designed to safeguard the interests of white consumers; little was said or done about the interests of white producers.

Increasingly, state and local governments found themselves forced to confront the implications of an aspect of marketing about which the act of 1755 had remained silent: the dominant role that bondpeople, more especially bondwomen, began to carve out for themselves in the vending of a wide range of fresh foodstuffs in Savannah. By 1755 this was already a firmly entrenched feature of the urban economies of Britain's sugar islands and was becoming a marked characteristic of the marketing of similar commodities in Charleston.[5] The steady growth of Savannah—by 1800 the city's population was estimated at 6,226 and said to include 3,216 Africans and African-Americans—provided an ever-expanding demand for fruit, vegetables, meat, fish, poultry, and dairy products.[6] To a remarkable degree, and by the late eighteenth century to many whites an alarming degree, this demand came to be satisfied by plantation bondpeople, often acting in concert with their urban counterparts.

If the garden plot quickly emerged as one of the most important expressions of the economic, social, and cultural aspirations of the lowcountry's enslaved population, then by the mid-1760s the marketplace in Savannah was well on the way toward becoming another. Like the markets in early-modern, provincial English towns on which it was modeled (and for that matter public markets in early-modern West Africa), Savannah's market fulfilled more than a purely economic function. Here, the cultures, as well as the economies, of countryside and town intersected.[7] As Bohannon and Dalton among others have pointed out, markets comprise "meeting places which can be used for political, religious, social and personal purposes." In the marketplace one could expect to meet and make friends, exchange news and information, and, if so disposed, recruit sexual partners. Gatherings at markets also offered the possibility of political organization, and from the standpoint of the governing classes it could be "politically advantageous to control the marketplace and hence to some degree the people in it."[8] This is precisely what successive state and Savannah city governments sought, but signally failed to achieve after the mid-1750s: effective political and economic control of those women and men who dominated the city's public market. By the early nineteenth century the mayor and aldermen of Savannah might be claiming that it was they who ran the city's public market, but in fact it was enslaved urban vendors acting in concert with plantation bondpeople and rivermen who organized and controlled it.

The act of 1755 that created a public market in Savannah made no mention of vending by bondpeople. But Georgia's first slave code, enacted in the same year and closely modeled on that drafted by South Carolina in the aftermath of the Stono Rebellion, decreed that bondpeople could not "buy, sell, or exchange any goods, wares, provisions, grains, victuals, or commodities of any sort or kind whatsoever" unless they resided or worked in Savannah and had the express consent of their owners to do so.[9] Like their counterparts in South Carolina, Georgia's planter-politicians had no wish to deny themselves the right to deploy their bondpeople as they wished, and this included the right to employ them as market men and market women. The possibility was there for bondpeople to market their own produce in Savannah, as well as that of their owners, and it was a possibility they were quick to exploit. Indeed, by the mid-1760s the Georgia grand jury was already complaining about the "large bodies" of bondpeople who were making their way to Savannah, often on Sundays, to dispose "of corn, wood and other commodities, without tickets from their masters."[10]

By 1774 the arrangements set out in the slave code of 1755, which were reaffirmed in those of 1765 and 1770, were deemed inadequate by the Commons House of Assembly.[11] The assembly might have been concerned by the number of bondpeople who were already plying goods in Savannah's public market, but it appears to have been even more disconcerted by the fact that it was proving virtually impossible to distinguish between those who had their owners' consent to be there and those who did not.

To make those bondpeople who had their owners' permission to vend goods instantly recognizable to public officials, as well as to potential customers who were legally forbidden to make purchases from unauthorized enslaved vendors, the government introduced a badge system similar to that already in operation in Charleston. Owners who wished "to let out or hire" their bondpeople "to sell Fruit, Fish, Garden Stuff or any other Commodities whatsoever in the Town of Savannah" were required to obtain a license. For their part, the bondpeople concerned "shall constantly wear a Publick Badge or Ticket." It was expressly forbidden to purchase goods from enslaved vendors who were not wearing the requisite badge or who could not produce a ticket from their owner or overseer.[12] With some minor amendments, these requirements remained in force through 1830.[13] They were requirements frequently evaded by owners, bondpeople, and white consumers alike.[14] In this respect, as in so many others, social and economic practice in lowcountry Georgia diverged sharply from the demands set down in the public laws of slavery.

The spatial arrangements and regulation of Savannah's public market, which was located at three different sites between 1755 and 1821,[15] would have been as instantly recognizable to the African-born men and women of the lowcountry as they would have been to contemporary Europeans.[16] As was the case in Savannah, many West African markets, including those at Wydah in the Kingdom of Dahomey, and Cape Corse in Guinea, were open six days a week.[17] Following the English model, the Savannah market was regulated by a clerk and commissioners appointed initially by the colonial government and subsequently by the city council. The clerk's salary, and such upkeep as the market required, were financed through the levying of a toll on the commodities offered for sale and eventually by the rental of market stalls.[18] These arrangements were broadly similar to those that characterized many West African markets. The Great Market at Wydah, for example, was presided over by an "officer who expect[ed] a toll from every vendor," and "the King appoints a Judge or Magistrate, who with four Officers, well armed, inspects the Markets, hears all Complaints, and in a summary way decides all Differences."[19]

Similarly, the spatial arrangement of the goods offered for sale in Savannah's public market was carefully delineated, which may well have reflected the experience and input of West Africans as much as that of Europeans. When the market moved back to Ellis Square in 1821 the "four covered," or outside, portions of the new building, described by a contemporary as "a wooden shed, about twenty-five feet wide," were reserved "for the sale of vegetables, dressed meat of all kinds, dressed poultry, and everything else that could not find a place elsewhere." The central "uncovered quadrangular space" was where "live poultry, fish, oysters, shrimp, crabs, and everything else that comes out of the water" were sold.[20] The Great Market of Wydah, which at some fourteen acres was of a rather different order of size from that in Ellis Square, was organized in a similar fashion. Different sections of the market were devoted exclusively to the sale of particular commodities. The same was also true of markets "throughout the Gold Coast."[21]

By the late eighteenth century white commentators were beginning to identify a pattern of public marketing in Savannah that closely resembled that of early-modern England and West Africa, as well as the other plantation colonies: the predominance of women vendors. The preeminent role of women in public vending was significant for several reasons, not least because, as Alice Clark suggested many years ago, "it must certainly have favoured the formation of a feminine public opinion on current events, which prevented individual women from relying exclusively upon their husbands for information and advice."[22]

By the late eighteenth century, what was true of early-modern England and West Africa, and for many years had been a feature of Charleston's public market, was equally true of Savannah.[23] As Barbara Bush has pointed out, we cannot be entirely certain "whether the importance of the slave woman in . . . internal marketing systems . . . was a direct African retention or a result of the new roles she was forced to adopt as a result of enslavement."[24] However, it is indisputable that there were quite remarkable similarities between the marketing activities of women in many West African economies and those of enslaved women in the towns of the lowcountry and the sugar islands.

European visitors to early-modern West Africa frequently remarked on the extent to which women assumed the main responsibility for marketing.[25] This was the case at Cape Corse and Wydah, and at Egga women were said to be "the chief if not the only traders."[26] Indeed, at the Great Market at Wydah only "the Slave-Trade is carried on by Men; all other Goods are disposed of by the Women."[27]

European travelers offered few explanations for the prevalence of women vendors in West African markets. Barbot, for instance, commented merely that women were "looked upon as fitter for [marketing] than the men."[28] Their "extraordinary Art in setting-off their Wares" and the reputation they enjoyed as "excellent Accomptants [accountants]," probably meant that it was "with good Reason . . . that the Men, rely on their Management."[29] More recently it has been suggested that the dominant role of women may have originated in the "need to adapt marketing and trading to the dangers of moving through the countryside" during times of war. Tribal wars did not totally negate the necessity of marketing and "at times when it was unsafe for men to move away from farms . . . women were relatively immune from attack."[30]

European commentators had no need to tell their audiences that women played a similar role in the public markets of early-modern England. In the sixteenth century the duties of the farmer's wife were said by one male author to include going "to the Market to sell butter, cheese, mylke, egges, chekens, kapons, hennes, pygges, gees, and al manner of Corne. And also to bye al manner of necessary thinges belonging to a houshold."[31] English women undertook, or were required by their male kin to assume, the main responsibility for vending those commodities that they often grew, raised, or manufactured themselves within the household economy. This did not preclude the possibility of women marketing goods that they and their husbands had produced jointly, nor did it preclude the possibility of men vending fruit, vegetables, poultry, and dairy products. The one marketing activity in early-modern England that was generally gender specific, and restricted to men, was butchering.[32]

A similar pattern characterized marketing in many parts of West Africa. Around Wydah, for instance, women made "Beer, and dress Victuals, which they carry to Market to sell." Among the Mandingo people, "the Rice is the Women's property; who, after setting by a sufficient Quantity for the Family use, sell the Remainder. . . . The same Custom they observe with regard to the Fowls, of which they breed great Numbers." On the Gold Coast it was the usual practice for women to "bake the Bread" and make "a sort of Biscuit" as well as "round twisted Cake, called *Quanqais*," which they "sold in the Markets."[33]

But despite the preponderance of women vendors in local markets, there were some gender distinctions. Among the Akan, for instance, it was held that "it is the business of a woman to sell garden eggs and not gunpowder." [34]

By the late eighteenth century, gender differentiation in marketing and trading was as clearly evident in Savannah's public market as it was in that of Charleston and those of the sugar islands. During the colonial period white reporters had relatively little to say about the market and did not comment on the gender of those who brought, vended, or purchased goods there. By the 1780s and 1790s, however, far more was being committed to paper about two closely interrelated facets of the market's operation: gender specialization and the preponderance of enslaved female vendors. Bondwomen and a smaller number of free African-American women virtually monopolized the vending of cakes and confectionery in Savannah's public market. Indeed, by the mid-1810s, if not earlier, the city's African-American market women were being referred to collectively in some quarters of white society as "Cake Wenches." [35] The baking and sale of bread, on the other hand, whether by bondpeople, free African-Americans, or Europeans seems to have been a predominantly male occupation.

Men also predominated in the butchering and sale of meat in the public market. In theory, these two activities could be carried out by bondpeople only in the presence of a white person; in practice, many white butchers were willing to run the risk of a fine by allowing their bondpeople to work unsupervised. [36] This failure to observe the law provided an outlet for meat that, if white complaints are to be believed, plantation bondpeople had appropriated from their owners or from neighboring planters. [37] It is also evident that some white butchers were perfectly happy to offer for sale "meat that they did not butcher," which they might have acquired from plantation bondpeople. [38] Although other commodities offered in the public market might be sold by either sex, by the late eighteenth century the great majority of those doing the selling were women.

The preeminent position enjoyed by bondwomen, and to a lesser extent by free African-American women, as traders in Savannah's public market is evident from the comments and, increasingly, the complaints made by white observers. [39] However, because they included occasional as well as full-time vendors, the exact number of these women cannot be easily determined. The problem is further compounded because none of the lists of authorized vendors and their owners, which were almost certainly compiled annually by the market commissioners, appears to have survived.

A rough idea of the number, but not the gender, of authorized vendors at the turn of the eighteenth century may be gathered from the orders for badges placed by the Savannah City Council. In August and September 1787, for instance, the council paid Robert Greer £12.14.0 for making 135 badges, of which 125 were sold for £15.10.0 (specie) and £108.10 (paper). Three years later the council agreed that ninety badges, not to "exceed the sum of nine pence each," should be made by Greer. In 1793 the city purchased 170 "Negro Badges" from John Hacler. John Gibbons, the treasurer of the city council, recorded in 1802 only that $281.50 had been received from the sale of badges. A decade later 166 badges were ordered by the city council at a cost of $41.50, and 108 were sold for the sum of $442.50.[40]

Slaves authorized as vendors in the public market wore the same, or very similar, badges as those displayed by bondpeople who had their owners' permission to be hired as laborers and porters or to drive carts, wagons, and drays around the city. The city treasurer's accounts do not identify either the number or the gender of those in each of these categories. Neither do they distinguish between those bondpeople who were resident in Savannah and those who were not. The buying and selling of goods in Savannah's public market, and somewhat less formally in the city's streets and alleys, by bondpeople came to involve two not always entirely discreet activities: marketing and professional trading.[41] Neither of these activities divided neatly along gender or residential lines.

Commodities produced by plantation bondpeople in their own time reached the lowcountry towns in one of three main ways. They might be carried there in person by those, or representatives of those, who had grown, raised, hunted, or made them; they could be collected by urban vendors; or they could reach the city as a result of the links established between rural bondpeople and the captains and crews of river and coastal trading vessels.[42] Whether plantation bondpeople took their own produce to sell in Savannah, Sunbury, or Darien, and how often they did so, depended on three main considerations: the practical, rather than the legal, constraints placed on their mobility; their proximity to urban markets; and the amount, as well as the type, of produce to be transported there.

It was with a view toward securing racial, rather than purely economic, control that the public slavery laws prohibited bondpeople from leaving their owners' property, for whatever purpose, without a ticket. That statute remained on the books throughout the antebellum period, but as virtually every white person and certainly every bondperson in the lowcountry must have appreciated, it was one that could not be strictly enforced. In practice owners and overseers could do virtually nothing to stop their bondpeople from leaving the confines of the plantation after nightfall. Many owners appreciated the futility of trying to prevent their bondpeople from visiting Savannah, Sunbury, and Darien, but they sought to ensure that such expeditions were made with their knowledge and only at times that suited them. Given the demands of the working week, Sunday was the day that those plantation bondpeople who were able to do so made their way to the lowcountry towns to do their marketing—with or without their owners' permission.

With varying degrees of success, some owners and overseers adopted a carrot-and-stick approach to Sunday marketing. On the Butler plantations during the 1820s, for instance, "a certain number" of bondpeople were "allowed to go to [Darien to trade] on Sundays . . . but must be home by 12 o'clock, unless by special permit." How those bondpeople were chosen, and who did the choosing, is unknown. It is also not clear what happened to those who returned late. However, if they came back "intoxicated (a rare instance)" they were put "into stocks, and not allowed to leave home for twelve months." The other forms of punishment mentioned by Roswell King, Jr., Pierce Butler's overseer, included "Digging stumps, or clearing away trash . . . in their own time" and "the lash, least of all." King noted that from the bondpeople's standpoint "the most severe" punishment was "confinement at home six months to twelve months."[43]

Plantation owners wanted to exert some control over the visits of their bondpeople to urban markets; so, too, did the public officials of those towns. Again, this reflected a concern with racial, rather than purely economic, control. An unlimited influx of plantation bondpeople into Savannah on weekends (even if they possessed tickets from their

owners and had no motive other than to trade) greatly alarmed the
city authorities, but in practice there was little they could do to prevent it. They did, however, try to ensure that only two bondpeople per
plantation were allowed to visit the city over the Christmas period, a
time when Savannah's white population was considered particularly
vulnerable to a concerted attack by bondpeople.[44]

The constraints that owners and the Savannah City Council sought
to impose on plantation bondpeople may have worked in some or even
in many cases. Nevertheless, the bondpeople's place of residence was
far more important than official sanctions in determining patterns of
marketing; the frequency of visits to Savannah, Darien, or Sunbury;
and the range of goods taken there. In the case of handicrafts, for example, the time taken to reach urban markets was of little consequence;
for most fruits and vegetables, dressed poultry and game, dairy products, fish, and meat, where a premium attached to freshness, time was
a critical factor.

Access, even if only intermittently, to boats or canoes, horses, mules,
and wagons was obviously important. Greater distances could be traveled than if the journey had to be made on foot, and a larger volume
of goods could be transported there and back in a single visit. Many
plantation bondpeople owned boats and canoes, usually of their own
manufacture, and marketing was one of the principal purposes for
which these vessels were employed. This was the only way that Darien,
Sunbury, and St. Marys could be reached from the Sea Islands.[45]

Most of the rural bondpeople employed on a full- or a part-time
basis by their owners as market men and market women had access to
horses, mules, or oxen, wagons and carts. With or without their owners'
blessing, these could have been used to carry to market at least some of
the surpluses produced in the slave quarters. Given the purchase price
of horses and mules (in the early nineteenth century a "decent" horse
could cost up to $150 and a "good" mule "60 or 70 dollars") it is highly
unlikely that, even if their owners had been agreeable, most bondpeople
could have afforded to buy them.[46] But the fact that many plantation
bondpeople did have access to horses and mules on weekends is suggested by R. Q. Mallard's comment that on "Saturday nights the roads
[in Liberty County] were . . . filled with men" visiting their wives who
lived on other plantations. Some of these expeditions, he continued,
were made on foot but many others were made on horseback.[47]

The speed with which fresh produce could be conveyed to Savannah, Sunbury, or Darien by wagon or cart, the distances that could be covered before that produce perished, varied according to the availability and quality of the tracks and roads that had to be navigated en route to market. Early Georgia, with its heavy dependence on navigable waterways, was not renowned for the abundance or the high standards of its roads. Road improvements, which often involved the compulsory employment of bondmen, were made, and by the 1820s, if not earlier, "many" of the "one-horse, two-wheeled vehicles" which "brought to the [Savannah] market all kinds of country produce" had traveled "a distance of fifty miles or more, and [been] two days and a night on the way."[48]

Some bondpeople rowed or paddled to market; others rode there; many had no option but to walk to Savannah, Darien, or Sunbury carrying their produce as best they could.[49] Walking to market would have been familiar to most West African women. In the Gold Coast, for instance, women "will repair . . . daily to the Market, some from five or six Leagues Distance, like Pack-Horses, with a child perhaps at their Back, and a heavy Burden of Fruits etc on their Heads. After selling their Wares, they buy Fish and other necessaries they want, and return home as loaded as they came."[50] As was the case in the sugar islands, many African and African-American women in the lowcountry, and no doubt some men also, walked as far as fifteen or twenty miles to market: not every day, but circumstances permitting, probably once a week. Often they carried their wares West African fashion in baskets or on "wooden trays" that they balanced on their heads. According to a report from early nineteenth-century Barbados, the loads carried in this manner by women could be as much as "51 pounds full weight."[51]

Referring specifically to the lowcountry, Georgina Bryan Conrad commented that "in carrying bundles, baskets, or buckets, [bondwomen] always balanced them on their heads." Frances Kemble remarked that the "erect and good" posture of bondwomen stemmed from "the habit they have of balancing great weights on their heads." One woman known to Kemble was "extremely lame, which she accounted for by an accident she met with while carrying a heavy weight of rice on her head."[52]

Regardless of how they transported their produce to the lowcountry towns, rural bondpeople had a considerable choice when it came to disposing of it. Arguably their most attractive option was to negotiate terms with those whose livelihood largely depended on such transactions: the predominantly female vendors, or traders, who operated on a full- or a part-time basis in the public market. In many cases these transactions involved negotiations between female suppliers and female vendors, and subsequently between those vendors and female customers. This aspect of enslaved women's lives in the urban economies of the sugar islands has attracted some interest in recent years, but with the notable exception of Philip D. Morgan's work on Charleston, little detailed research has been undertaken on the scale and significance of bondwomen's trading activities in the southern towns either before or after 1830.[53]

Savannah's public market was a supremely important context for the forging of networks between female vendors, as well as between female vendors and their customers. It also enabled important links to be forged between urban and rural bondwomen. The public market was a profoundly significant forum for the conduct of what F. G. Bailey has described as "the small politics of everyday life."[54] Women exchanged news and gossip on a regular basis and in the process forged their own opinions about acceptable patterns of female and male behavior—with a minimum amount of interference from either white or African-American men.[55] By the late 1780s the independent Afro-Baptist churches were also emerging as important forums for the creation of women's networks. But the churches differed from the public market in at least one critical respect: the extent of the authority exercised over women by male pastors and deacons.

Little is known about the precise form of the transactions and discourses conducted between plantation bondpeople and Savannah's market traders. However, if they followed the Charleston model, negotiations over the sale of produce were somewhat less than orderly. According to some white accounts, Charleston's market women engaged in fierce competition and were prepared to go to almost any lengths to secure the wares they sought. In the early 1770s one commentator claimed:

> The country negroes take great pains, after having been first spoke to by [these] women, to reserve whatever they chose to sell to them only, either by keeping the particular articles in their [canoes], or by sending them

away, and pretending they were not for sale; and when they could not
be easily retained by themselves, then I have seen the wenches so briskly
hustle them about from one to another, that in two minutes they could
no longer be traced.

It was quite common, this reporter continued, for market women "to
surround fruit carts, in every street, and purchase amongst them, the
whole contents."[56]

Savannah's market women may have conducted themselves in a
similarly competitive fashion as they sought to obtain the best quality
commodities at the lowest prices, but it is also possible that they negotiated and maintained regular links with particular plantation bondpeople, which would have been mutually advantageous. Neither is there
any firm evidence that they colluded in price-fixing, at least not in the
prices they paid their suppliers. But if white commentators are to be
believed this was not true of the prices they demanded of their white
customers: they marked up their prices knowing full well that their captive market would either have to pay up or go without.[57] Whether they
asked lower prices of favored African and African-American customers
who were buying for their own use, rather than for their owners', is not
clear from the surviving evidence.

In addition to buying goods brought to them by plantation bondpeople, Savannah's market traders could obtain their wares by two
other means. First, as was true in Charleston as early as the 1730s,
they might form mutually beneficial ties with the captains and crews
of the trading vessels that docked in Savannah.[58] Second, again as in
Charleston, they might go out into the countryside to seek for the produce and commodities they wanted. They traveled by boat, on foot,
or in drays, wagons, and carts, which they might own, or which they
borrowed or hired from the bondmen and free African-American men
who virtually monopolized the transportation of goods in and around
Savannah.[59] Quite possibly market traders were included among those
"evil disposed persons" who "infested . . . the Savannah river in the
neighborhood of the City of Savannah." These "persons," who probably included bondpeople and poor whites hoping to secure country
produce as cheaply as possible for their own consumption or to sell in
places other than the public market, lived in "huts, or camps, arks, or

floating houses" and "under the pretence of being engaged in fishing [were] in the habit of trading with negroes."

In 1831 the state government decreed that it was illegal for anyone to live in such accommodation unless he or she was actively "engaged in fishing, in the carriage or transporting goods or produce to or from market." The anchorage of any "ark, flat, or floating house" within twenty miles of Savannah was expressly forbidden. Moreover, extensive powers of search and seizure were granted to "patrols and any civil officers," who were authorized to search any of these vessels whenever they pleased. If their searches revealed "any rice in the rough state or clean, or Indian corn or pease, exceeding in quantity one peck . . . or any spirituous liquors exceeding in quantity one gallon for each occupant" the same would be construed as "evidence against the inhabitant or inhabitants . . . of trading . . . with negroes without a ticket from the owner."[60]

The relationships that were formed between plantation bondpeople and Savannah's market traders might not always have been entirely placid, nor easily established and maintained, but in an economic sense the interaction between rural producers and urban vendors was always mutually advantageous and mutually empowering. Each group provided the other with a profoundly important source of disposable income; each increased the economic options open to the other; each significantly enhanced the other's living standards.

Rural bondpeople bringing their produce to Savannah, Darien, or Sunbury could negotiate with urban retailers in precisely the same way that they did with country storekeepers. The public market dealt principally in the fresh produce and handicraft that plantation bondpeople had to dispose of, and not the commodities they wished to purchase. The white or free African-American shopkeeper, not the market vendor, furnished the sugar, molasses, coffee, and sometimes the liquor, as well as the footwear, fabrics, and ready-made clothing they sought in exchange for their surplus produce. Most shopkeepers were perfectly happy to do business with them.[61]

If they so chose, plantation bondpeople could also sell their produce directly to white consumers. They might do this in or very near the public market, where they could be assured of a steady stream of customers. On the south and west side of Ellis Square, for instance, produce was "sold from the carts where they were parked."[62] Alternatively, but far more time consuming unless they had established regular contacts, bondpeople might take to Savannah's streets and alleys in search of customers. This was most likely to be done by bondmen and bondwomen who did not possess a ticket or badge and who wished to avoid the attention of the market authorities. One visitor to the city in the early years of the nineteenth century commented that on Sundays "the poorer sort [of bondpeople] traverse the streets [of Savannah] with brooms and various other manufactures of their own."[63]

Some bondpeople went from house to house in an attempt to peddle their wares. In 1775, for example, an anonymous correspondent to the *Georgia Gazette* reported that on the previous Sunday "three Negro Fellows" had come to "[my] house in town, and offered some geese and turkeys for sale." As "there was reason to think they had stolen them, the poultry was detained till the Negroes should produce a ticket . . . which they have not yet done." The rightful owner could reclaim these fowls "by applying to the printer and paying the expense of advertising."[64]

Not all white consumers who were approached by bondpeople with something to sell were as suspicious as this anonymous advertiser. On the contrary, relatively few seem to have been unduly worried by the provenance of the goods offered to them by bondpeople. The only thing potential customers had to fear was being caught red-handed by the city authorities or by a white person who was willing to inform on them. Should they find themselves charged with illicit trading, the testimony of their enslaved trading partners was inadmissible.

There is ample evidence that throughout this period bondpeople without tickets or badges experienced few difficulties in disposing of their wares in the lowcountry towns. There is no record of the number of unauthorized vendors who were apprehended and whipped, but the names of their owners and those who purchased goods from them appear periodically in the Savannah City Council minutes. The tip of what in all probability was becoming an increasingly large iceberg by the late eighteenth century is suggested by the fact that between July and October 1791 the council fined seven owners, including "Free London," sums ranging from one shilling and sixpence to ten shillings and eight pence for allowing their bondpeople to sell "small wares" and poultry "without a Ticket or Badge."[65] Not atypically, around the turn of the eighteenth century, in a single month, August 1805, the owners of thirteen bondwomen and one bondman were fined for the same offense.[66]

By the late 1810s and early 1820s fines for selling without a badge appeared less frequently in the city council minutes. This was probably because the practice had become so commonplace that it was proving virtually impossible to enforce the law. And given the dependence of white consumers on African-American producers and vendors for perishable foodstuffs enforcement was not altogether desirable. Periodically the city council did attempt to clamp down on unauthorized vending by fining more owners and, presumably, punishing more bondpeople. At times it even tried to shame those whites who traded "illicitly" with bondpeople by publishing their names in the local press.[67]

Fines, notices in the press, and the punishment of bondpersons who were vending illicitly may have had the desired effect on some individuals for a short time, but in the long run such approaches made virtually no difference. Indeed, what had, by the early years of the nineteenth century, become an inescapable fact of Savannah life was recognized by a state law of 1818 that permitted bondpeople to sell goods valued at less than one dollar "without a ticket."[68] This same law allowed bondpeople in Liberty, McIntosh, Camden, and Glynn counties, but for reasons that are obscure, not in Chatham County, to dispose of "poultry at any time without a ticket."[69]

Some of the unauthorized vendors whom the Savannah City Council sought so unsuccessfully to curb had no intention whatsoever of returning to their owners once they had completed their business. From the 1760s onward, selling goods and negotiating for the sale of their labor in Savannah offered fugitive bondpeople the prospect of securing for themselves a coveted, albeit precarious, independence.[70]

The commodities offered for sale by runaways, who might be from the countryside or reside in Savannah, depended on what they could collect, gather, or manufacture. In 1774, for example, James Bulloch reported that two of his bondmen, Morris and July, who had "absented themselves for several weeks," were supporting themselves partly by "cutting and selling grass . . . about town." Hagar, who ran away from James Johnston in 1789, had "been seen . . . selling water melons near [Savannah]." John McKinnon was more than a little surprised in

1814 when quite by chance he encountered one of his bondwomen, Betty, who had "absconded . . . for several months," on her way to Savannah "with a basket, some huckle-berrys and a quart measure."[71] Twenty-year-old Adam kept himself by "cutting grass" and "bringing up oysters." Artisanal skills and the possession of tools offered other possibilities. When Will, a Virginia-born bondman, ran away in 1769 he took with him "tools for making bowls etc."[72] Will was not exceptional. Throughout this period many other fugitive bondmen sought to sell their skills in Savannah (see chapter 5).

Sometimes, as in Will's case, runaways were sufficiently fluent in English and sufficiently confident to try to sell their wares themselves, often by trying to persuade their prospective white customers that they were free men and women. It is also possible that someone like Will, who had been brought from Virginia, had no family members or friends in Savannah to whom he could look for help and was understandably reluctant to trust strangers. Some runaways, however, did have family or friends in the city who were happy to help them vend their wares and who often acted as go-betweens for fugitives and their customers. Adam, for example, was believed by his owner, Balthasar Shaffer, to have "lately joined up with his correspondents in town" for his "business" of "bringing up oysters."[73] Bob, an African-born runaway aged between twenty-five and thirty, was thought to be "harbored on some of the islands, a fishing for others to sell."[74]

As a white commentator pointed out in 1820, it was probable that at one time or another every white Savannahan had wittingly or unwittingly purchased goods from an unauthorized African or African-American vendor.[75] What this particular commentator did not add was that at times these goods almost certainly included some items that the purchasers knew or suspected had been appropriated by the bondpeople from their owners or other whites. Anthony Philips, Mark George, Lawrence Driscoll, and Pierre Thomasin, for example, could have been in little doubt about the source of the oil they purchased in 1806 "from the Negro slaves employed by the constables [of Savannah] to light the public lamps."[76] In the same year Charles Frushet was indicted by the Savannah City Council for "buying corn from Mr. Nix's Negroes at a late hour of the night, knowing it to be stolen," but the charge could not be made to stick.[77] For many white commentators, cases such as these two merely confirmed their belief that, as in the countryside, much of the vending conducted by bondpeople in Savannah involved "stolen" goods.

Beginning in the mid-1730s, with Pastor Bolzius's comments about the behavior of the South Carolina bondmen and bondwomen who assisted with the building of the Salzburger settlement of Ebenezer, many white Georgians, like their counterparts in the plantation societies of the southern mainland and Caribbean, were utterly convinced that West Africans had a predilection to steal. Elizabeth Cosson, who arrived in Savannah in the early 1770s, summed up the prevalent white opinion on the eve of the Revolutionary War when she commented that "the poor negroes are so disonest [sic] that they steal all things they can come at[.] I am told by Mr Wright and Mr Crane that they cannot bring up Pigs or Fowls but they will steal them unless there is an honest White person to look after them. . . . It is also said that they steal most things out of the Garden and break throu [sic] to steal the Beef out of the sellor [sic]." [78]

Sixty years later Emily Burke expressed a similar sentiment when she claimed that there was a "universal want [among planters] of confidence in the honesty of bondpeople. The fear of theft haunts the slave holder at all times and in all places." Indeed, she asserted, so great was this "fear" that "when night comes every movable article of property must be put under lock and key. Even the fowls have to be all collected together every evening." Such, she concluded, was "the propensity for stealing among the slaves . . . that even the dead are often exhumed for the purpose of securing their grave clothes." [79]

Few whites sympathized with Pastor Bolzius's belief that very often the appropriation of goods by bondpeople reflected their maltreatment by "Foolish masters." [80] The possibility, which was hinted at by Elizabeth Cosson, that the thefts so frequently complained about might stem from desperate need rather than greed was simply not contemplated by planters, especially during the decades following the American Revolution when they were increasingly keen to depict themselves as the benevolent providers of all the material needs of their bondmen and bondwomen. [81] From their standpoint, an increasingly attractive explanation of bondpeople's alleged predilection to appropriate goods was the untrustworthy character of West Africans.

That bondmen and bondwomen did indeed appropriate items from their owners or other whites, that they were widely believed to be doing so, and that they were sometimes encouraged to do so by their actual or potential white trading partners is evident from surviving accounts of the trials of bondpeople, published advertisements for runaways, and notices placed in the Savannah newspapers by whites who had "stopped" bondpeople in possession of goods ranging from bank notes and jewelry to gunpowder and grindstones.[82] The automatic assumption was that these and other items must have been stolen. If that was indeed so, then some commodities, such as food and clothing, were probably taken for the personal use of the bondpeople's families; other goods might have been taken with a view to selling or exchanging them. The distinction is not always clear-cut. In 1804, for instance, four bondmen and one bondwoman were tried and found guilty of "killing a sheep" belonging to William Savage. If they were in fact guilty as charged, they might have been seeking food for themselves and their families or looking to sell all or part of the carcass.[83]

During the course of a burglary, two bondmen, Frank and Abram, came across some goods they could use themselves and at least one item that presumably they hoped to sell or barter. Frank and Abram were tried in 1797 by a court in St. Marys on a charge of "breaking open the House of William Mowbray." Mowbray alleged that in addition to "a silver pencil case" the two bondmen had taken most of his clothes, "a considerable part of his Wife's apparel with some Blankets," and a "Hat belonging to his child." Some days later Frank was taken into custody because Mowbray had encountered him "in the street [wearing] his Waistcoat." Frank subsequently confessed to the court that he had "Mr. Mowbray's Goods in his possession" and Abram, who in all probability hoped to be able to fence it, was found with the "silver pencil case." The court duly sentenced both men to death.[84]

The fact that some bondpeople returned items they found, many of which they or their family members and friends could have used or sold, was seldom remarked on by whites. Between June 1809 and August 1813, for example, the *Georgia Republican* published thirty notices that were equally divided between those describing bondpeople who had been "stopped" in possession of various goods and those who had found lost property and turned it over to their owners. The items returned by bondpeople, whose names were never published, ranged from gold and silver watches to "a bag of Greenseed Cotton," "a Silk Handkerchief," and "a man's saddle." In two cases, one of which involved "Two Bills of One Hundred Dollars each," money was returned by bondpeople.[85] It may, of course, be argued that these items were turned in because they were of little use to the finder (although this argument loses some cogency with regard to money). Or perhaps the certainty of a monetary reward for "his honesty" was preferable to the uncertainty and possible difficulties that might be encountered when trying to dispose of the articles.

By the turn of the eighteenth century, what many whites chose to regard as the universal dishonesty of slaves was perceived in a rather different light by bondmen and bondwomen. As Charles Ball's comments indicate, from the bondpeople's perspective the ownership of the commodities they had produced for their owners was a highly debatable point. According to the laws drafted by whites, those items belonged as of right to the owner. But, asked Ball, did not the enslaved producers have a moral right to those same goods, to the fruits of their labor? On at least one occasion, when dealing with the captain of a trading vessel, Ball answered his own question in the affirmative and went ahead with his trade. According to this interpretation, the appropriation of goods one had produced or raised oneself, which included virtually every crop and animal on most plantations, was not construed as theft. But to appropriate items from other bondpeople in the slave quarters was. The moral economy that was being forged by bondpeople in lowcountry Georgia during the second half of the eighteenth century drew a clear distinction between "theft" and "stealing."[86] As John Brown explained, "I never considered it wicked to steal, because I looked upon what I took as part of what was due to me for my labor." He was "sure that, as a rule, any one of us would have thought nothing of stealing a hog, or sack of corn, from our masters, [but] would have allowed [ourselves] to be cut to pieces rather than betray the confidence of our fellow-slave[s]."[87] To most whites, such a distinction, if they were even aware of it, was entirely academic, utterly irrelevant. Certainly it did not stop some of them from dealing in what they knew or assumed to be "stolen" property.

The significance of Savannah to the bondmen and bondwomen of lowcountry Georgia as an outlet for the commodities they produced in their own time, or acquired by other means, mirrored that of the city's population growth. The living standards of plantation and urban bond-people, producers and vendors, were significantly enhanced by the economic links they had been instrumental in forging between countryside and town. And by the late 1760s and early 1770s the lowcountry towns offered bondpeople another way in which they could earn cash and at the same time enjoy an important, if often uncertain, independence. All except the very young and the very old among the lowcountry's enslaved population had this commodity at their disposal: their labor. By the mid-1770s self-hire had emerged as an integral component of the Savannah labor market. For owners in town and countryside alike it was an increasingly worrisome one.

5 ❧ Self-hire in Savannah

THE POPULATION growth and economic diversification of Savannah, and to a lesser extent of Darien and Sunbury, after the mid-1750s provided bondmen and bondwomen with ever-increasing opportunities to negotiate terms for the sale of their labor as well as their surplus produce. As in the countryside, engaging in one of these income-generating activities did not rule out the possibility of engaging in the other on a different, or even on the same, occasion. By the mid-1770s urban as well as plantation bondpeople had carved out for themselves the option—the right—of selling their labor, but it was a right they could not take for granted.[1] There were to be some broad similarities, as well as some profound differences, between self-hire in the towns and self-hire in the countryside.

Self-hire in the lowcountry towns, especially that involving skilled and semiskilled bondpeople, was greatly facilitated by the adamant refusal of owners to accept any restrictions on the kinds of work that might be undertaken by their bondmen and bondwomen, and their equally strong insistence that they be allowed to hire out their enslaved workers as and when they pleased. But during the 1750s this resolution had by no means been assured. The notion that all forms of urban employment should, without restriction, be open to bondpeople did not go uncontested.

By the early 1740s the trustees had conceded, albeit grudgingly, that in the context of plantation agriculture enslaved Africans would prove far more remunerative than any form of white labor currently available.[2] But it was for precisely this reason that they believed the ban on chattel slavery ought to be maintained. In their opinion, the experiences of the other plantation colonies amply demonstrated the degree to which the competition of enslaved labor eroded the living standards of white workers and, as a result, deterred prospective European migrants. The trustees insisted that what the Georgia of the 1740s needed, if only for military reasons, was more, rather than fewer, white settlers— because only they could be depended on to defend the colony.[3]

In 1755 Georgia's continuing vulnerability to Spanish invasion and its limited population growth after two decades of settlement prompted the planter-politicians who dominated the assembly to agree that under certain circumstances carefully recruited bondmen might be drafted into the militia and, if absolutely necessary, serve as combat troops.[4] In the event, such legislation, which reflected the sheer desperation of the planter elite as it wrestled with the problem of how Georgia's burgeoning plantation economy might best be protected, was never implemented. However, the emergency that prompted planters to even contemplate the arming of bondmen also served to keep alive the argument that it was imperative to build up the colony's white population by encouraging, or at least not actively discouraging, European migration to what was still a highly exposed frontier society. By 1758 the issue was clear-cut. In the broader public interest of trying to attract more immigrants by safeguarding the living standards of those white workers already in the colony, would the planters be willing to forego some of the undoubted economic benefits that accrued to them from the flexible employment of their bondpeople?

Predictably, by the end of the 1750s it was the white artisans and craftsmen who were insisting that the urban employment of bondpeople in various skilled and semiskilled occupations should be severely restricted. After less than a decade of facing entirely unregulated competition from bondpeople, they needed little persuading that, as the trustees had predicted, their living standards suffered as a result. In 1758 they pressed the assembly to protect their interests. Some eminent planters grumbled about "the Greediness and insatiable Thirst after Gain of a few Tradesmen," but for essentially pragmatic reasons felt they could not simply dismiss the latter's demands out of hand.[5] The result was legislation that, on the face of it, made most of the concessions demanded by white "Tradesmen," but that in reality scarcely threatened the freedom of owners to deploy their bondpeople as they wished in Georgia's embryonic urban economies. Ironically, those who pressed for government intervention in 1758 were to be those who eventually stood to lose most by it.

The steps taken by the assembly to placate those who were complaining about the intense competition they were encountering from enslaved workers were modest in the extreme. The act of 1758, ostensibly "to encourage Tradesmen to Settle in the several Towns" of Georgia, stated that bondpeople could be employed as "Shipwrights, caulkers, Sawyers [and] Coopers" in Savannah, Augusta, Frederica, and Ebenezer and apparently conceded that they should ply no other trades in these four towns. This did not necessarily mean that all other skilled and semiskilled jobs would be reserved for whites. Partly to curry the support of those craftsmen and tradesmen who owned or aspired to the ownership of African or African-American apprentices, but mainly to protect the interests of those planters who might wish to hire out their enslaved artisans in the towns, a rider was added declaring that those owners whose bondpeople had "been brought up" to their "Trade" and had followed it for at least a year would not be "debarred the privilege & benefit of such negro or other slaves work." The only legal obligation under which masters were placed was that of issuing their bondpeople who "worked out of their respective Houses" with "a Tickett [*sic*] in Writing." It was forbidden to employ a bondperson who was not in possession of such a document.[6] In effect, free and enslaved craftsmen and artisans would continue to compete in virtually every branch of the skilled and semiskilled labor market.

For white artisans and craftsmen, the most ominous provision of the act of 1758 was that it established maximum wages for certain kinds of work. The assembly took the not entirely disinterested view that if left to their own devices, if not made subject to competition from bondpeople, some whites might be tempted to "make Exorbitant Demands for their respective Work." To protect the owners of skilled and semiskilled bondpeople, and in the process the interests of white consumers, the act provided for nonelected commissioners who would meet annually "to Limit rate and appoint the Price of the work of all Carpenters Joiners Bricklayers and Plaisterers [*sic*] either by the day week or

Month." If the tradesman in question held out for a higher rate, then his prospective customer was free "to engage and employ . . . negroe or other slave Artificers without Limitation."[7] Before 1758 the maximum wages of white craftsmen and artisans had been fixed de facto by the notional wages of their enslaved competitors. The de jure arrangement of 1758 further eroded these whites' already weak bargaining position and tightened the planter elite's grip on what might be described as the formal market for skilled and semiskilled labor in the lowcountry.

The act of 1758 was allowed to lapse in 1763 because the assembly saw no good reason to reenact it and apparently was under no great political pressure to do so. The defeat of Spain and the end of the Seven Years' War may have diminished the force of the argument that Georgia needed, if only out of military necessity, to attract white migrants who could be called on to defend the colony against external aggressors. From the perspective of those who had a vested economic interest in the employment of skilled and semiskilled bondpeople, and this included everyone who sought the cheapest form of labor as well as those who owned such workers, the de facto regulation of white wages might not be as precise a way of controlling the skilled and semiskilled labor market, but ultimately it achieved the same ends as the act of 1758.

There is no extant record of the reactions of white artisans and craftsmen to the disappearance of the act of 1758 from the statute book. For some, of course, it meant the relief of not having their fees fixed by commissioners; for all it meant a return to unregulated competition, not only with each other but also increasingly with enslaved artisans and craftsmen who might be hired out legally by their owners or who sold their skills on their own behalf. The pressure that white tradesmen had brought to bear on the assembly in 1758 had backfired and, if nothing else, perhaps demonstrated the futility of looking to a planter-dominated government for help in safeguarding their standards of living.

The assembly's inaction in 1763 provoked no public protest from skilled and semiskilled white workers. This did not mean that the employment of bondpeople, particularly skilled bondpeople, in Savannah was removed from the political agenda. On the contrary, this subject would continue to figure prominently in the ongoing debate about the quasi-autonomous economic activities of bondmen and bondwomen.

Increasingly, however, it was a debate that focused on the interests of those who owned skilled and semiskilled bondpeople rather than on the economic interests of white tradesmen.[8]

White carpenters and other "mechanics" organized themselves and were incorporated as the Savannah Association of Mechanics in the early 1790s. But despite meeting regularly thereafter, not until the 1830s did they orchestrate political campaigns designed to protect their livelihood against the city's comparatively small number of free African-American artisans and craftsmen and the mounting competition from bondpeople that came in one of two forms.[9] First, they, and indeed skilled and semiskilled free African-Americans, were forced to compete with bondpeople who were employed or hired out by their owners. Second, they had to compete with those who, usually unbeknownst to their owners, negotiated on their own behalf for the sale of their labor.

No occupational censuses were taken of the lowcountry's enslaved population during this period, but advertisements for the return of fugitive slaves suggest the growing range of skills bondmen had at their disposal. Between 1763 and 1821 advertisements for fugitive bondmen referred to wagoners, coopers, carpenters, blacksmiths, tailors, and weavers, as well as other occupations. During this time period the percentage of advertisements in which the bondperson's skill was mentioned increased by 50 percent. Unfortunately, the number of advertisements that mention the skills of fugitive bondwomen is too small to support any conclusions about changes in the types of skills they might have learned. Bondpeople also held jobs other than those mentioned in the published advertisements for fugitives. Estate, city, and government records, as well as notices placed in local newspapers by owners seeking to hire out their bondpeople and by those in search of a particular skill or service, reveal examples of bondmen who worked as chimney sweeps, joiners and cabinetmakers, butchers' assistants, and barbers.[10] In addition to the vendors, washerwomen, and ubiquitous "House Servants" mentioned in the advertisements for female runaways, some bondwomen were also employed, in town and countryside alike, as cooks, seamstresses, nannies, and wet nurses.[11]

In the towns and the countryside of lowcountry Georgia, as in all the plantation societies of the southern United States and the Caribbean, gender was the principal determinant of occupation.[12] Skilled and semiskilled work was monopolized by men. Neither rural nor urban records reveal any bondwomen who worked as coopers, carpenters, blacksmiths, or the like. These jobs were effectively restricted to bondmen. In both town and country many, but not all, household jobs were reserved for women. On large plantations, for instance, upward of 10 percent of bondwomen might be employed as cooks, maids, washerwomen, nurses, midwives, and seamstresses.[13] However, in the countryside the vast majority of enslaved women worked as field hands, and there was a very real sense in which they were tied to the rice, indigo, and, by the late eighteenth century, cotton fields. In Savannah and the other lowcountry towns some bondwomen worked as vendors, but most were employed in their owner's home or were hired out to work in somebody else's home as domestic servants of one sort or another.

On one level, what was true of bondwomen was true of bondmen also. Throughout this period somewhere on the order of 80 to 85 percent of bondmen apparently worked in unskilled jobs: as field hands in the countryside, as porters and day laborers in Savannah, Darien, and Sunbury. But there was a crucial difference. Whether occupation necessarily conferred the same prestige and authority in the quarters as it did in white society is highly debatable, but insofar as it is possible to talk of an occupational elite among bondpeople in lowcountry Georgia, then that elite was predominantly male. When it came to selling their labor, members of that male elite enjoyed options that were effectively closed to bondwomen and, it must be added, to the majority of bondmen. Those bondmen who had been trained for more than one type of work were in a particularly advantageous position when it came to maximizing the opportunities for securing an income through the sale of their labor.

In 1763 the planter-dominated Georgia assembly had unequivocally declared its opposition to any attempts to curb the employment of skilled or semiskilled bondpeople in the lowcountry towns. They never entertained the possibility of restricting the use of unskilled bondpeople either in Savannah or in any of the lowcountry's other, smaller, towns. By the mid-1770s, however, mainly because of the activities of bondmen and bondwomen in Savannah, they were forced to address the need to try to control the employment of unskilled bondpeople in the urban economies.

In 1774, for the first but certainly not the last time, the Georgia government turned its attention to the regulation of unskilled labor in Savannah. The de jure attempt to establish maximum rates for the work undertaken by certain white artisans and craftsmen had been abandoned by the planter elite in 1763 at absolutely no cost to itself; eleven years later the elite sought to further tighten its control of the urban labor markets by legislating maximum "wages" for unskilled bondpeople, a policy that had the additional effect of establishing the going rate for unskilled white workers. In 1758 some assemblymen had complained about the rates demanded by white "Tradesmen"; in 1774 they seem to have been far more concerned by the "wages" being demanded by bondpeople who were negotiating on their own behalf for the sale of their labor.

Owners demanded maximum flexibility in the deployment of their bondpeople, skilled and unskilled alike, in the urban as well as in the rural economy; merchants and shippers sought the cheapest form of labor to fetch and carry goods, to load and unload trading vessels. By its very nature, and completely unlike the situation in the countryside, the unskilled work demanded of urban bondpeople outside their owners' homes was immensely difficult to supervise, financially and in other ways.

The transportation of goods to and from the docks, the packing and unpacking of cargoes, often brought the bondpeople concerned into contact with several different employers during the course of their day's work. It was impracticable for owners to negotiate terms with each and every prospective employer of their bondpeople, and until 1774 bondmen and bondwomen were left very much to their own devices. Usually they were instructed by their owners to return at the end of each day, or week, with a certain amount of money and then sent out to earn it by whatever means they could.[14] They might also be expected to feed and clothe themselves out of the money they made.

This system was analogous to the task system in that the sum stipulated by the owner represented a task, or a set of tasks, to be completed by the bondperson on any given day or during any given week or month. The tacit understanding was that anything the bondperson was able to earn over and above that sum was his or hers to keep. But what if bondmen and bondwomen were unable to earn the minimum sum demanded by their owners? As Pastor Bolzius was informed by a group of bondpeople he met while en route to Charleston, those who found themselves in this situation sometimes felt that the only way they could avoid a flogging was by resorting to theft. Many owners, they told him, neither knew nor cared how the money handed over to them had been made.[15]

In 1774, principally because of the belief that unskilled urban bondpeople were overcharging for their work, and consequently had cash at their disposal to spend on alcohol and other "evil Courses," the assembly followed the example of Charleston and fixed the rates of pay for the kinds of jobs bondpeople most commonly undertook in Savannah. These ranged from nine pence for every "Hogshead of Rum, Pipe of Wine or Hogshead of Sugar" taken from "the Top of the Bluff" to "the Strand or any place between that and Saint Julien Street" to one shilling and sixpence for delivering the same items "to any part of the Town on the North line of the Common." [16]

Unskilled bondpeople could also be hired and paid by the day. The payment for a whole day's work, from dawn "until Dusk," was set at one shilling and sixpence; for half a day's work one shilling; and for "the fourth part of a day" sixpence. Bondpeople who worked "on Board any Ship or Vessel" would be paid two shillings a day, and the "Owner . . . to furnish necessary Provisions." Any bondperson who refused to work for these rates was liable to receive a maximum of thirty lashes "on the Bare Back." [17] These pay scales, which set no limits on the number of tasks a bondperson might need or wish to undertake on any given day or during any given week, were periodically reviewed and amended.[18] Beginning in 1774 the de jure regulation of the rates received by unskilled bondpeople also ensured the de facto regulation of wages paid not only to unskilled whites but also to those bondpeople who did not have their owners' permission to hire out their labor.

The fixing of pay scales was twinned with another provision that sought to ensure not only that Savannah's unskilled slave labor market would be restricted to those men and women who did have permission to work but also that they could be easily identified as they went about their business. Many white Georgians were fearful that, regardless of whether they had their owners' consent, the bondpeople who worked in Savannah might well take advantage of their comparative freedom of mobility to foment organized rebellion. The problem the assembly sought to resolve in 1774 was how best to minimize the threat of racial disorder while retaining the economic advantages reaped by owners and white employers from the flexible deployment of bondmen and bondwomen in the urban economy.

As with the pay scales drawn up in 1774, the assembly took a leaf out of the South Carolina book and introduced a badge system, identical to that for vendors, which would allow those bondpeople who had their owners' permission to work for hire to be readily identified. The onus was placed on owners to purchase annually from the city authorities a badge that had to be worn at all times by those of their bondpeople who were permitted to work in Savannah.

In 1774 the public authorities charged a flat rate of ten shillings per badge, regardless of the bondperson's occupation. That sum remained unaltered until 1787, when owners were required to pay a fee of one shilling and sixpence for registering each bondperson whom they wished to hire out and twenty shillings sterling per badge. Three years later the Savannah City Council introduced a sliding scale that linked the cost of a badge to the bondperson's occupational skills. Owners who hired out bondmen, or allowed their bondmen to hire themselves out, as cabinetmakers, carpenters, caulkers, bricklayers, blacksmiths, tailors, barbers, bakers, or butchers were required to pay twenty shillings per badge. For other "mechanics or handicraft tradesmen" the figure was set at ten shillings. A badge for "a porter or other daily labourer" cost seven shillings and sixpence.

These fees were revised in 1792 when the cost of a badge for each of the bondpeople who fell into the first category was reduced to fifteen shillings. The second category remained unchanged and the third was lowered by sixpence. An important innovation in 1792 was that owners were required to buy a badge, which cost three shillings and sixpence, for each of their bondpeople, mainly bondwomen, who were "hired for domestic service by the month or week." [19] No doubt most owners took these charges into account when determining the amount of money they demanded for those of their bondpeople who were hired out. Finally, as with the purchase of commodities from bondpeople, prospective employers were forbidden to hire any bondperson not displaying the requisite badge. In 1783 the fine for hiring unlicensed help was set at ten shillings per day per bondperson.[20]

The Savannah records did not distinguish between those badges made for enslaved vendors and those made for men and women whose labor was for hire. And in the absence of anything approximating an occupational census of lowcountry bondpeople it is impossible to determine precisely how many bondmen and bondwomen fell into the second of those categories.[21] A rare estimate of the number of bondpeople "that live by themselves & allow their Master a certain Sum for Work" was made by the Rev. Samuel Frink in 1771. Frink claimed that 40, or almost exactly 5 percent, of Savannah's 821 bondpeople were authorized by their owners for hire.[22]

The regulations concerning the hire of unskilled bondpeople proved just as difficult to enforce, and for similar reasons, as those that sought to control the vending of goods. To a considerable extent, the income of those bondpeople without a badge who sought work depended on two considerations: their own willingness, or desperate need, to undercut the prices that authorized bondmen and bondwomen were legally permitted to charge and the willingness of whites to break the law and employ them. From the mid-1760s owners constantly complained that their bondpeople were being illegally employed in Savannah. More often than not, these complaints concerned bondmen and bondwomen who had taken flight from the countryside and made for Savannah, either in the hope of escaping by sea or by eking out a free, but precarious, existence in town.

Throughout this eighty-year period, and in keeping with the pattern elsewhere on the southern mainland, there was a conspicuous imbalance between the number of advertised male and female runaways.[23] Before the American War of Independence only 13 percent of runaways were women, a proportion that increased to 23 percent during the two decades after the war. Twenty years later it remained at almost exactly the same level. These proportions of male and female fugitives did not reflect a similar gender imbalance in the enslaved population as a whole. As Peter H. Wood has remarked of South Carolina, bondwomen were "more likely than men to visit . . . and return of their own accord in a pattern less likely to prompt public advertising." [24] It is probable that, mainly because of the constraints imposed by motherhood and occupation, precisely the same was true of lowcountry Georgia.[25] Rather more difficult to explain is the virtual doubling of the proportion of advertised women runaways following the Revolutionary War. Perhaps, as a result of wartime dislocations and separations, more women were actually absconding than had been the case during the colonial period. Or perhaps owners were more disposed to advertise for the return of their bondwomen, especially during the immediate postwar years when they were particularly hard-pressed for workers. The eventual closing of the African slave trade might also have played a part in convincing owners to do all they could to retrieve their runaways.

The assumed motives and destinations of runaways varied in much the same manner as they did elsewhere in the eighteenth- and early nineteenth-century South. However, after the Revolutionary War owners became rather more willing to express an opinion on this subject, a possible indication of their growing familiarity with their bondpeople. The published comments of owners who knew, or thought they knew, the intentions of their fugitive bondmen and bondwomen suggest that, overall, destinations did not change dramatically between the 1760s and the early 1820s. Two notable exceptions are the steady increase in men who were assumed to be returning to "former residence" and women who were trying to reach "husband/family."

During the postwar years a higher proportion, but not markedly dissimilar proportions, of bondmen and bondwomen were said by their owners to have taken flight in order to be reunited with a family member or to return to a former residence. This no doubt reflects the growth of family and kinship networks in the lowcountry and the continuing propensity of owners to separate partners and split families. The addition of the Chesapeake to the list of destinations after the Revolutionary War underscores the growing significance of the internal slave trade for the lowcountry and the unquenchable desire of bondmen and bondwomen to return to their former homes.

Before, after, and during the Revolutionary War the backcountry and Florida were attractive to those who sought their escape from the lowcountry and their liberation from chattel slavery. However, proportionately fewer bondwomen than bondmen were said by their owners to be making for these destinations—again almost certainly reflecting the constraints of maternity and occupation.

Savannah proved a magnet for fugitive bondmen and bondwomen alike. But if owners were correct in their assumptions, a noticeably higher proportion of bondwomen were already in, or were believed to be making for, that city. Until the end of the eighteenth century at least one-fifth of all female fugitives fell into this category; by the early 1820s this had increased to just over one-quarter. There is some suggestion, though, that the gender gap was closing: between the 1780s and the early 1820s the proportion of bondmen believed to have Savannah as their destination increased from just under 15 percent to almost 19 percent.

Fugitive bondpeople made for or remained in Savannah for different reasons. Some saw only the river and the port—the prospect of being able to make their escape from the lowcountry by sea. For them Savannah was a springboard to freedom; they had no intention of staying in the city for any longer than necessary. Some were seeking to be reunited with family members and friends who lived in Savannah; others relished the prospect of carving out for themselves a quasi-independence in the town, of blending into the black urban crowd. Whatever the attractions held by Savannah, and clearly they were many, fugitive bondpeople, particularly those without family or friends to whom they could turn for material support, had to consider the question of how to secure their livelihood. In theory, their labor was the commodity all of them had at their disposal; in practice, successfully negotiating for the sale of that commodity would be determined by linguistic ability, occupational skills, and gender, as well as by the willingness of white Savannahans to employ them. Fugitive bondpeople seldom found the latter in short supply.

Bondmen and bondwomen displayed as much ingenuity in negotiating for the sale of their labor in Savannah as they did for the sale of their produce. Polydore, who absented himself from Levi Sheftall in 1785, had "worked as a porter" in the city and clearly did not rule out the possibility of continuing in that line of work because he took with him "his porters ticket no. 16 or 17 when he went away.["] [26] Jack, a mulatto in his midtwenties, was thought by his owner to have "procured a forged free paper," which he might use to try to secure employment as a coachman until he could "get on a vessel for some eastern or northern port." [27] Another bondman named Jack, who absconded in 1819, was said by his owner to be "an excellent scribe" who was in possession of a pass that he had forged for himself. [28] At least one master thought his bondperson had managed to obtain a pass, or ticket, from a white person. John, who ran away from Christopher Hall in late 1796 or early

1797, had been "seen several times talking with a White Man [on] the evening before he went off." According to Hall, the man in question "had been a companion with [John] in gaol and it is supposed he has given him a pass." [29] Hall did not mention, probably because he did not know, whether John intended to use his pass to try to escape from the lowcountry or whether he would try to pass as free in Savannah.

There is no way of knowing whether John paid for his pass, and if so how much, but one bondman who did, although not with money, was John Brown. Brown managed to obtain "a forged pass from a poor white man, for which I gave him an old hen." [30] That bondpeople who could write might forge tickets and freedom papers for their compatriots is suggested by an advertisement placed in the *Daily Savannah Republican* on 2 February 1818 by Morgan Mara of Liberty County. Mara noted that two of his bondmen, Ned and Trim, who he did not indicate were related by blood or marriage, were "likely" to be in possession of forged documents. He believed that Ned, who "can write," had probably "forged a pass for Trim and himself."

Literacy was not the sole preserve of bondmen; bondwomen too were able to forge passes. In 1807 Jane Morrice commented that Holland, who was "well known in Savannah as a washerwoman . . . may have forged a pass and will endeavor to pass herself as a free woman." In the same year an African-born woman named Mary, who had "been in the country about seven years" and was "used to house work, as a cook and washer etc and has occasionally worked in the field," was thought by her owner, Edward Stebbins, "to have a forged pass." [31]

Many owners knew that, with or without forged papers, their bondpeople had a sufficient knowledge of the workings of white society, a sufficient command of the English language, and were glib enough to persuade prospective employers that they either were free or had permission to hire out their labor. Like many other owners, James Cochran was convinced that two of his bondpeople, Wilkes and Peg, would resort to one or the other of these ploys. Both of them, he claimed, were "very artful." [32] The increasing frequency with which the words "artful" and "plausible" occurred in the published advertisements for runaways is indicative of the extent to which lowcountry planters shared Cochran's conviction that some whites might be duped into illicitly employing their bondmen and bondwomen.

There was no significant gender differentiation in the depiction of runaways as "artful" or "plausible." The increasing application of these epithets during the early national period, together with increasing references to runaways' "look" or "countenance," might have reflected a growing acquaintance of lowcountry planters with their bondpeople. It might also be taken as firm evidence of growing white concerns about what they correctly perceived to be the assertiveness of bondpeople, an assertiveness that had been heightened during the Revolutionary War.[33] Those concerns were further fueled during the 1790s by the Santo Domingo revolution, a firsthand experience of which was brought to the lowcountry by French émigrés and their bondpeople.[34]

When readers of the lowcountry's newspapers were presented with images of runaways as "artful," "plausible," and "surly" they were being reminded and warned of the need to be alert, to be constantly on their guard. The message was clear: bondpeople should not be taken at face value and they were never entirely to be trusted. But after the American Revolution white Georgians were simultaneously presented with another, and from their perspective rather more comforting, stereotype: the "downcast," "modest," "smiling" bondperson. This was not necessarily an imagined personality, nor was it necessarily at odds with the image of the "artful," "surly," "impertinent" bondperson. The downcast look the owner saw might have reflected an internalized deference and compliance that "arose from a plantation slave community that identified white culture with the whip." But as Eugene Genovese has pointed out, there is another possible explanation. That same look, he argues, "betrayed not any fear but smouldering anger and resentment."[35]

Whether they were seeking work in Savannah or their escape from the lowcountry, fugitive bondpeople frequently proved to be as "smart" and "intelligent," as "artful" and "plausible" as their owners intimated they would be. They changed their clothing and their names in an attempt to disguise themselves; they were often able to talk their way out of trouble and sometimes out of the lowcountry. Those who chose to remain in, or make their way to, Savannah found it comparatively easy to talk themselves into jobs.

All but the most naive of white employers must have suspected that many of the bondpeople without badges who approached them in search of work, or whom they approached with the offer of a job, were fugitives. But often the white person's need dovetailed with that of the bondperson: the bondperson needed work; the prospective employer wanted to obtain the services he or she sought as cheaply as possible. For whites, given the fairly slight risk of being caught by or reported to the Savannah authorities, the financial incentive was compelling. The risk was considerably greater for the bondperson, especially for those who were said by their owners to be "known in Savannah." Their employers were unlikely to turn them in, but there was always the chance they might be challenged by the Savannah city guard or recognized by a white person who knew or suspected them to be fugitives. When these situations arose bondpeople needed to be as "artful" as possible, to have the presence of mind and the ability "to tell a plausible story." If they were unable to carry this off they were virtually guaranteed a flogging, if not from the city guard then almost certainly from their owners. Advertisements placed by the likes of Thomas Johnston and Gardener Tufts promising that if their runaways returned "of their own accord they will be forgiven" provided a chilling reminder, as if bondpeople needed any reminder, of what was likely to happen if they were apprehended.[36]

The enslaved population of lowcountry Georgia knew full well the dangers they ran, the potentially enormous physical cost to themselves if they fled but were unable to make good their escape. Similar costs were likely to be paid by bondpeople who harbored or helped family members, friends, or even strangers they knew to be fugitives. Yet there is little evidence that the awareness of those costs persuaded bondpeople to inform on runaways. Neither did offers of financial rewards up to one hundred dollars, although more usually in the range of five to fifty dollars, sums it might take bondpeople days, weeks, or even months to earn.

The skills and services offered in the Savannah labor market by fugitives or by bondpeople who had not run away but who sought to secure an independent income encompassed every branch of slave employment. Some indication of the occupational skills offered by bondpeople who worked without a badge, whether residents of Savannah or runaways from the countryside, may be gathered from the records kept by the Savannah City Council of the fines imposed on owners whose bondpeople had been caught working without permission. Between

1791 and 1793, for instance, occupations included barbering, butchering, and carpentry.[37] Advertisements placed in the press by owners of runaways suggest that bricklayers, painters, coopers, wheelwrights, sawyers, bakers, tailors, joiners, and cabinetmakers also sought to sell their skills in Savannah.[38]

Many owners believed that their bondpeople, especially if they were well known in the town or were without occupational skills, were likely to seek more anonymous employment in and around Savannah's docks. Or they might, regardless of whether they had any prior experience, seek work as boat hands or sailors. If the claims of owners are to be believed, bondmen had little trouble finding whites who were willing, even eager, to employ them in these capacities.[39]

Owners advertising for the return of runaways who they knew or suspected were working in Savannah or on the trading vessels that plied the Savannah River seldom knew who was employing them. Edward Warren was a rare example of an owner who knew, or believed he knew, the name of the person who had illicitly hired one of his fugitive bondpeople. His bondman Poladore, he claimed, "has been employed on board of the Augusta boat last week, on a part thereof by a Mr. Jordan, and contracted to go on a voyage with him to Augusta."[40] More often, owners of runaways issued a general warning to the effect that they would not hesitate to bring to bear the full force of the law against any person or persons discovered to be employing their bondpeople. Ann Elon spoke for many owners when she asserted that "several persons have made a practice of employing my two bricklayer fellows Bob and Smart without my consent to work at their trade, whereby I have been materially injured, I do hereby forewarn for the future, all persons from employing them in any manner whatsoever without first applying to me, otherwise they may depend on being prosecuted to the utmost extent of the law."[41]

The effectiveness of such threats is highly dubious. They may have deterred some employers, but it is abundantly clear that many whites simply ignored them. Between September 1791 and October 1793, for instance, only fourteen owners were fined by the Savannah City Council for permitting their bondpeople to work without a badge. Five of the bondmen concerned were plying a trade (four were working as barbers, one as a carpenter); one was employed as a butcher, another as a fisherman. Only two were said to be working as porters. The work being undertaken by the remainder was not mentioned, which strongly suggests that it was unskilled.

The extant records of the bondmen and bondwomen who were picked up and taken to Savannah's jail between April 1809 and May 1815 indicate that on only fifty-seven occasions were charges brought for vending or working without permission.[42] By the 1820s comparatively few fines were being levied by the Savannah City Council on owners for permitting their bondpeople to work without a badge. In May and June 1823, for instance, only three were fined; in February 1825, four; in May 1827, five.[43] Neither the Savannah jail book nor these later city records indicate what type of work was being performed by the bondpeople concerned.

In many respects the situation regarding the illicit hire of enslaved labor paralleled illicit vending by bondpeople. Savannah's streets and wharves were virtually impossible to police effectively, and the city authorities could not rely on white citizens to turn in bondpeople who were seeking to negotiate for the sale of their labor. Quite the contrary, in fact. By the early years of the nineteenth century self-hire was as much a fact of Savannah life as the vending of goods.

Owners who advertised for the return of their fugitive bondpeople assumed that the men and women concerned would encounter few difficulties in finding work in Savannah. But the opportunities for self-hire in Savannah were shaped by an important consideration: gender. This, more than anything else, determined the types of occupational skills that could be offered to prospective white employers. The vast majority of rural and urban bondwomen in the lowcountry worked in unskilled capacities. Even the possession of domestic skills—the ability to cook; to wash, iron, make, and mend clothes—did not necessarily mean fugitive women would find it easy to negotiate for the sale of their labor in the lowcountry towns. At best, all they could hope for in Savannah was occasional employment as washerwomen, seamstresses, and domestics. And in their search for such work they were likely to encounter stiff competition from Savannah's resident bondwomen and, particularly as washerwomen and seamstresses, from the town's free African-American women, the majority of whom were employed in these two occupations by the early years of the nineteenth century.

Moreover, it was most unlikely that whites who could afford to hire domestic labor would take an unknown bondwoman into their home, at least not on a permanent basis, without some recommendation from a previous employer. It was simpler, and safer, for whites to advertise for help in one of the local newspapers.[44]

In town and countryside some bondmen worked in domestic capacities, as cooks, butlers, valets, barbers, grooms, and coachmen. But they had an option that was essentially closed to bondwomen: if unable to secure employment in their area of expertise, they could head to Savannah's wharves, seeking work as porters and carters or trying to persuade a ship's captain to hire them. Theoretically, there was nothing to prevent bondwomen from doing exactly the same. But in practice it was a very different matter: these types of work were clearly delineated as being men's work. The Savannah wharves and docks, the shipping waiting to be loaded or unloaded were men's sphere, not women's. Bondwomen, who were well known for their ability to carry large loads to and from the public market, might have tried and even managed to get occasional work fetching and carrying goods around Savannah. But for the heavier types of labor associated with porterage, white employers would almost certainly try to negotiate terms with a bondman.

Employment prospects for bondwomen in the lowcountry towns were far more limited than they were for bondmen. Friends and family members might have offered material support, however minimal, to women fugitives from the countryside; women who normally resided in Savannah might have looked to vending as a viable means of securing a regular income. But by the mid-1810s at least one white commentator was claiming that many bondwomen were securing incomes in Savannah through the sale of their bodies. In a scathing critique of the sexual mores of African and African-American women "ANTI-MULATTO," the pseudonym adopted by an anonymous correspondent to the *Savannah Republican* in 1817, claimed that prostitution was rife in the city.[45] However, "ANTI-MULATTO" offered no substantive evidence in support of this allegation, nor do the city council records or the Savannah jail book. None of the bondwomen lodged in the jail between 1809 and 1815 was charged with prostitution.

As in all the slave societies of the New World, sexual liaisons between white men and African-American women were formed in Savannah and elsewhere in the lowcountry. However, insofar as the early national lowcountry is concerned their number, duration, and significance are highly debatable. To ensure economic survival or because of their vulnerability to sexual harassment by white men, some bondwomen may have felt they had little choice but to enter into essentially casual, exploitative relationships. On the other hand, some relationships appear to have been long-standing and, it seems reasonable to suggest, may have reflected mutual affection rather than purely material considerations. Given the total absence of personal testimony dating from these years, the ways in which bondwomen viewed their relationships with white men must remain a matter for conjecture.

The income that bondpeople might expect to earn by negotiating for the sale of their labor varied enormously. For porters and laborers the rate they could ask was set by law. For all bondpeople hired out by their owners, the money they were able to keep for themselves depended on the amount demanded of them by their owners. Their income was also affected by the number and kind of jobs they were able and willing to undertake for any given time period. This in turn depended on the demand for their services. For those working at the wharves and docks, this could vary according to the amount of shipping that cleared the port of Savannah. The income of bondpeople who were hired out by their owners and wore the requisite badge might be threatened by those, including runaways, willing to sell their labor at a lower rate than that fixed by law. There was almost certainly competition, and the potential for conflict, between these two groups, but unfortunately the records shed no light whatsoever on this issue.

One of the few extant accounts of the income earned by an urban bondman who had his owner's permission to hire out his services is that penned by William Grimes. Obviously it would be foolhardy to extrapolate a universal pattern from Grimes's testimony, but his experiences were probably not unique. In the early nineteenth century Grimes, who at that time was owned by Archibald Bulloch, was "left, by my master's order, to work out and pay him three dollars per week, and find myself."

Grimes found various kinds of employment in and around Savannah, some of it temporary, some of it more permanent. He began by

working "on board the *Epervier* . . . for . . . about a month." The vessel's
owner, a Mr. Irving, paid him "one dollar for each day I worked there."
After he left Irving's employ Grimes "worked about town for a few
days," doing precisely what he did not say. His search for work took him
out of Savannah, to the plantation owned by a Mr. Houstoun, where
he got a week's work "mowing." The rate he negotiated with Houstoun
was also a dollar a day. The arrival of the *James Monroe*, "a national
vessel," in Savannah offered Grimes his next chance of employment.
The captain employed him "as cook and steward" for seventy-five cents
a day. But compensation came in another form: he did not have to pay
for his own food. Grimes did not record how long he served on board
the *James Monroe*. The last job he mentioned involved another change
of employer and employment. This time he found work as a carriage
driver for "Mr. Burrows a brother-in-law of my master." Burrows appears to have paid him on a monthly basis at the rate of "twenty dollars
a month."[46]

Assuming that Grimes worked a six-day week and had no other
sources of income during the time he was hired out, his disposable income once he had settled with Bulloch ranged from $1.50 to $3.00 per
week. Except for the time he worked on the *James Monroe*, Grimes had
to use a portion of this money to buy food for himself. Some owners
demanded more than three dollars a week from their bondpeople who
were hired out. Charles Ball, for instance, encountered some bondmen in Savannah "who went out to work, where and with whom they
pleased, received their own wages, and provided their own subsistence."
One of these men told Ball "that he paid six dollars on every Saturday evening, to his master." But even so, the man in question "was
comfortably dressed, and appeared to live well."[47]

Grimes's income, which varied from job to job, and the sum demanded each week by his owner, may or may not have been typical,
but in all probability one aspect of his experience would have been entirely familiar to most of the bondpeople who sought employment in
and around Savannah: his flexibility. Or to put it another way, bondpeople in Grimes's position could not afford to be choosy about the type
of work they did. Given that he had to pay his owner and maintain himself out of his wages, Grimes had little choice but to take on whatever
jobs he could find. He was nothing if not adaptable.

The incomes of bondpeople in Savannah varied considerably, as did the sources of those incomes. Some earned money from the sale of their labor, some from the sale of goods. But however they may have obtained it, many bondpeople had money to spend, even if in comparatively small amounts and only occasionally. Despite all the legal obstacles placed in their way, it proved—to the increasing consternation of some whites but to the great satisfaction of others—comparatively easy for bondpeople to find ways of spending their hard-earned income in Savannah.

By the turn of the eighteenth century, bondpeople, in their capacity as consumers, were a force to be reckoned with in the Savannah economy. Urban retailers were never entirely dependent on their enslaved customers, but many of them secured a tidy income from their usually illicit dealings with bondpeople. This was an income they were loathe to forego as, through the first third of the nineteenth century, the purchasing power and spending habits of bondpeople came under increasingly heavy scrutiny, and attack, from other quarters of white society.

6 🌿 Patterns of Expenditure in Savannah

WHETHER THEY secured their cash income through the sale of commodities, their labor, or both, bondpeople found that the lowcountry towns, but especially Savannah, offered more ways to spend their money than did plantation stores or country storekeepers. Of course, the material needs of urban and rural bondpeople did not differ significantly. On the contrary, the basic necessities were essentially the same. Whether urban or rural, and regardless of the size of the property on which they lived, the vast majority of bondpeople had to make some financial provision if they were to augment the basic subsistence provided by their owners. They had to find the means to secure the additional foodstuffs and clothing they needed, and wanted.

Neither was there any difference in the yearning of urban and rural bondpeople, skilled and unskilled, young and old, men and women for the one thing their disposable income could seldom buy: their freedom from chattel slavery. Money could be useful, if not always absolutely necessary, for bondpeople who sought to escape or to pass as free in Savannah or elsewhere in the South. For a price, paid either in cash or commodities, bondpeople might secure forged passes and freedom papers from compliant whites. But however hard they worked in their own time, however much they grew in their gardens, however often they negotiated for the sale of their labor, however much they scrimped and saved out of their meager earnings, however many goods they were

prepared to appropriate and sell, manumission was the one commodity
they were rarely able to acquire—on any terms, at any price. A handful of bondmen and bondwomen were able to purchase their freedom,
sometimes for a nominal sum that bore no relation to the bondperson's
market value, but throughout this eighty-year period they were the
exceptions.[1]

One of the first recorded manumissions in Georgia, that of Phillis
and her four children in 1755, required that Phillis pay "five shillings
lawful money of Great Britain" to her owner, Joseph Butler.[2] There is
no extant record of how long it took Phillis to earn this money, how
she managed to do so, or why Butler was willing to manumit her for
what to him was such an insignificant sum. Joseph Habersham, Jr.,
demanded rather more from Lovett, "formerly the property of Joseph
Clay & then John Glen," when he manumitted her in 1771. The exact
connection between Lovett and Habersham, when and under what circumstances they met, and why he agreed to help her in her dealings
with Glen are not recorded. But probably after representations from
Lovett, Habersham bought her from Glen for five pounds, a sum she
agreed to pay in order to secure her freedom. Habersham's rider to the
instrument of manumission stating that any children born to Lovett in
the future would also be free was, from a legal standpoint, unnecessary:
they would automatically assume their mother's legal status.[3] Habersham probably took this for granted; Lovett may have been less willing
to do so and insisted upon a written, and what she must have hoped
and assumed would be a legally binding, guarantee that any children
subsequently born to her would be free.

In an equally rare number of cases, manumission cost rather more
than five shillings or five pounds. In 1799, for instance, a bondwoman
named Iris somehow managed to acquire five hundred dollars in order
to secure her own release and that of her daughter from Elias Robert.
A few years later Cleopatra, who had already bought her own freedom, was able to save enough from her work as a washerwoman and
seamstress in Savannah to purchase the release of her two children.[4]

Sometimes bondpeople acquired their freedom after their owner's
death. In 1792, for instance, Alexander Carley, a Savannah carpenter,
signed a document in which he promised to give Elsey and her four
children "their full and absolute Manumission and Freedom . . . Im-

mediately from and after my Decease." He noted that this was because of Elsey's "faithful service . . . and for other causes and considerations," which he did not itemize. They may have included sexual "service . . . causes and considerations," but of that we cannot be certain. Regardless of the precise service that Elsey had rendered, Carley was unwilling to give this "faithful" bondwoman and her children their unconditional freedom during his lifetime. Elsey paid Carley "Five Shillings Sterling Money" in order to secure her freedom together with that of her children. What she got for her money was the written promise of her eventual manumission: together with all of her children she remained obligated to work for Carley until his death.[5]

A few other bondpeople also secured their manumission on terms that involved a continuing obligation to their owner, albeit of a different kind than that demanded of Elsey and her four children. Bryan Morel, for instance, agreed to free two of his bondpeople, Clarinda and her husband, George, provided they agreed to continue taking care of his house. In addition, Clarinda was required to cook, wash clothes, and raise poultry for Morel's benefit.[6] For an unspecified length of time, until Morel died or could be persuaded to change the arrangement, Clarinda and George's enslaved status had been converted into another form of servitude, into quasi-freedom. Clearly, such a status, the demands Morel continued to make on them, had significant implications for the organization of their working lives, for the income and thereby for the standard of living they could achieve for themselves. Yet this was a price Clarinda and George were willing to pay not only for themselves but also for any children who might subsequently be born to them. We know nothing about whether Clarinda was, in fact, of childbearing age, but if she were any children born to her as a free woman would automatically follow her status. Like Lovett, and for that matter every other bondman and bondwoman in the lowcountry, she must have been acutely aware of this circumstance.

The financial obligations of former bondpeople, the requirement that they must pay for their freedom, could continue for many years after the death of their former owner. In some cases this reflected a concern on the part of the owner to make adequate financial provision for his dependents, particularly his wife. In 1801, for example, Hermon Hertson of Chatham County drew up his last will and testament in which

he manumitted "my Negroe men named Fortune and Chance." But as
with Clarinda and George, their freedom was conditional. In this case
it was dependent on their ability and willingness to "pay unto my said
Wife weekly and every week after my decease the Sum of Two Dollars [each] so long as she my said wife shall live." If they "shall neglect
or refuse to pay . . . unless in case of extreme illness then the manumission hereby granted is become forfeit and of none effect."[7] Like
Clarinda and George, Fortune and Chance had been released from
chattel slavery but bound in another form of servitude. No doubt they
considered two dollars a week a comparatively small price to pay for a
legal freedom they would gain in full on Mrs. Hertson's death.

David Johnston, a Chatham County planter, stopped some way short
of enabling four of his bondpeople, two men and two women, to secure
even limited freedom after his death. What he did do, though, was try
to kill two birds with one stone. His prime interest was in the well-being
of a Mrs. Ann Courteny, who may have been a family member, a friend,
or a sexual partner. His wish to provide for Mrs. Courteny should he
predecease her prompted him to devise an arrangement whereby the
bondpeople concerned would be allowed to earn an income for the rest
of their lives. In his will Johnston stipulated that "immediately after my
death" one of the women, Jenny, was to be sent "to Mrs Ann Courteny
there to continue and work four days every week for [her] benefit and
two days every week for herself." This arrangement "must continue till
the death of one of the partners." Should Jenny outlive Mrs. Courteny
"then she shall pay four days reasonable hire to my Executors every
week during her life and two days for herself." Johnston made the same
provision for the other three bondpeople, Grace, Roger, and Sampson,
except that he did not name their employer. They were to work "by the
direction of my Executors."[8] Why Johnston did not simply bequeath
these bondpeople to Mrs. Courteny or instruct his executors to sell them
and make over to her the proceeds accruing from their sale is unknown.
Whatever his reasons, Johnston did at least ensure that these four bondpeople would have the opportunity to earn a legitimate income through
the hire of their labor. What he did not guarantee under the terms of
his will was their freedom from bondage.

It is evident that on rare occasions miscegenation was a vitally important factor in shaping the testamentary provisions of lowcountry

owners. Most children born of sexual liaisons between white men and African-American women in lowcountry Georgia remained in bondage for the rest of their lives; a very small proportion were given their unconditional freedom, usually on the death of their white fathers. In even rarer cases white fathers not only acknowledged the fact of paternity in their last wills and testaments but also sought to make some financial provision for their mulatto children. Francis Harris, a Savannah merchant, was one such.

In his will Harris declared unequivocally that he wanted to try to ensure that "a Mullatto [sic] Boy named Jack, the son of my Negro Wench called Betty," and probably his own child, would be in a position to support himself when he grew to adulthood. Harris sought to guarantee this by requiring that Jack remain in bondage until he was twenty, during which time he should be taught a trade. He stipulated that his executors must not only maintain Jack "out of my Estate" but also ensure that he "learn some good and sufficient Trade and Occupation." Of course, the same outcome could have been achieved by Harris had he chosen to manumit Jack and appointed his executors, or others he trusted equally as well, to act as the boy's guardian until he came of age. But, for reasons he did not elaborate on, Harris rejected this course of action. Moreover, he said nothing at all in his last will and testament about Jack's mother, Betty. In the absence of evidence to the contrary, it must be assumed that she remained enslaved.[9]

A minuscule number of bondmen and bondwomen were manumitted without any financial strings attached; an even smaller number received their freedom and a legacy, in the shape of cash, land, or even bondpeople, in their owners' wills. Owners who fell into the second of these categories were few and far between. They included not only white fathers who, like Harris, were willing to make financial provision for their mulatto children but also those who publicly acknowledged those children as being their offspring. In 1790, for example, Moses Nunes "of Savannah" declared in his last will and testament that he was the father of four of the children who had been born to his bondwoman "Mulatto Rose." Nunes did not see fit to manumit Rose and the four children during his lifetime, but he insisted that this be done immediately upon his death. Moreover, he made financial provision for each of them in his will. Rose received an enslaved boy and a bondwoman "during her natural life" and an annuity of "ten pounds specie." To his three natural sons he bequeathed land, bondpeople, and money. He left his daughter "one hundred pounds specie . . . and a Silver Tankard," but neither land nor bondpeople.[10]

The manumission of bondpeople was a comparatively rare occurrence in lowcountry Georgia throughout this eighty-year period. And after the Revolutionary War it became progressively more, rather than less, difficult for owners to manumit their bondpeople. The commitment of elite white Georgians to the institution of slavery hardened in the aftermath of a war that revealed to them in the most unambiguous terms the extent of their bondpeople's longing for freedom. After the war, and the dashing of the ill-founded hopes that many bondmen and bondwomen had entertained that the British might prove to be their liberators, that longing continued to be expressed by bondpeople who fled in search of their freedom.[11] During the 1780s it was a longing that was also expressed in more organized and violent ways. For elite whites, and probably for many nonelite whites also, the maroon community that established itself in the swamps not too far from Savannah during the mid-1780s and supported itself partly by raiding outlying plantations, presented an appalling specter not only of black freedom but also of the prospect of a racial war that might engulf them.[12] The black revolution in Santo Domingo, which brought many white émigrés and their bondpeople to the lowcountry with their firsthand experiences and accounts of that uprising, further enhanced those fears.[13]

During the 1780s and 1790s many lowcountry planters might have come to believe the image of themselves as benevolent, paternalistic masters who tended to all the material and spiritual needs of their bondpeople. This self-serving ideology provided further justification for strenuously resisting the manumission of those who were increasingly depicted as childlike dependents. Although manumission was never totally forbidden in Georgia, if only because of the property rights involved, in 1801 it was made more difficult by the planter-dominated state government. In that year legislation was enacted that deemed it unlawful for bondpeople to be manumitted "in any other manner or form, than by application to the Legislature."[14] A comprehensive survey of lowcountry wills gives no indication that many more than the handful mentioned above ever seriously considered manumitting any of their bondpeople. Nevertheless after the passage of the 1801 act, any owner who contemplated freeing some or all of them would have to go to the trouble and expense of securing a separate legislative act of manumission for each bondperson.

The comparatively small number of free African-Americans resident in the lowcountry between the 1750s and 1830 testifies to the virtual impossibility of bondpeople being able to buy their freedom from slavery, as well as to the reluctance of their owners to offer them this most priceless of gifts. In 1817, for instance, 401 names, including those of children, were listed in the Savannah Register of Free Persons of Color.[15] In that same year 105 free African-Americans were liable to pay taxes in Chatham County.[16] Two years later 66 free African-Americans were registered in McIntosh County, 35 of whom were resident in Darien.[17] According to the 1820 census, the enslaved populations of Chatham and McIntosh counties stood at 9,542 and 3,715, respectively. In the five lowcountry counties as a whole in 1820, there were 25,961 bondpeople, but only 805 free African-Americans.[18] As they must have been the first to acknowledge, the bondpeople of lowcountry Georgia had little incentive to work and save in the hope that one day they would be able to purchase their freedom. The cost to those who struggled against the most daunting odds to obtain what they regarded as the most precious commodity continued to be measured in essentially nonmonetary terms.

Whether they lived in the countryside or in one of the lowcountry towns, bondpeople had every reason, need, and incentive to spend their disposable cash incomes in ways that would make their daily existence more comfortable and more tolerable. With one notable exception, housing, the spending habits of bondpeople who resided in Savannah and Darien and those who visited these towns on their own or their owners' business were comparable. Expenditure in the towns, as in the countryside, fell into five broad, and to some degree overlapping, categories: food, clothing, "luxuries," recreation, and religion. To all intents and purposes, housing expenditures were confined to urban bondpeople and reflected the extent to which the practice of self-hire offered many bondmen and bondwomen the opportunity of securing a degree of residential privacy. This was a privacy for which they had to pay—and like so many other rights they sought, it was something they could never take for granted.

Theoretically, urban bondpeople who had permission to sell goods or their labor were supposed to return to their owners' residences every night. From the mid-1750s onward the sale or rental of any form of accommodation to them was prohibited by law. In practice, however, many owners did not bother to try to enforce the requirement that their bondpeople return home every evening, and some white landlords were not averse to letting rooms, or even entire houses, to bondpeople, assuming always that they could pay for them.[19]

The degree of residential independence enjoyed by bondpeople in Savannah as a result of their own efforts and exertions (which in itself testifies to the amounts of money they were able to earn) was remarked on as early as 1768. In that year, less than two decades after chattel slavery was first introduced to Georgia, one Henry Preston complained to the Georgia grand jury that in his opinion far too "many Negroes . . . are allowed to live so much at large . . . by which means a door is open to robberies and other bad practices."[20] Three years later a grand jury composed of different personnel from that which had convened in 1768 endorsed Preston's comments when it presented as one of its "grievances" the fact that bondpeople were "permitted to Rent houses in the lanes and invirons [sic] . . . of Savannah" where "meetings . . . are very frequent [and] spirits are sold."[21] Accommodations rented by bondpeople, it was held by the jurors, might also be used by them for such nefarious purposes as gambling and prostitution—and for the even more dangerous purpose of plotting rebellions.

An almost identical complaint to that made in 1768 appeared in the list of "grievances" presented by Georgia's grand jurors in 1781. No doubt wartime disruptions and dislocations had heightened this grand jury's sensitivity to what it described as "a dangerous tendency, the number of Negroes who are suffered to erect and inhabit houses in and about the town of Savannah and parish of Christ Church, and who harbour, and even protect with fire arms, Negroes who run away from their owners."[22] The "dangerous tendency" was not to be stopped in its tracks, or even seriously deflected, by either private or public action in the immediate postwar period. On the contrary, it was a tendency that continued to grow during the last two decades of the eighteenth century, and it clearly reflected the growing assertiveness and spending power of Savannah's enslaved population.

By the early 1790s the practice of renting accommodations to bondpeople had become so extensive, and clearly so worrisome to the Savannah authorities, that the city council decided steps had to be taken to try to stamp it out. More effective policing of Savannah's streets might help achieve this end, but the city council placed its greatest faith in what it assumed would be the most effective weapon in its arsenal: hitting the pocketbooks of errant white landlords. However, perhaps because of a lack of political courage, the council never fixed financial penalties at a level high enough to act as a deterrent to white landlords, which was, of course, greatly to the benefit of bondpeople who sought residential autonomy. Moreover, even when landlords were called to account, making the charge stick often proved difficult for the council. Indeed, given that bondpeople could not testify against whites, the astute landlord had every chance of avoiding, if not detection, then certainly conviction of this offense. The fact that bondpeople were seen entering or leaving the premises, however frequently, was not in itself proof that they were renting the property. The absence of written records such as receipts or rent books could make it virtually impossible for the city council to prove the charge of illicit renting. This is precisely what the council discovered during the early 1790s when it tried to clamp down on the renting of accommodations to bondpeople.

In a single month in 1791 nine whites were summoned before the council to answer charges of letting property to bondpeople. The defendants included one of Savannah's most eminent citizens, Dr. Noble Wimberly Jones; the case against him could not be proved beyond reasonable doubt and was thrown out.[23] Three years later another leading Savannahan, Dr. John Brickell, appeared before the council to answer the same charge. As with Jones, "the charge not being substantiated [he was] discharged without a fine."[24] Clearly, the threat of a fine did not deter enough landlords; in 1800 the Savannah City Council enacted an ordinance that forbade not only the renting of "any house, room or store" to a bondperson but also the renting by whites of "houses for the occupation of slaves."[25] There is no suggestion that this legislation made any significant difference to the attitude of white landlords and, thereby, to the degree of residential independence sought and secured by many bondpeople in Savannah. During the early nineteenth century the ordinance of 1800 remained on the statute books, but insofar as trying to implement it through the prosecution of landlords was concerned, it soon became of comparatively little consequence to those whites who had property in Savannah to let and to those bondpeople who sought to rent it from them.

Given the essentially clandestine nature of the leasing arrangements entered into, it is virtually impossible to determine precisely the going rate for rent. But whatever was charged, bondpeople who could afford to pay the rents for rooms and houses in Savannah depended on the complicity of white landlords. The same was true of their dealings with the city's retailers who, by law, could trade only with those bondpeople in possession of a ticket from their owner. For those bondmen and bondwomen, including of course most runaways, who had no ticket, when it came to the purchase of even the most basic items of food and clothing, they had two choices: find someone who was in a position to do their shopping for them or locate a retailer who was more interested in making a profit than in observing the law. By all accounts, there was a plentiful supply of the latter in Savannah.

The steady growth of Savannah's enslaved population, and that of the surrounding countryside also, after the mid-1750s provided the city with an ever-increasing supply of produce and cheap labor—and retailers with an ever-increasing pool of prospective customers. From an estimated 200 in 1751, Christ Church parish's African and African-American element grew to 1,800 in 1771.[26] By 1790 Chatham County's total enslaved population was approximately 8,201, a figure that grew to 9,049 in 1800, 9,748 in 1810, and fell back slightly to 9,542 in 1820, and 9,052 in 1830.[27] Savannah's African and African-American population increased from 821 in 1771, to 1,104 in 1791, to 3,216 by 1800. By 1821 it was said to total "probably 3,500."[28]

Assuming, for the sake of argument, that each bondperson in Chatham County spent just one dollar a week in Savannah's stores and shops, which by 1798 probably numbered well in excess of one hundred, the significance of their purchasing power for the health of the city's retail sector becomes immediately apparent.[29] From the retailer's perspective a single bondperson's expenditure on any given day, or in any given week, was probably modest in the extreme and certainly would not have made the difference between bankruptcy, staying in business, or making a fortune. A Habersham, a Bulloch, or a member of any other of the lowcountry's premier families might patronize a store and spend on a single purchase of food or clothing what a bondperson might require a year or more to earn. In terms of individual spending, all but those who occupied the lowest rungs of white society enjoyed a greater spending power than did the great majority of bondpeople. For Savannah's retailers it was not the few cents or dollars that the individual bondperson, or enslaved family, had to spend that was the issue: it was the sheer number of bondpeople in and around Savannah who might be persuaded to visit their establishments, the sheer volume of trade they represented collectively, that was so very important to the shopkeepers. This was an income they were determined not to forego.

Savannah's white retailers, especially the city's grocers and clothiers, had every financial incentive to ignore the law and deal with bondpeople, regardless of whether they could display the requisite ticket or note from their owner. Peter H. Wood has suggested that in the case of early eighteenth-century Charleston "white merchants [could be] hurt by the enterprise of slaves around the marketplace."[30] In fact, by the late eighteenth century, if not earlier, precisely the reverse was true in both Charleston and Savannah.[31] Generally speaking, enslaved producers and vendors in the public market, who dealt mainly in fresh foodstuffs, did not compete with white retailers for the business of either white or enslaved consumers. Urban bondpeople who sought fresh food did so in a public market dominated by enslaved and free African-American vendors; rural bondpeople supplied much of that food and had no need to buy it. The utensils, clothing, and fabrics sought by bondpeople, whether resident in Savannah or in the countryside, were very much the preserve of white retailers. If there was competition to sell these commodities to bondpeople, to secure as much of their disposable income as possible, then it was a competition waged almost exclusively between white shopkeepers.

Some Savannah retailers did uphold the law. Some turned away bondpeople who could not produce the requisite ticket from their owner or who offered goods of a suspect nature, and turned in to the authorities those who tendered what seemed to be bank notes of unusually large denominations for a bondperson to be in possession of. In 1802, for instance, one Savannah shopkeeper confiscated "A Bank Bill" from "a black man named Harry" because the latter "offered it . . . for less than its value." Initially Harry claimed that "he received it in payment for his wages, but afterwards that he found it." The retailer, Joseph Davies, was convinced that the note had "come illegally into his possession" and declared in the pages of a local newspaper that he would return it to its rightful owner "on evincing his claim and paying expences."[32]

It was not unusual for whites who had lost sums of money, or for owners and others who believed that bondpeople had robbed them of the same, to advertise in newspapers for its return and to warn local retailers to keep an eye out for bondmen and bondwomen who offered them bank notes of suspiciously large denominations. In 1815, for example, an anonymous advertiser in the *Georgia Republican* reported the loss of "a green silk Purse, containing from fourteen to sixteen hundred dollars, in Charleston, Northern and Savannah bills." Local shopkeepers were "requested to stop all large bills offered by negroes." The following year Edmund Blunt announced in the local press that he had been robbed of "five hundred and eighty six dollars, principally in 50 and 20 dollar bank notes of the State Bank of North Carolina, numbers not recollected." He assumed that a bondperson, or bondpersons, had stolen the money and asked that should "a negro attempt to pass bills of the above description, the person to whom they may be offered will please detain the negro."[33]

Bondpeople who offered bank notes, especially of large denominations, to retailers were immediately suspect. Clearly, whether they had earned them, appropriated them, or simply found them in the street, changing or spending the paper money could prove problematical. But not all white Savannahans were as upstanding as Joseph Davies. On the contrary, the city's retailers, and many other whites, appear to have been quite willing to ignore the public laws of slavery and relieve bondmen and bondwomen of their money, coin or paper, regardless of how they might have acquired it.

Neither the city council, owners, or white commentators paid much attention to bondpeople who shopped in Savannah, sometimes during the day and sometimes in the evenings, for what were two of their most important priorities: food and clothing. Insofar as purchases of either of these commodities attracted any significant white attention, it was the variety and the quality of the garments that some bondpeople were able to afford. In the hierarchical and status-conscious society of the lowcountry, visible signs of social rank were profoundly important. The way in which a person dressed reflected and reinforced that individual's social position. In theory, people could be instantly identified, in the sense of social rank, by the clothing they wore. Racial, as well as social, order and ordering demanded that bondpeople dress according to their humble status, that they not attire themselves in a manner that made a mockery of their lowly status while simultaneously challenging the status claimed by their white "superiors."

Highly reminiscent of the sentiments expressed in Charleston thirty years earlier, there were grumbles in 1775 that certain bondmen and bondwomen in Savannah were clothing themselves in a manner scarcely befitting their servile status. The Georgia grand jurors that year demanded the passage "of a law for preventing the excessive and costly apparel of Negroes and other slaves in Savannah."[34] Such a law was never enacted and, for the next half century, the expenditure of urban bondpeople on clothing attracted comparatively little white attention.[35] This was in marked contrast to the situation in Charleston. There, in the immediate aftermath of the Vesey Rebellion, some white commentators demanded the enactment of a state law that would prescribe the quality of the clothing to be worn by bondpeople on the grounds that "the expensive dress worn by many of them [is] highly destructive of their honesty and industry and subversive of that subordination which policy requires to be enforced."[36]

With the city's steady growth, Savannah offered bondmen and bondwomen increasing opportunities to purchase food and clothing, of varying quality and styles, from white retailers. The latter, who stood to gain financially from such transactions, saw little harm in them. The sale of a waistcoat or a dress to a bondperson, the purchase of a few pounds of molasses seemed unlikely to bring the lowcountry's slave system tumbling down around their ears. But the possibility of purchasing food and clothing was not all that Savannah offered to bondpeople who were resident in the city or to those who periodically came in from the countryside. Bondmen and bondwomen could also spend their money on recreational pursuits, which generally speaking were in short supply in the countryside. For a mixture of pragmatic and, by the turn of the eighteenth century, religious reasons some of these pursuits came to be regarded by a growing number of whites as infinitely more dangerous than bondpeople's purchases of food and clothing.

Various recreational activities, which had to be paid for, were available to bondpeople in Savannah. For those of a mind to do so, fortune-tellers could be consulted. These clairvoyants, themselves often enslaved, earned an income by depriving other bondpeople of theirs. Not surprisingly perhaps, they tended to tell the bondpeople who consulted them that which above all else they wanted to hear: that sooner or later they would secure their freedom from chattel slavery. William Grimes, for instance, recalled that he "would often go to the fortune teller," who charged him twenty-five cents per consultation, a sum that could amount to as much as one-fourth of his daily income. The woman in question "would tell me what my fortune would be. She told me I would eventually get away, but that it would be attended with a great deal of trouble." [37] In the event, the woman proved to be correct on both counts. William Grimes did secure his freedom: like so many others, he did so not by purchasing it from his owner, but by successfully escaping to the North.

Horse races, a possible source of income through vending or gambling, or simply a source of entertainment, were available in Savannah and Sunbury. [38] By 1818 the Savannah race course had gained a notoriety in some quarters and was coming under the increasingly close scrutiny of Chatham County's grand jury. It was, the jurors asserted, "a serious evil to the community . . . the source of every species of vice." Two vices associated with race days particularly disturbed the jurors: heavy drinking and gambling. [39]

The visits paid by bondpeople to fortune-tellers and their attendance at horse races were probably regarded by most white Savannahans as harmless enough pastimes, although they reinforced the image of bondpeople as financially irresponsible beings. The activity that many whites most definitely did not consider harmless, quite the opposite in fact, was one they believed virtually every bondperson engaged in as often as he or she could: visits to Savannah's bars, taverns, and unlicensed "dram shops."

Both in the towns and in the countryside, it was widely believed

by whites that bondpeople made money for one purpose and one purpose only: to drink it away. And for some elite whites, Savannah's
drinking establishments presented a prospect even more worrying than
drunken, uninhibited, possibly violent behavior. Bondpeople, they suspected, might do rather more than get drunk in the city's bars and
taverns. Here were prospective meeting places for the bondpeople who
sought to fence stolen property, secure a forged pass, or even gain passage from Georgia and the nonelite whites who, for a price, might provide these services. Here were establishments where bondpeople and
whites could and did meet and fraternize on a regular basis; establishments whose racially mixed, but predominantly male, clientele might
well be attaching rather more significance to social rank, to class, than
to race. Bars, taverns, and "disorderly houses," together with whites
who retailed liquor in their stores, attracted ever-increasing attention
from elite white commentators. For rather different reasons, by the
late eighteenth century these establishments and their racially mixed
patrons were also beginning to come under growing fire from another
quarter: the Baptist and Methodist churches.

State laws and local ordinances governing the sale or gift of alcohol
to bondpeople by whites were simple. From the mid-1750s, gifts and
purchases of alcohol were expressly prohibited unless the bondperson
had written permission from his or her owner to receive same. The periodic revision of these laws and ordinances is indicative of the extent to
which they were breached in town and countryside alike. In 1808, for
instance, the state government declared that it had become "the custom with tavern keepers and retailers . . . to encourage . . . slaves . . .
to sell unto them a quantity of provisions and other commodities, and
in return, to pay unto them spirituous liquors etc." In a vain attempt
to eradicate this practice, the law was changed to require anyone who
"wished to keep a store, shop or tavern, and are retailers of spirituous
liquors and other commodities" to swear an oath affirming that they
would desist from selling hard liquor to bondpeople.[40]

By 1800 twenty-nine men, but only one woman, Barbara Ouncill,
were licensed "to retail Spirituous Liquors under a quart or in any quantity in Savannah."[41] These innkeepers and retailers could be policed
with comparative ease by the city authorities because of the notices they
were legally obliged to display above their doors.[42] The proprietors in

question, if not their white clientele, might have been cautious in their dealings with bondpeople simply for fear of being fined or, a more serious consequence, for fear of losing their liquor license. What remains unknown, possibly because it was not known to the Savannah authorities between the 1750s and 1830, is the precise number of unlicensed establishments in the city or the number of whites who bought alcohol quite legitimately from wholesalers, retailers, and tavernkeepers only to resell it at a profit to bondpeople. A very rough sense of their minimum number may be gathered from the fines levied on offenders by the Savannah City Council.

Selling liquor without a license and "entertaining" bondpeople were not necessarily the most common of the illicit interracial economic encounters in Savannah, but they were the most vigorously prosecuted by the city council during the first third of the nineteenth century. In 1822, for instance, eighteen whites were fined by the Savannah authorities for illicitly "entertaining" bondpeople, an offense that often involved selling or giving them alcohol. In 1823 that number had increased to twenty-four; in 1824 it fell back to twelve; and in the following year it increased to fourteen. But during this four-year period when sixty-eight individuals were fined, there were a total of ninety-two prosecutions. Obviously there were repeat offenders. Some whites were making far too much money from the sale of alcohol, not always to an exclusively enslaved clientele, to be deterred by fines of up to $30. From the perspective of the city authorities, one of the most notorious offenders was Mrs. Mary Garnett. Between 17 October 1822 and 17 October 1825 she was fined on twelve different occasions for "entertaining" bondpeople or retailing liquor without a license. Her total fines amounted to $270.[43]

The prosecution by the city council of whites who "entertained" and sold liquor to bondpeople reveals the ease with which those bondmen and bondwomen who sought alcohol in Savannah could find it.[44] What these records do not confirm, however, is the belief of many white commentators that liquor was the only item for which bondpeople spent their disposable income. That bondpeople in the towns and countryside of lowcountry Georgia drank alcohol is indisputable; that they drank constantly, to the excess claimed by some whites is far more debatable.

By the turn of the eighteenth century the Chatham County grand jury seldom met without complaining that "on Sundays and other days" parts of Savannah were notorious for their "scenes of drunkenness and disorderly behavior." The streets were full "of Drunken & riotous Negroes & people of Color."[45] If this was indeed the case, one might have expected the charge of being drunk and disorderly to have appeared next to the names of a great many of the bondmen and bondwomen who were lodged in the city jail. But this was not so. Between 1809 and 1815 there were 932 instances in which the Savannah watch and private individuals, other than the bondperson's owner, took bondmen and bondwomen to the jail for "safe-keeping." Some of these cases may have involved drink, but even if they all did this meant that an average of only three bondpeople a week were being taken to prison for drink-related reasons. In fact, during this entire six-year period there was only one prisoner, a bondman, who was said by the jailer to have been drunk. Moreover, these same years saw only sixty-four bondpeople, including sixteen women, taken to jail on the charge of "Rioting" or "Riotous behavior," which may have been another way of saying they were drunk and disorderly.[46]

Some bondpeople, like some whites, in the lowcountry undoubtedly drank to excess, and those who did so regularly were likely to be punished by their owners. This might entail a whipping or, as was the case on some plantations, a form of punishment devised exclusively for drunkenness. Such chastisement might contain within it an element of attempted humiliation as well as physical punishment and discomfort. W. W. Hazzard, for example, declared that on his estate "Drunkenness, if riotous, would be punished by lying in stocks all night and drinking a pint of warm water."[47] Many bondpeople, both in the towns and in the countryside, drank alcohol only occasionally and in moderation. As Charles Ball commented, the purchases of plantation bondpeople might include "an occasional bottle of rum."[48] Liquor provided urban and rural bondpeople with some degree of comfort, consolation, and solace after their day's or week's work, but, it may be posited, seldom if ever at the expense of feeding and clothing themselves and their children.

The fines levied by the Savannah City Council on the likes of Mary Garnett were a direct political response to the continuing stream of complaints aimed in the council's direction by grand juries, which seldom met without calling for steps to be taken against "the numerous drinking shops, in different parts of this City, occupied by Negroes, both free and slaves, which dram shops are constantly the scene of nightly disorder & the resort of the lowest & most abandoned of mankind."[49] By the late eighteenth century, however, these allegations of persistent and widespread drunkenness on the part of bondpeople, and strident demands for action on the part of the city authorities, involved rather more than a pragmatic interest in seeking to regulate and control the behavior of bondpeople. Increasingly, they reflected a religiously in-spired concern not only with the consumption of alcohol by bondpeople but also with virtually every facet of their quasi-independent economic activities. By the early years of the nineteenth century those activities, particularly in Savannah, had become the subject of a wide-ranging and often acrimonious debate. By the 1820s, through their activities as quasi-autonomous producers and in the role they had assumed for themselves as urban consumers, the bondpeople of Savannah and its hinterland were figuring prominently on the city's domestic political agenda. And to all intents and purposes they themselves were respon-sible for setting that agenda. This may not have ranked high, if indeed at all, in their own assessment of the gains that accrued to them from their economic activities, but it was no less of an achievement for that.

By the turn of the eighteenth century some white Savannahans were already beginning to complain that economically, through the market-ing activities of bondpeople in the city, they were virtually enslaved to their bondpeople. What increasingly began to dawn on white Savan-nahans during the next quarter of a century was that what was true of the city's markets was also true of the city's domestic politics. This particular form of dependence and the bitter divisions it exposed in Savannah's white society are the focus of the next chapter.

7 ❧ White Critiques of the Informal Slave Economies, 1785–1830

FROM THE EARLY 1760s onward there had been periodic complaints, mainly from owners and mainly for essentially practical reasons, about the quasi-autonomous economic activities of bondmen and bond-women. Similar complaints continued to be voiced during the half century after the American Revolution, and were to be stimulated by events outside as well as inside the lowcountry. Neither Santo Domingo nor the Prosser and Vesey rebellions went unnoticed in lowcountry Georgia.

Beginning in the mid-1780s, however, white and black perceptions of the informal slave economies that had taken such deep root in Georgia's coastal counties began to be informed by new religious imperatives. A systematic and increasingly acrimonious debate on the necessity and desirability of those pursuits was generated within and between the white and black communities. By the 1820s this debate had produced what, on the face of it, were some strange alliances.

The roots of this specifically religious concern with the activities and conduct of bondpeople were located in the rapid growth of the Baptist and Methodist churches in the lowcountry during the years after the Revolutionary War. Lowcountry Georgia was not immune to the forces demanding social and moral reform that were unleashed by the Second Great Awakening.[1] On the contrary, the Baptist revivals that began in the Savannah area in the mid-1780s, and gathered pace and strength after the great revival of 1802, attracted a significant number of new church members and revitalized the old.[2]

The moral, social, and, increasingly, economic demands being made of the lowcountry's inhabitants, free and enslaved, by the spiritually reborn were quite explicit: society as a whole must go through the cleansing process of rebirth and regeneration. And, if necessary, the forces of government as well as those of the church must be directed toward the attainment of that end. Nowhere was this spiritual and moral decay more in evidence, nowhere was the need for action more urgent, than in Savannah or, as Henry Holcombe called the city in 1812, "This emporium . . . Satan's strong hold."[3]

The whites' religiously inspired concern with what they depicted as the irreligion and immorality of bondpeople, particularly as evidenced by their conduct in Savannah on the Sabbath, had a practical objective. Whether by the spiritual rebirth of bondpeople and their owners, by government dictate, or a combination of both, the proposed reformation of African-American behavior was intended to secure more obedient, and consequently more productive, workers. Few whites in the lowcountry would have quarreled with that objective. What many did quarrel with, however, were the costs to themselves of a course of action that sought not merely to regulate but to rigorously suppress many of the "spare-time" activities of bondpeople.

Drinking and gambling were widely regarded as two of the more common leisure time pursuits of poor whites and bondpeople, in Savannah and in the countryside. The demand that these activities be immediately and ruthlessly stamped out met with little opposition. Urban and rural owners alike had long complained about the comparative ease with which their bondpeople were able to secure hard liquor. And in 1808 and 1810 the proprietors of "dram shops" and others who retailed alcohol found no support when the fines for selling liquor to bondpeople were increased.[4] Likewise, the Savannah ordinance of 1818 that sought to prevent bondpeople from gambling met with no significant opposition.[5]

Implementing these laws was to prove another matter entirely, but no influential voices were raised suggesting that such legislation was either unnecessary or inappropriate. When it came to drinking and gambling, pragmatism and a religiously inspired concern with the morality of poor whites and bondpeople were in perfect harmony. This was not to be the case with the marketing activities of bondmen and bondwomen, particularly those that took place in Savannah on Sundays. During the first third of the nineteenth century those activities, and many of the spending habits they were reputed to support, bitterly divided the lowcountry's white society.

By the early 1790s some white commentators were beginning to complain that bondmen and bondwomen virtually controlled the supply of certain basic foodstuffs, but especially poultry, eggs, fruit, and vegetables, to Savannah's white consumers. Their concern was not so much that these goods were being sold on the Sabbath as it was that the bondpeople's monopoly of them was so complete that they could charge their white customers whatever they liked, whatever the market would bear. It was by no means unknown, claimed these critics, for enslaved vendors "to nearly double [the] former or real value" of the items they offered for sale. Their argument was simple: white consumers were being held to ransom by bondpeople, and this altogether intolerable situation must not be allowed to continue. In 1795 the Savannah City Council responded to this mounting criticism, not by trying to do the impossible, totally prohibiting the vending of foodstuffs by bondpeople, but by passing an ordinance that sought to further tighten the controls on market men and market women.[6]

This legislation, which acknowledged the city's dependence on bondpeople for an assured and convenient, although assuredly not always cheap, supply of essential foodstuffs, may have prompted a degree of caution on the part of enslaved vendors; if so it did not become a permanent feature of their marketing activities. Within a few years white commentators were again complaining of "the daily practice of forestalling at the markets" by urban bondpeople who bought "fresh butter within market hours and afterwards [exacted] exorbitant prices from the citizens." Indicative of their importance as vendors, Savannah's "huckster women" were singled out for particular attention in 1812 when, it was claimed, they virtually monopolized the supply of "eggs, chickens, vegetables and fruit."[7]

Periodically, as in 1795, 1812, and 1818, the Savannah City Council sought to curb the prices charged by enslaved vendors.[8] However, a combination of bondpeople's ingenuity and ineffectual policing virtually ensured that these measures would fail to secure the desired objective. In practice, there was little that the public authorities or white Savannahans could do (other than going without) to prevent what some depicted as the "great injustices" and "great inconvenience" of being forced to buy goods, "not always of the best quality," from enslaved vendors "at two or three hundred per cent in advance."[9]

Most of the purely pragmatic criticism of the vending activities of bondpeople in Savannah centered on how the interests of white consumers might best be protected. Little was said about safeguarding those of white producers and retailers. In fact, there are few surviving complaints from the latter groups about the competition they were experiencing from bondmen and bondwomen. The most significant organized protest, which reflected a mutuality of interest between farmers, planters, and some retailers, came in 1822 when Savannah's butchers petitioned the city council "to prevent slaves from butchering and selling meats in the [Public] Market on their own account and for their individual benefit."

The nub of the butchers' complaint was that bondpeople were underpricing them by selling "small meats . . . unfairly acquired." Indeed, it was claimed, bondpeople "have become so bold as to enter pastures . . . and with a boldness unprecedented, carry off [cattle in] droves." These animals were "shot down, carried to the market and sold; no marks or brands asked for, or taken."[10] The city council responded to the petition by discussing an ordinance that would have prohibited "slaves from butchering and selling meats on the Market on their own account."[11] Such an ordinance, had it been enacted, would have made it more difficult, but not impossible, for bondpeople to dispose of their own hogs and cattle, as well as those that Savannah's butchers believed they had stolen. But, for reasons that are not clear, the city council took no action in 1822, and it was not until the mid-1850s that the demands of the city's white butchers were satisfied.[12]

A second long-standing concern about the marketing activities of bondmen and bondwomen featured prominently in the butchers' petition and was, in a sense, its raison d'être: the belief that permitting bondpeople to engage in any quasi-independent trading activities was tantamount to encouraging and condoning theft. As with the reputed proclivity of bondmen and bondwomen to drink and gamble, there was little disagreement among white critics about their propensity to steal in order to obtain goods with which to trade. Pragmatism and, by the turn of the eighteenth century, evangelical Protestant religious morality ensured that increasing attention would be paid to what had always been regarded in some quarters of white society as one of the most pernicious aspects of the lowcountry's informal slave economies.

In 1817 pragmatic and religiously inspired anxieties about the economic activities of bondpeople merged for the first time in print in a series of articles published in the *Savannah Republican*.[13] The anonymous author of these pieces, who adopted the pseudonym "ANTI-MULATTO," iterated what by the mid-1810s was the familiar charge that enslaved vendors in Savannah monopolized the supply of certain commodities for which they overcharged their white customers. The novelty of "ANTI-MULATTO"'s argument, which was highly critical of the residential independence enjoyed by bondpeople in the city and their propensity to fritter away much of their income on alcohol, was the attention it paid to Savannah's market women and, in particular, to their sexual mores.

By the early years of the nineteenth century whites who complained about the monopoly enjoyed by enslaved vendors in Savannah sometimes noted, almost in passing and usually without offering additional comment, that bondwomen predominated in the city's public market.[14] For "ANTI-MULATTO" these market women posed an invidious threat to the social and moral fabric, as well as to the economic interests, of white society.

According to "ANTI-MULATTO" the first thing a bondwoman did when given permission to vend goods was to look for "a paramour (white, black or yellow), hire a hovel [and] open a huckster shop," the proceeds from which kept "the male partner . . . in a state of intoxication." But far more serious as far as "ANTI-MULATTO" was concerned was the manner in which the sexual behavior of these "abandoned and unprincipled" women was "too apt to vitiate the morals and dilapidate the constitutions of young [white] men."[15]

It was unthinkable to "ANTI-MULATTO" that any white man, of whatever social rank, should choose "to wallow in the filth and reeking obscenity of African harpies."[16] He thought that those who did form liaisons with African and African-American women must have been subjected to intense and shameless sexual temptation; nevertheless he was adamant that they were guilty of conduct that, by undermining marriage and the family, was threatening the very basis of the lowcountry's white society. It was, he insisted, incumbent on all white men, of every rank in society, to remember their moral obligations and social responsibilities and to desist from any and all sexual relationships with African and African-American women.[17]

As for the women themselves, "ANTI-MULATTO"'s solution was perfectly simple: the city council should refuse badges to all "Cake Wenches." Moreover, no bondperson, male or female, should be allowed to rent rooms or houses "for the accommodation of the tastey white souls that feed on the fragrance of muskey blankets." Bond-people ought also to be banned from following "any calling or profession by which idleness may be encouraged." Such steps, concluded "ANTI-MULATTO," would ensure that "all those who live by directly or indirectly robbing society would now have to turn to honest avocations enriching the country's revenue and arresting disgraceful disease."[18]

With one notable exception, "ANTI-MULATTO"'s withering critique of Savannah's market women touched on practical and moral issues that continued to figure prominently in subsequent critiques of the quasi-independent economic activities of the lowcountry's enslaved population. His indictment of the sexual mores of bondwomen contained within it a fairly explicit critique of the sexual conduct of white men, which the latter preferred not to debate, at least not in the pages of the lowcountry's newspapers. During the next few years the relationship between the informal economic activities of bondwomen and the sexual and social morality of white society identified by "ANTI-MULATTO" did not reappear on the agenda for public discussion.

Ever since the 1760s there had been those who, for a mixture of essentially practical reasons, had sought to curtail the economic activities of bondmen and bondwomen, in the countryside and in the towns. During the early years of the nineteenth century, however, intense attention came to be paid not only to the goods bought and sold by bondpeople but also to the one day of the week when, in the lowcountry towns at any rate, many of their trading activities took place: the Sabbath. By the mid-1810s an increasingly articulate Sabbatarianism was making itself heard in the lowcountry; by the early 1820s Sunday trading was beginning to emerge as the central issue in Savannah politics. The same was true of many other towns and cities in the early Republic.[19] In Savannah, however, Sabbatarianism comprised one of the main ingredients of a wide-ranging, and increasingly bitter, debate that touched on virtually every aspect of the informal economic lives of bondpeople. The political triumph of Sabbatarianism promised, or threatened, a reordering of those lives in the countryside as well as in the city of Savannah.

The legal requirement that the Sabbath be kept in Georgia dated back to 1762. In that year the Commons House of Assembly enacted a comprehensive statute that not only prohibited "worldly labour," the marketing of "any Wares, merchandize, fruits, herbs, Goods or Chattels," travel, and "Publick Sports [and] pastimes" on Sundays but also insisted that "all and every person" observe "the Lords day . . . by exercising themselves thereon, in the duties of Piety and true religion publickly or privately." The act would be enforced by the "church wardens and Constables of each Parish," who were required to patrol the streets of Savannah and Georgia's other towns on Sunday mornings and afternoons "in the time of divine service . . . and apprehend all offenders."[20]

The fear of fines ranging from two shillings and sixpence to ten shillings sterling for breaking the Sabbath, and for those who could not afford to pay such fines the humiliation of being "set publickly in the Stocks for the space of Two Hours," may have persuaded some to comply with the law. But in the colonial period there continued to be complaints, usually from private individuals or public officials rather than from the churches, about "Disorderly" behavior on Sundays, especially in Savannah. These complaints were as likely to be made about the behavior of poor whites as they were about that of bondpeople. In 1767, for instance, twenty-one of Georgia's magistrates signed a letter to the *Georgia Gazette* in which they declared it to be their "indispensable duty" to be "vigilant and strict" in seeking out and prosecuting "all persons" thought "guilty of excessive drinking, blasphemy, prophane [sic] cursing and swearing, lewdness, [and] prophanation [sic] of the Lord's Day."[21]

Nine years later, as the Georgia Patriots stood poised to do battle

with Britain for their political independence, Gov. Archibald Bulloch
felt that at such an "important juncture" it was imperative "to concili-
ate the divine favour and protection." In part, he held, this necessitated
"taking proper notice [of] the tumultuous meetings of Negro Slaves, in
and about the Town of Savannah, & their practice of buying & selling
[on] the Lord's Day."[22] In all probability, Bulloch was rather more worried about what might ensue from these "tumultuous meetings" than
he was by Sunday trading per se.

After the American War of Independence, protests about the breaking of the Sabbath, and in particular Sunday trading, increased in direct
proportion to the growth of evangelical Protestant Christianity in the
lowcountry. By the turn of the eighteenth century these protests were
being made with increasing frequency by Chatham County's grand
jurors as well as by the Baptist and Methodist churches. Indeed, after
1800 it was a rare grand jury that did not "present as an evil," or "as
a grievance," the "violation of the Lords Day" in Savannah.[23] The behavior of whites, particularly those who did business with bondpeople
on Sundays, was of as much concern to successive grand juries as was
the conduct of bondmen and bondwomen who lived in Savannah or
visited the city on Sundays to trade.

The character of the complaints made by the grand jurors of Chatham County did not change appreciably through the first thirty years
of the nineteenth century, and neither did their insistence that the
city council take steps to remedy the situation. Constant references
were made to the manner in which the "Morals of the people" were
being corrupted by "the general profanation & violation of the Lords
Day." On most Sundays, it was claimed, "Assemblages of Drunken &
riotous negroes" were to be seen in the streets of Savannah.[24] Much
of the blame for this alleged state of affairs was laid at the door of
tavernkeepers and other white retailers because of their willingness to
put profit before morality. Grand jurors in 1805 claimed that several
"Dram Shops, and other disorderly Houses" in and close to Savannah, were opened by their owners "on the Sabbath day" not only for
the retailing of liquor but also "for the avowed purpose of Gambling."
Their proprietors, who were "without the Habit of Industry," were held
largely responsible for corrupting "the Morals of the people" and for
encouraging "Negroes to plunder their owners."[25]

The Chatham County grand jurors continued to complain about the
extent of the drinking and gambling that went on in Savannah on Sundays, but by 1808 they were also paying increasingly close attention
to Sunday trading. This, after all, was what brought many bondpeople
into the city on Sundays in the first place and provided them with the
wherewithal that, the grand jurors were convinced, they were so eager
to drink and gamble away. While the "higher orders of Society" spent
part of their Sundays "in our Churches [being] taught to reverence
God," asserted the grand jury in 1808, "the multitude" were "crying
Small wares about our Streets. Market is filled with Boys and Negroes,
engaged in different kinds of games, forgetful alike of the laws of God
and of their Country." [26] Such behavior, it was claimed, was "an offence
against the religious feelings of this community" and a "stigma on the
moral character . . . of our city." Only the "interposition [of the] legal
authority," represented by the city council, could "remedy [such] evil"
and secure the reformation of the manners and morality "of the lowest
& most abandoned of mankind." [27]

The strident complaints and demands for government action that
were made by successive grand juries during the early years of the nineteenth century paralleled and stemmed from those being directed by
the leaders of the evangelical Protestant churches to their members.
By the mid-1810s the evangelical objective was not the regulation but
the total suppression of Sunday trading, and thereby all the moral and
social ills that were believed to derive from it. An ever-growing, and
increasingly shrill, Sabbatarianism was also evident in the published
minutes of the annual meetings of the lowcountry's Baptist associations.
In 1815, for instance, the published minutes of the Georgia association
included a circular letter on the importance of observing the Sabbath.[28]
Sometimes, as in 1825, an attempt was made to reach an even wider
audience by publishing circular letters in the local press.[29] This literature might not have been read by all church members, but its contents
were almost certainly conveyed to them, African, African-American,
and white, by their pastors and deacons.

By 1820 the Savannah City Council and the city's shopkeepers, who
since the 1760s had been conducting what they viewed as harmless,
if not always strictly legal, transactions with bondpeople, were coming
under intense pressure to put an end to Sunday trading. In 1820 the

council bowed to that pressure by stipulating that although the city's public market would be open for business "on every Sunday of the year," between November and April it would not be allowed to continue "beyond the hour of nine on the morning." Simultaneously, the council declared that retail stores must also close at the same time on Sundays.[30] But even this was not enough for the Sabbatarians. They continued to argue vociferously for a total ban on a practice that was as convenient for bondpeople as it was profitable for Savannah's shopkeepers. Politically, both sides in the ensuing battle had precisely the same objective: to secure control of the city council.

Compared with what was to come during the 1820s, Savannah's political life during the first two decades of the nineteenth century was relatively tranquil. Annual elections for membership on the city council came and went without generating any significant controversy. Elections were contested, but it was seldom that, as in 1820, more than about eighteen men stood for the fourteen places available.[31] Lists of candidates and the votes they secured were published in the local press, but little was said about the specific policies of those who stood for office. The Savannah electorate seemed content to elect and reelect a city council dominated by lawyers, merchants, and doctors, most of whom were members of the Episcopal church.[32]

During the early 1820s the older order came under increasingly heavy attack. Savannah politics began to be characterized by a bitter power struggle that generated, among other things, a good deal of written propaganda concerning all aspects of the informal economic activities of bondpeople. The latter were at the heart of the political divide in the city—the issue that split the white electorate into warring factions. For the first time in lowcountry Georgia some whites began to argue that the informal economic activities of bondpeople might, provided they could be carefully regulated, actually be beneficial to their owners as well as to white society as a whole.

The tone for the debate that culminated in the rancorous city council election of 1829 was set nine years earlier when two anonymous authors, "HONESTUS" and "HUMANITAS," crossed swords in the pages of the *Georgian* and the *Savannah Republican*.[33] "HONESTUS" took an uncompromising line and "denounced, with great severity, the practice of permitting shops to be kept open on Sunday mornings." "HUMANI-

TAS," who declared himself to be a member of the city council, believed that "in the plenitude of his scrupulous piety" his opponent may well have overlooked his own transgressions on the Sabbath. Had he, asked "HUMANITAS," "never taken his glass of wine, and even sent for it on the Sabbath—received, paid for, and read business letters and newspapers—purchased from those very Negroes their several articles of traffic—had an expensive dinner (both as to time and cost) cooked on that day *with many other practices* equally as pernicious as those he exclaims against?"

Rather more germane, perhaps, was the explanation "HUMANITAS" offered his readers for why he supported the continuance of Sunday trading. "Benevolence and charity," he held, demanded that this practice not be curtailed. The regulations drawn up by the Savannah City Council permitted "only two Negroes from each plantation" to visit Savannah on Sundays "to dispose of the products of their industry and economy during the week; and procure with their proceeds the necessaries and comforts of life." On weekdays plantation bondpeople were forbidden by their owners "to leave their work." Why, he asked, did "HONESTUS" think it necessary "to proscribe that unfortunate race, to deprive them of the inducements to industry, and to deny them the means of enjoying the necessaries and comforts of life?" Moreover, after they had completed their business, plantation bondpeople had it in their "power to hear from the sacred desk, the word of God disseminated in a language suited to [their] capacity."

Further, he argued, even if Sunday trading were totally prohibited, plantation bondpeople would still make their way to the city in search of trading partners. Once in Savannah, he continued, they would almost certainly be able to find "unprincipled men . . . at every corner. . . . who would encourage a species of traffic, calculated to corrupt the morals of Negroes and endanger the interests of their masters by promoting drunkenness and purchasing stolen produce." Surely, "HUMANITAS" concluded, it was very much in the interests of plantation owners and city dwellers alike to persist with the present arrangements which posed "No serious danger" to Savannah's white inhabitants.[34]

"HUMANITAS" did not rule out the possibility that Protestant Christianity, if presented to bondpeople by white ministers, might prove to be a powerful weapon in the attempt to secure docile and productive bondpeople who would be perfectly content to remain tied to their plantations. The main thrust of his argument, however, and one that was endorsed later in the decade by Roswell King, Jr., was not specifically religious in its orientation, but was predicated on the assumption that bondpeople subscribed to precisely the same economic values and aspirations as their owners. According to this line of argument, the encouragement of "industry" in the slave quarters, to permit bondpeople to market their surpluses and accumulate amounts of property, albeit meager amounts, must surely redound to the owner's benefit. As King put it, on the Butler estates "Every means are used to encourage [bondpeople], and impress on their minds the advantage of holding property. Surely, if industrious for themselves, they will be so for their master. . . . No Negro, with a well stocked poultry house, a small crop advancing, a canoe partly finished, or a few tubs unsold, all of which he calculates soon to enjoy, will run away."

King, who boasted that "In ten years I have lost, by absconding, forty-seven days out of nearly six hundred Negroes," had conveniently forgotten the alacrity with which the bondmen and bondwomen of the Butler plantations had made for the British forces during the War of 1812 in search of their liberation from chattel slavery.[35] In the lowcountry, as elsewhere on the southern mainland, the decision to run away, as well as the destinations of fugitives, were informed by many considerations, but family and kinship assumed a much higher priority than property in the shaping of that decision. Bondpeople ran away in search of loved ones from whom they had been forcibly separated; others chose to remain with their loved ones rather than seek their personal liberation from chattel slavery. Roswell King failed to appreciate, or was reluctant to acknowledge, that the industry and property of which he spoke represented accumulation for the sake of survival, rather than an unthinking internalization of the economic ethos of the master class.

They might not have concurred with all the sentiments expressed by "HUMANITAS," or with the essentially pragmatic argument advanced by King in 1828, but through the first half of the 1820s successive Savannah City Councils steadfastly resisted any and all suggestion that the ordinance permitting limited trading on Sundays be rescinded. But the pressure continued to mount and in 1826 the council was forced to take action, not on the issue of Sunday trading but against those who retailed liquor in Savannah. In that year the cost of liquor licenses was increased dramatically, a move that prompted a group of Savannah storekeepers, including some of the city's most eminent men, to organize themselves politically.[36]

The city council's prime target may well have been the proprietors of less reputable "Dram shops," many of whom had been fined during the past few years for the illicit sale of alcohol to bondpeople and others on Sundays. But several of Savannah's shopkeepers who also retailed liquor felt they were being unduly penalized. In August 1826 "the Grocers" called a meeting to determine what action, if any, they should take.[37] Under the leadership of George Shick, a Baptist, they quickly agreed to press for the repeal of the ordinance on the grounds that "it is not alone the interests of the grocers, but of every white citizen whatever may be his occupation" to prevent the imposition of "exorbitant taxes upon the business part of the community particularly." The Grocers decided that their case could be best advanced if they secured a voice on the city council, and they proposed a slate of candidates to contest the upcoming aldermanic elections. The fourteen men they nominated ran as the Grocer's Ticket, which campaigned and won under the slogan, United We Stand, Divided We Fall.[38] Five weeks after the election the offending ordinance was amended. Those who retailed liquor in amounts "not less than a quart" were now required to pay only twenty-five dollars for their licenses; those who sold liquor to be drunk on their premises paid thirty dollars.[39]

In 1826 Savannah's Grocers won a signal political victory. But the city's retailers were not in total agreement about the increasingly thorny question of Sunday trading. That several put religious morality before profit is evident from the fact that in April or May 1827 "sundry store keepers and others" petitioned the city council "requesting the Stores and Markets in this City to be closed on the Sabbath." The petition apparently has not survived, but some indication of its contents may be gleaned from the minutes of the city council meeting held on 10 May 1827 at which it was discussed at some length. It seems that the petitioners based their case on the by now familiar argument that Sunday trading constituted "a violation of the laws of the State, and of the Commands of God."[40] The committee the council appointed to look into the matter reported back three weeks later, after it had "collected information from various sources." Its report expressed sympathy with the objections to Sunday trading raised by the petitioners, but took the view that there were insufficient "reasons to warrant any further interference with the long established and necessary usages of the city which the memorialists pray be prohibited by Ordinance."

The "reasons" cited by the committee, which on 24 May were endorsed by the council by a vote of seven to four, were essentially pragmatic.[41] First, it argued that it was only by opening the market and retail stores for a few hours on Sunday that the people of Savannah and "the slaves of adjacent plantations" could be certain of obtaining "wholesome" food for immediate consumption. The practice of opening the market at all on Sundays, they claimed, had begun because meat and fish bought the previous day "cannot . . . be kept in a sound state for use on Sunday." Given that the local climate "has not changed the necessity of the case . . . is as urgent now as it ever has been."

The committee's second argument was that keeping the market open until nine o'clock on Sundays could scarcely be said to "violate the Sabbath" to the degree claimed by the petitioners. After all, vendors and customers alike could still attend church if they so desired and, the committee insisted, "it may with truth be said that our streets are as free from any impropriety of conduct during divine worship as those of any City on the Atlantic Coast."[42]

Finally, the committee argued, given the attitude of most planters, Sunday was, as it had always been, "the only day" when bondmen and bondwomen could visit Savannah to trade. Apparently the petitioners thought that owners might be persuaded to allow their bondpeople to conduct their business in the city on Saturdays, but the committee claimed to have received "information from several sources, that many planters would reject such an arrangement as wholly incompatible with their interests." If plantation bondpeople were not allowed to trade in Savannah on weekdays, they would surely continue to make their way to the city on Sundays.

The committee was convinced that the total prohibition of Sunday trading would mean that "illicit trading would be carried on to [a] late hour on Saturday Evening [and] thro' out the day on the Sabbath, notwithstanding the . . . hopes of those who think it can be prevented by ordinance." The policing problems would be enormous, and, the committee concluded, it was in the interest of white Savannahans and planters alike "that the trade between the Shopkeeper [and bondpeople] should be openly carried." If not, it was only to be expected that there would be an "increase in those articles by which [planters] already suffer much inconvenience and losses." Moreover, white Savannahans "would have to contend against the evils that would naturally spring from large assemblies at night of slaves belonging to the adjacent plantations."[43]

The memory of the Vesey rebellion in Charleston five years earlier was still very fresh in white minds, and the message the committee hoped to get across to the full city council was clear: one way to avoid a similar occurrence in Savannah was by offering bondpeople legitimate opportunities to trade, even if this meant having to keep the public market and retail stores open for a few hours on Sundays. In effect, the committee suggested that attempts to ruthlessly suppress the bondpeople's right to trade in Savannah on the Sabbath would not be the most effective means of trying to maintain racial order and might in fact prove counterproductive. The pragmatic solution, the compromise, they proposed was intended to placate as many interests as possible: Savannah's retailers and consumers, the city's Baptist and Methodist congregations, and, not least of all, Chatham County's enslaved population.

In the spring of 1827, at the time it received the committee's report, the city council was clearly divided on the issue of Sunday trading, and those divisions were nowhere more evident than in the way in which the council disposed of cases involving alleged breaches of the ordinance of 1820. In May 1828, for instance, a Mr. M. D. Howard appeared before the council on a charge of "trading with negroes on Sunday after nine o'clock." On the face of it, the case against him was clear enough: the city marshall testified that "he had seen several Negroes in his shop 6 or 7 minutes after nine o'clock." For his part, Howard denied trading after 9:00 A.M. and claimed that he "was merely making change, and delivering articles which had been previously sold." George Shick sprang to Howard's defense and proposed that the case be dismissed because "it was impossible to drive Negroes from a shop at the very instant of the striking of the clock." Shick added that he had often shut his shop door, in order to get them out sooner and to prevent others from coming in. Moses Sheftall seconded Shick's proposal, and after a vote had been taken the case against Howard was dismissed.

On the same day the council considered the case of a Mrs. Donager who, the city marshall claimed, had "several Negroes in her shop [in Battle-Row] near 10 o'clock." The Council agreed that Mrs. Donager was "a very poor woman," but disagreed as to how much she should be fined. Once again Shick took the lead by proposing that she pay a one-dollar fine on the grounds that this "might be collected—a larger one could not be." Alderman Williams, who had voted in favor of the committee report of the previous year, complained that such a "trifling" sum amounted to "an inducement . . . to individuals to break the ordinance"; in effect it was "giving the license to sell on Sunday for $1." He proposed a five-dollar fine, and argued that even if Mrs. Donager was unable to pay "it would still be held over her in admonition." As in the previous case, Moses Sheftall supported Shick, but this time they were defeated and Mrs. Donager was duly fined five dollars.[44]

In the summer of 1829 the city council was presented with yet another petition on the subject of Sunday trading, this time from "the Citizens of Savannah." This "Memorial," like that drawn up by the city's Grocers two years earlier, does not seem to have survived. However, it may be safely inferred from the comments of the three-man council committee appointed to consider it that the petitioners were concerned first and foremost with the religious reasons that in their view demanded the keeping of the Sabbath and the total repeal of the ordinance of 1820.

Aldermen D'Lyon, Cuyler, and Welman, who prepared a report for consideration by the full council, were in total sympathy with the petitioners. They agreed "that a strict observance of the Sabbath day is a sacred duty enjoined upon us by divine command" and that the ordinance of 1820 was "injurious in its effects, and destructive of the best interests of the Community." In their opinion, those who sought to defend even the limited Sunday trading permitted by that ordinance "must . . . rest their argument on the absolute necessity of such provisions as it contains" because "Religion commands . . . that the Sabbath should be observed as a day of rest."

The committee thought that the case of "absolute necessity" made by the proponents of Sunday trading could be easily disposed of. Their claim that "the poorer class of white persons, who generally receive their weekly wage on the evening of Saturday" needed "a short time on Sunday morning" to do their shopping was scarcely tenable "so long as a public market is kept open." It seemed to the committee that "the only serious ground" upon which the ordinance could be defended was that Sunday was the only day of the week when plantation bondpeople could trade in Savannah. But, the committee claimed, local planters were prepared "to allow a portion of their slaves to visit the city . . . in weekly rotation . . . to obviate the inconvenience at present resulting from their trading on the Sabbath day."[45]

D'Lyon, Cuyler, and Welman tried to cast doubt on the motives of Savannah's shopkeepers, who, they alleged, professed concern for the welfare of plantation bondpeople but whose chief interest was in the profits they made on Sunday mornings. And where did most of those profits come from but "from the sale of liquor"? It was the case, the committee contended, but without offering one shred of evidence in support of its allegation, that bondpeople spent "more than half their money [on] ardent spirits." Shopkeepers had every reason not only to lobby in support of the ordinance of 1820 but also to keep their shops open long after the 9:00 A.M. deadline. The money they made on Sunday mornings meant that fines of five or ten dollars were meaningless.

The committee noted that it had been rumored that if the council repealed the ordinance of 1820 some retailers would move their businesses "into the country, in the neighborhood of the plantations, and carry on a trade with the negroes, greatly to the injury of their owners." The committee did not entirely rule out such a possibility, but felt confident that if this did happen it would be comparatively easy to police such establishments. Many lowcountry planters would not have shared that confidence.

Cuyler, D'Lyon, and Welman thought it significant that the defenders of Sunday trading had not presented a petition of their own to the council. Their silence, together with the fact that "a large and respectable number of citizens" were demanding the repeal of the ordinance of 1820, led them to believe that the repeal was "desired by the majority of our constituents."[46] D'Lyon proposed a bill to this effect on 28 July.[47] For some council members his draft legislation did not go far enough toward ensuring the total observance of the Sabbath, and D'Lyon agreed to withdraw it "on the understanding that it could be offered at any subsequent stage of the proceedings."[48] No doubt because of the impending city elections, which all parties concerned hoped would provide them with a clear mandate, the council took no further action on the committee's report.

As Alderman D'Lyon pointed out, the proponents of a limited amount of Sunday trading did not petition the city council in July 1829. However, adherents to that position more than made up for their previous silence during the weeks leading up to the council elections. Those elections, held in September, hinged on the single issue of Sunday trading.

Together with the city's Baptist and Methodist churches, Savannah's newspapers provided the most important vehicle for the rallying of public opinion. One of the first shots fired in an increasingly acrimonious election campaign appeared in the pages of the *Argus* on 23 July. An anonymous author, "VOX POPULI," sided with those who sought to prevent Sunday trading, mainly on the familiar grounds that the "little *comforts*" sought by bondpeople in exchange for their produce consisted principally of whiskey.[49] The debate intensified during the next few weeks and took a new turn when the People's Ticket was announced at the end of August.[50] "VERITAS" complained that the "Ticket" had been "got up for a particular purpose, and a majority may be *presumed* to be *pledged to a certain course*. . . . Their minds are made up. . . . They are not capable . . . of rendering an impartial verdict."[51]

Another correspondent to the *Argus*, who signed himself "A FRIEND TO LIBERAL PRINCIPLES, MORALITY, AND RELIGION, IN THEIR PROPER PLACE," was outraged by what he depicted as an untoward religious meddling in Savannah's secular affairs. He alleged that a group of men, "wedded to a certain religious institution [the Baptist church] in our city," had "unanimously resolved to vote for *no* candidate who would not *pledge* himself" to voting for a total ban on Sunday trading. It was intolerable, this author continued, that any church should "be permitted to be turned into a political engine . . . to combine its united power and influence, and dictate to us not only *who shall be our rulers, but how those rulers shall vote*." A group of men who believed themselves "more holy and sanctimonious than their neighbors" ought not to "be allowed to cram down the throats of independent men, . . . *their notions of who is a man of* VIRTUE, MORALITY *and* ORDER and what are the fit qualifications for an Alderman."[52]

An essentially similar line of argument was advanced by "Q" in a letter to the *Savannah Republican.* Sunday trading, he claimed, could scarcely be considered "obnoxious" for the simple reason that "long before the churches are open the shops are closed, the market is cleared, and every vestige of worldly traffic is removed from observation." It seemed to him that if "a few *sectarian reformers*" were allowed to have their way, Savannah's aldermen would be elected not because of their "willingness and ability to advance [the city's] *temporal concerns*" but because of "their pliancy in yielding to certain restrictions." "Q" asserted that church leaders and their congregations should confine themselves to "argument and exhortation" and "never mingle in the strife of party contest, nor prostitute the holy influence of religion to the purpose of interest, or ambition." This *"pious tampering"* in Savannah's secular affairs must at all costs be resisted; it was "an attempt to unite religion and politics, and revive an influence which has ever been withering to the liberties of the people."[53]

The opponents of Sunday trading who sought the total observance of the Sabbath in Savannah fought back in the pages of the city's newspapers. The People's Ticket was warmly supported by "PHILO-REPUBLICAE" and "SENEX" in articles published in the *Argus,* and in the *Savannah Republican* "ONE OF THE PEOPLE" declared that the issue was simple: should Savannah retain an ordinance that was contrary to state law and was it "in *principle correct* to encourage the worst species of traffic on the holy day"?[54] The Savannah electors gave their answer on 7 September when a total of 348 votes were cast. Ten of those who had run on the People's Ticket, but significantly not Levi D'Lyon, were voted into office.[55] George Shick, a leading member of the Independent Ticket, retained his seat on the council with 218 votes, as did Moses Sheftall, who secured 162 votes. John B. Gaudry and Samuel M. Bond, with 270 and 164 votes, respectively, were also elected.[56]

The Savannah City Council election of 1829, which clearly demonstrated the twin impact of quasi-autonomous black economic endeavor and evangelical Protestant Christianity on the politics of the lowcountry, marked a vitally important step in the attempt not only to curtail the marketing activities of bondmen and bondwomen on Sundays but also to ensure the wholehearted observance of the Sabbath. The piercing Sabbatarianism that was such a prominent feature of the 1829 Savannah aldermanic election found its most explicit political expression in a city ordinance "for enforcing the observance of the Sabbath." With one or two exceptions, work or trade of any kind was forbidden in Savannah on Sundays, as were any "public sports or pastimes," including "hunting and fishing . . . singing, fiddling or other music for the sake of merriment." [57] Like all the previous legislation that had sought to regulate or restrict the informal economic activities of bondpeople, this ordinance would prove virtually impossible to enforce. Little was resolved by the Savannah election of 1829, and the trading activities of bondmen and bondwomen, especially on Sundays, remained a divisive, and at election times often violent, issue in the city's economic, political, and religious life for the remainder of the antebellum period.[58] Moreover, it was an issue on which there was by no means unanimous agreement in the slave quarters of the lowcountry.

8 🌿 African-American Christianity and the Informal Slave Economies, 1785–1830

DURING THE decades after the Revolutionary War increasing white critiques of the informal economic activities of bondmen and bondwomen, especially in Savannah, met a favorable response from some elements in the slave quarters of the lowcountry. Indeed, the Sabbatarianism that enjoyed such political triumph in the Savannah City Council election of 1829 was not imposed on an unwilling and hostile enslaved community: it was rather warmly embraced by many bondpeople and free African-Americans. Nevertheless, this impulse, with all its implications for the bondpeople's right to use Sundays as they pleased, was by no means uncontested by the bondmen and bondwomen of the lowcountry.

Bondpeople's Sabbatarianism was firmly anchored in the spiritual, moral, and social imperatives that informed the quite remarkable growth of African-American evangelical Protestant Christianity in lowcountry Georgia during the decades following the American Revolution. The content and appeal of the evangelical Protestant Christianity initially presented to bondpeople by white Baptists and Methodists, but increasingly by African and African-American preachers, have been brilliantly illuminated by the work of Sylvia Frey.[1] Two of her findings have a particular bearing on the present discussion: the rapidly growing number of bondpeople everywhere in the early national South who chose to become members of the Baptist and Methodist churches and the fact that in most racially mixed churches they comprised a significant proportion of the total membership. As Frey argues, "black Christians were major participants in the shaping of southern religious life" and in what she appropriately describes as "the transformation" of that region's "religious cultures" in the years following the American Revolution.[2]

During the quarter of a century before the American War of Independence bondwomen and bondmen had secured the right to use Sundays as they wished and won highly significant marketing rights. They had firmly established themselves as income producers and as consumers. By the mid-1780s some were beginning to claim another right: to have religious beliefs, practice public worship, and organize their own churches. The assertion of this right, the fusion of religious and economic morality wrought by the bondpeople's "critical appropriation" of evangelical Protestant Christianity, was to entail several potentially profound consequences for their informal economic activities. It may not have added an entirely new dimension to patterns of bondpeople's expenditure, but it certainly gave an entirely new meaning to that expenditure, to the financial choices being made by those bondmen and bondwomen who embraced evangelical Protestant Christianity and elected to become church members. It entailed new choices for converts as to the most appropriate ways in which to spend their own time, especially their Sundays. Their enthusiasm to impose their choices, their religious imperatives, on nonbelievers stood to fundamentally reshape the moral economy of the slave quarters, to fundamentally alter both the meaning and the modus operandi of lowcountry Georgia's informal slave economies.

During the early national period, the bondpeople of lowcountry Georgia were making different religious choices, and those differing choices were not entirely unwelcome to the master class: anything that divided the enslaved community was bound to work to the advantage of owners.[3] If whites could gain control of the African churches then, from their viewpoint, so much the better. This they signally failed to do; white involvement in the creation of the African churches was never successfully translated into anything approximating total control.

From the outset, African-American Baptist leaders fully appreciated the practical necessity, if not the spiritual desirability, of forging links with their white coreligionists, and they chose to affiliate themselves with the Baptist associations formed in the lowcountry. As with white and, by the early nineteenth century, racially mixed congregations, each of the African churches sent two delegates, usually the pastor and a deacon, to annual meetings devoted to formulating church policy, including guidelines for the moral conduct of its membership.[4] But interracial discourses on this subject were not limited to two or three days a year; the dialogue continued in a less formal vein throughout the year. African-American Baptists appear to have played a central and continuing role in defining the rigorous standards of morality demanded of all church members—standards that through the first quarter of the nineteenth century their white coreligionists sought to impose by political means on the lowcountry as a whole.

Within the formal structure of the African-American churches and less formally in the quarters, these moral demands were made more often than not by African-American preachers and exhorters, not by white clergy. As Sylvia Frey has argued, growing numbers of bondwomen and bondmen found within this evangelical message a profoundly significant sense of spiritual independence, a sense of meaning for the present and hope for the future.[5] The willingness of so many African-American Baptists to lead their lives according to the exacting moral standards demanded of them was to be crucially important in shaping and reshaping many facets of their lives—not least in enhancing individual and collective concepts of self-worth, dignity, and purpose. At the same time, perhaps, it fostered a sense of spiritual and moral superiority over the unregenerate, regardless of their color, gender, or status.

The impressive growth in the number of African-American Methodists and, more especially, African-American Baptists in early national Georgia is well documented. In the lowcountry, for instance, there was at least a tenfold increase in the membership of the Baptist Church between the mid-1780s and 1829. By 1829 the five African churches affiliated with the Sunbury association reported a total membership of 4,264. Even more remarkable is the fact that by the 1820s, if not before, African-American Baptists comprised at least 70 percent of the total membership of the association.[6]

As was the case at the Sunbury Baptist Church, organized in 1806 with an initial membership of two whites and sixty-eight people of color, some African-American Baptists worshiped alongside their white coreligionists. However, the vast majority, certainly of those who lived in or close to Savannah, elected to worship in their own independent churches. Andrew Bryan led a tenacious struggle to secure that right during the 1780s and early 1790s, and the support he received from some of Chatham County's most influential citizens was by no means an unimportant factor in securing and retaining that right.[7]

The opening of the First African Church in Savannah in 1787, with an initial membership of around 300, was followed fifteen years later by the creation of two more independent African churches: the Second African, also in Savannah, and the congregation that organized itself at Ogechee, fourteen miles to the south of the city.[8] In 1819 churches were formed in the immediate neighborhood of Savannah at Abercorn and White Bluff, but in terms of membership the two Savannah churches remained preeminent. Between 1803 and 1829 their combined membership increased from 600 to 3,397, and together they accounted for between 70 and 80 percent of the total membership of the five African churches affiliated with the Sunbury association.[9]

The African-American Baptists who were concentrated in and around Savannah comprised an ever-increasing proportion of the local enslaved and free African-American population. There is no extant record of the age, gender, or place of residence of these church members, but it seems reasonable to suggest that the catchment area of Savannah's independent African churches was comparable to that of the city's public market. That is, church members living within a fifteen- or twenty-mile radius of Savannah could, depending on the transportation available, make their way to the city in time for at least one of the three services held in the African churches on Sundays or for "the LORD's Supper," which was celebrated "quarterly."[10] In 1812, when the membership of the first African Church stood at "about 1500," "many" of the members were said to "belong to the plantations in the neighborhood of Savannah, and some are a number of miles out in the country."[11] Some bondmen and bondwomen had access to horses or mules, and carts; many made the journey on foot; others "paddled down and up the [Savannah] river on the Sabbath mornings and evenings" in "cypress log dugouts, called by the Indian name canoe."[12]

The first of the Sunday services in Savannah's independent African

Baptist churches, a prayer meeting, was held "at sunrise"; the second and third, which involved preaching, began at ten o'clock in the morning and three o'clock in the afternoon. How bondpeople who came in from the countryside intending to participate in more than one of these services occupied themselves in the intervening time is not clear. They may well have gathered together informally, inside or outside the church, to pray or sing together, or simply to talk, to exchange news and information. No doubt some took advantage of the time between the dawn and ten o'clock services to do their trading.[13]

Sunday was not the only day of the week when church members gathered together in Savannah. Until 1792 it was the "custom" of African-American Baptists to hold an additional meeting in the town on Thursday evenings, but these were "frowned upon of late by some despisers of religion [and] set aside."[14] A state law of 1792, enacted in the aftermath of the Santo Domingo revolution, prohibited bondpeople from being out on the streets after 8:00 P.M. in the winter and 9:00 P.M. in the summer, and these curfews meant that evening services were rarely held in the churches, "unless some of the white ministers preached to them."[15] That this legislation did not deter bondpeople from congregating together elsewhere after the curfew is suggested by a complaint made in March 1794 by the Chatham County grand jury. On this occasion the grand jurors presented "as an evil" the fact that between five hundred and six hundred bondmen and bondwomen "at a time" met in Yamacraw, on the outskirts of Savannah, "under a pretence of Public Worship."[16] Ten years later the city council was still complaining about similar gatherings and sought to ban all weekday "assemblies or meetings of negroes for religious worship." Sunday services "in meeting houses," which could be policed with comparative ease by the city authorities, were permitted by the law of 1792 but only between the hours of ten in the morning and five in the afternoon.[17]

In theory, by 1820, with the founding of churches at Abercorn and White Bluff, most of Chatham County's bondpeople were within reach of an independent African-American Baptist church. Between 1790 and 1830 the enslaved population increased by just under 1,000, from 8,201 to 9,052, and the number of free African-Americans, concentrated mainly in Savannah, from 112 to 426.[18] Some bondmen and bondwomen may have crossed over from South Carolina to attend church in Savannah, and the Ogechee church may have attracted some members from neighboring Liberty County, but in all probability Chatham County accounted for virtually the entire membership of the lowcountry's five independent African churches. Assuming that this was the case, the proportion of the county's bondpeople who chose to become affiliated with these churches increased from around 9 percent in 1800, to roughly 35 percent by 1820, to somewhere on the order of 47 percent by 1830.

Rather more difficult to enumerate with any degree of certainty are those bondmen and bondwomen who joined the racially mixed Methodist congregation in Savannah and the smaller number who worshiped alongside their owners in the city's Presbyterian, Episcopal, Lutheran, and Roman Catholic churches. Yet it is clear that unlike the situation in Charleston and Georgetown, South Carolina, the African and African-American population of Savannah and its environs found the Baptist church far more attractive than the Methodist.[19] In 1790, for instance, there were only 184 African-American Methodists recorded in the entire state of Georgia. They accounted for a mere 8 percent of all Georgia Methodists.[20] As William Capers commented, during the early years of the nineteenth century "there were very few negroes who attended the Methodist preaching" in Savannah. The "one side of the gallery appropriated to their use . . . was always the most thinly seated part of the church." Capers concluded that in part this reflected a preference for "the economy and doctrines of the Baptist Church," but he recognized that even more significant than this was the fact that the two independent African churches in Savannah were precisely that: they had "pastors, and deacons, and sacraments, and discipline all of their own."[21]

The choices open to prospective church members elsewhere in the lowcountry were far more restricted. True, depending on where they lived, by the 1820s bondpeople in Liberty and McIntosh counties could opt to become members of the Baptist churches in Sunbury, Darien, and Pleasant Grove.[22] The Congregationalist church at Midway attracted a growing number of African and African-American members during the first quarter of the nineteenth century. However, the fact that between 1800 and 1830 at least 450 bondpeople, including young children who had no say in the matter, were baptized and admitted to full communion in the Midway Church must be put in the context of a Liberty County population, which during these years grew from 3,940 to 5,602.[23]

In the other lowcountry counties, whose combined enslaved population increased from 5,952 in 1790, to 6,906 in 1820, and 13,107 in 1830, the possibilities of church membership and attendance were virtually nonexistent. As Julia Floyd Smith has observed, before 1830 and the plantation missionary movement, "the large majority of rural slaves . . . remained outside the reach of the institutional church."[24] This did not mean that plantation bondpeople who lived at some remove from Savannah were unaware of the fundamental tenets of evangelical Protestant Christianity. As Jonathan Clarke explained in 1792, white ministers as well as some of Savannah's African-American Baptists preached in the countryside. Jesse Peter, for example, had "three or four places in the country where he attends preaching alternately."[25] But in a purely institutional sense, in terms of church attendance and the discipline church membership entailed, African-American Christianity in the lowcountry was concentrated in and around Savannah and, to a lesser extent, around the smaller towns of Sunbury and Darien during the half century after the American Revolution.

For plantation bondpeople who were unable or unwilling to attend Sunday services at Chatham County's independent African churches or in the racially mixed churches of Sunbury and Darien, communal religious observances might still take up part of their Sunday and some of their weekday evenings. Regular religious gatherings in the quarters, which some owners sought to confine to Saturday nights and Sundays, often supplemented or substituted for church attendance.[26] On the Butler estate during the late 1820s, for example, "a certain number of slaves" were permitted to go to Darien on Sundays to trade, and presumably, if they wished to, they could attend the town's Baptist church.[27] A few years later, however, Frances Kemble recorded that her husband's bondpeople were "only permitted to go to Darien to church once a month." On the intervening Sundays those of a mind to do so met at the house of London, the "head cooper, . . . who reads prayers and the Bible . . . and addresses them with extemporaneous exhortations." How long these meetings lasted, and how many bondpeople attended them, she did not say. What she *could* not say was what message, or messages,

London sought to convey in his "extemporaneous exhortations." This was not for lack of interest on her part. On the contrary, Kemble had "the greatest desire to attend one of these religious meetings, but fear to put the people under any, the slightest restraint."[28]

As had been the case in lowcountry Georgia since the 1750s and 1760s, less frequent gatherings of bondpeople continued to be held both on plantations and in the towns, usually at night, for the purpose of celebrating marriages and burying the dead. As Caroline Gilman commented, bondpeople's marriages "have all the varieties of our own," but regardless of the precise form of the wedding ceremony the postnuptial celebrations followed a very similar pattern. The guests "assemble together" and if they had their owners' permission "stay until twelve o'clock."[29] Owners might have been reluctant to allow their bondmen and bondwomen time off work to bury their dead, but there is ample evidence that Africans and African-Americans preferred to perform both first and second burials during the hours of darkness.[30]

The celebrations, and more especially the feasting and drinking, associated with marriages and burials involved the participants in the expenditure of money as well as time. It was the usual practice for the family members and friends of the deceased bondperson, or of the enslaved couple to be married, to provide food and drink for all those who attended the ceremony. And, as James Barclay commented of non-Christian marriages on lowcountry plantations on the eve of the Revolutionary War, this could involve the entertainment of "several hundreds [who] will flock together from the neighbouring plantations." Preparations for the wedding celebrations might include fattening "a number of land tortoises" and spending "what money they have got for their labour on Sundays . . . on rum." Sometimes, added Barclay, their owner "will allow them a hog or two to entertain the company."[31]

Expenditure for religious purposes did not begin with the penetration of evangelical Protestant Christianity into the quarters of the lowcountry. Evangelical Protestant Christianity certainly changed the meaning that attached to expenditure on marriages and burials, but there is no evidence that during the half century after the American Revolution the Christian performance of those ceremonials entailed any significant changes in the amount of time or money expended on them by bondpeople. As Caroline Gilman remarked in the late 1830s, a high priority still attached to the provision of suitable "refreshments" to those who attended weddings and burials, and this cost money. In the case of burials, the "refreshments" provided were "decorously distributed" to mourners and everyone present set a great deal of store on "this solemnity [which] is usually styled by the negroes 'a setting up.'"[32]

Church membership demanded of individuals and families that they make choices, some of which were probably easier to make than others, about the uses to which they put their own time and their patterns of consumption. Even before the strident Sabbatarianism of the 1810s and 1820s, the rural bondpeople's decision to attend church could mean that little, if any, of their Sunday was available for other, secular, purposes. For those who lived on the outer fringes of church catchment areas, most of their Sunday was likely to be taken up with traveling to and from services. Unfortunately there are no detailed records of church attendance, but if they attended church regularly, this meant finding time during the week for such activities as tending their gardens, hunting and fishing, and making handicrafts. Similarly, by choosing to attend church many plantation bondpeople effectively ruled out the possibility of securing a cash income by hiring out their labor for all or part of the Sabbath.

What those plantation bondpeople who attended church services in Savannah did not necessarily rule out before the 1820s was the possibility of combining their spiritual and material needs on their Sunday visits to the city. The fact that the public market and many retail stores remained open until 9:00 A.M. on that day offered an opportunity to trade as well as to worship. How many rural bondmen and bondwomen took advantage of this situation is impossible to ascertain, but the vigor with which Savannah's retailers defended their right to do business on Sundays is perhaps indicative of the volume of trade they conducted with the bondpeople who came into the town on that day. What is certain is that by the mid-1810s African-American Baptists were being exhorted by their own leaders, as well as by their white coreligionists, not to trade on Sundays. In 1815, for instance, the Georgia association minutes included a circular letter on the importance of observing the Sabbath. Nine years later the Sunbury association minutes contained a letter on the same subject, which in due course was reprinted in the

Darien Gazette.[33] Not every African-American church member was able to read these directives, but all would have been made familiar with their contents by their pastors and deacons.

By the early 1830s, regardless of their religious preferences, bondmen and bondwomen were legally debarred from trading with Savannah's retailers on Sundays.[34] In practice, however, it was possible for them to do so, provided they could locate shopkeepers who were willing to turn a blind eye to the law. And there had never been a dearth of those in Savannah. But rural African-American Baptists and Methodists who were committed Sabbatarians, and who could visit Savannah only on Sundays, were forced to reconsider their trading practices. It may have been that rather than break the Sabbath in Savannah they reoriented their trading practices in ways that involved them in more dealings, more negotiations, with their owners and, when within reach, with country storekeepers. Their urban counterparts were in a very different situation. It was perfectly simple for them to comply with the prohibition on Sunday trading: they had innumerable opportunities for trading on weekdays.

Regardless of whether bondpeople attended church on a regular basis, church membership involved adjustments in the budgets of rural and urban bondpeople. New imperatives attached to the expenditure of church members, to the financial choices they made. For example, the determination of African-American Baptists to construct their own places of worship, the building and maintenance of churches, which had not been a requirement for the organized religious practices of bondpeople before the Revolutionary War, involved congregations in expenditures that might take the form of cash or unpaid labor. Initially, contributions of land and capital from white benefactors, usually but not necessarily white Baptists, were important in the physical construction of the lowcountry's African-American churches, but once those churches had been built the financial responsibility for their upkeep devolved to their congregations.

By the early 1780s Baptist meetings, about which we know virtually nothing, were being held in the slave quarters of some plantations along the Savannah River.[35] Between 1785 and 1789, with or without the permission of their owners, African-American Baptists from different estates worshiped together irregularly at two locations, both of which were made available to them by sympathetic whites. The first meeting place was in a barn provided by Jonathan Bryan at his Brampton plantation, some three miles west of Savannah. The second, in Yamacraw, somewhat closer to Savannah, in the city's western suburbs, was "a rough wooden building" constructed by African-American Baptists on land made available to them by Edward Davis.[36]

Meetings continued to be held both at Brampton and at Yamacraw after 1790, the year in which Thomas Gibbons transferred to Andrew Bryan the rights to a lot in Savannah's North Oglethorpe Ward upon which was to be built the first independent African church within the city's boundaries.[37] In 1795 this "temporary shelter" was replaced by what came to be known as "the big meeting-house," a building constructed on a plot of land in Middle Oglethorpe Ward that Andrew Bryan, with the necessary legal assistance of two whites, William Bryan and James Whitfield, had acquired two years earlier from Matthew and Catherine Mott on behalf of his congregation.[38]

The site of the permanent meeting place for Bryan's flock had a 95-foot frontage that ran along Bryan Street and was 132.5 feet deep.[39] The money required to buy the land, which cost "thirty pounds, equal to $150," and to build the church, was given to Bryan "by his people, and friends."[40] Two white Baptists, Jonathan Clarke and Ebenezer Hills, who acted as "trustees" for the "subscription," opened the fund with a donation of £35.6.8. Unfortunately, there is no extant record of the money contributed by African-American Baptists.[41]

The church, which when completed measured forty-two by forty-nine feet, and "a small wooden building" next to it for Bryan's residence were constructed by the congregation. Both were "slow in building, as facilities for getting materials were difficult." Women church members might have helped with the construction of the church and given money for the purchase of the site and building materials, but the skilled work entailed in this enterprise was very much a male preserve. Indeed, the expertise of enslaved and free African-American sawyers and carpenters was invaluable. Timber for the frame of the church and for Bryan's house was "hewed out in the forest," and presumably cost the congregation little or nothing, and "the weather-boarding was all neatly planed smooth." Apart from wood, the only other material used in the building of the church, which "was very plain, without any attempt at architectural beauty," was glass for some "small windows." Whether out of choice or because of limited funds, "no part of the building was painted or whitewashed." The one "pretension to neatness," which involved an outlay of time rather than money, "was in the smoothing of the backs and seats and rounding and beading the edges and tops."[42]

The self-imposed financial contributions and obligations of members did not end with the construction of their churches. Sometimes congregations, or particular groups within a congregation, joined together to buy plate or other adornments for their church. In the mid-1810s, for instance, the First African Church in Savannah received a gift of silver plate, the value and provenance of which is not recorded, from its women members.[43] Some of these women might have enjoyed a certain prestige and influence within the church by virtue of their age or their piety, but as in the other African-American and biracial Baptist churches, the offices of pastor and deacon, with the formal authority they entailed, not least in the disciplining of congregations, were filled by men.[44] Nevertheless, this gift of plate, it may be posited, provided tangible evidence of a conscious and organized female presence in the First African Church. It is also indicative of something else: the extent to which bondwomen and free African-American women were empowered to make independent financial decisions or were able to influence those made by their families.

The financial contributions and choices of all church members —male and female, young and old—were not limited to building and adorning their churches. For example, from the outset African-American Baptist congregations did what they could to meet the expenses incurred by visiting preachers. The Rev. Abraham Marshall recorded that when he visited Savannah in 1788 and "baptized forty-five people of color . . . constituted them into a church [and] ordained them a Minister [Andrew Bryan]" those present "made up eight dollars for him in six and a quarter, twenty-five and fifty cent pieces, [and] gave him two loaves of bread and a bottle of wine."[45]

The financial arrangements between the pastors, deacons, and congregations of the independent African Baptist churches are obscure. All or part of the out-of-pocket expenses incurred by the former, including those they ran up when attending association meetings held at churches other than their own, might well have been met by their

congregations. Otherwise these men do not appear to have been supported financially by their congregations, at least not on any regular or
formal basis.

As a general rule, bondmen were not excused from their daily
work to take on full-time pastoral duties for which they or their
owners could expect to receive financial compensation from the church.
Free African-Americans, on the other hand, who through this period
monopolized the office of pastor in Savannah's independent African
churches, enjoyed far more flexibility in the time they were able to
devote to church affairs, and most appear to have been financially
self-supporting. Andrew Bryan, for instance, bought his freedom from
Jonathan Bryan for a nominal sum in the early 1790s and subsequently
managed to earn enough to buy that of his wife and child. He was said
not to make any financial demands on his congregation, but to be able
to maintain himself and his family entirely "by his own labor." When
he died in 1812 Bryan left an estate valued at a minimum of three thousand dollars.[46] By all accounts, Bryan's nephew Andrew Marshall, who
followed in his uncle's footsteps as pastor of the First African Church
in 1814 or 1815, was an eminently successful drayman.[47] Evan Grate, or
Great, an assistant pastor at the same church during the 1790s and subsequently a deacon of the Second African Church, gave his occupation
variously as pastor and as wagoner.[48]

The financial support given by the wives of pastors and deacons to
their husbands, and thereby to their churches, might also have been significant. For example, Evan Grate's wife, Mary, worked as a seamstress,
as did Henry Cunningham's wife, Elizabeth.[49] The evidence strongly
suggests that most free African-American pastors and deacons did not
have to rely on their congregations for financial assistance. If anything,
the reverse is more likely to have been true: when the need arose, pastors and deacons were in a position to contribute at least something
toward the material needs of their congregations.

Incidental expenses that were incurred on a regular basis by the
congregations of the independent African Baptist churches included
the annual contributions they made toward the cost of printing their
association minutes. In 1822, for example, the two Savannah churches,
together with those at White Bluff and Abercorn, contributed $10,
or just over one-fourth, of the total cost of printing that year's Sun-

bury association minutes.[50] By the mid-1820s the independent African churches were also making regular donations to the Sunbury association's domestic missions fund. In 1824 the Savannah churches subscribed $11.00, or roughly 15 percent, of the $77.50 collected for the fund, and no doubt the African-American members of the churches at Sunbury and Newport were responsible for at least some of the remainder.[51] In the following year the African churches accounted for an even higher proportion of the money paid into the fund: $10.00 of the $37.90 collected came from them. The pattern of subscriptions was similar to that of 1824. The First and Second African churches in Savannah contributed $2 and $3, respectively. The congregation at White Bluff gave $1, that at Abercorn $3, and that at Great Ogechee $2. As in 1824, the largest donation, of $21.50, came from Savannah's white Baptist church.[52]

On a per capita basis, the contributions made by African-American Baptist congregations toward the cost of printing the association minutes and to the domestic missions fund amounted to a virtually incalculable fraction of a cent and might seem totally inconsequential. And in a sense they were. However, this money, together with those sums required for the day-to-day running and maintenance of their churches, had to be earned.

If white commentators are to be believed, church membership, or more specifically church attendance, involved bondmen and bondwomen in an additional expenditure for clothing. Whereas standards of clothing did not necessarily correlate with church membership, there is evidence that from the outset African-American Baptists and Methodists attached a high priority to dressing themselves as well as they could when about the business of their Lord. In the late nineteenth century, for instance, some of the "old Christian sisters" who had witnessed the dedication of the First African Church in Savannah on its completion in 1795 recalled that on this momentous occasion the male church members were "clad in their best garments, the elder females with snow-white aprons and neck and handkerchiefs."[53]

A white resident of Liberty County related how on Sundays bondpeople were to be seen "clean and neatly dressed and . . . in their best" making their way to the racially mixed Congregational church at Midway, often "on foot carrying their shoes and stockings." They would replace their footwear only after they had washed their feet "in the waters at the causeway near the church; for they believe in treading the Lord's courts with clean feet!" As Eugene Genovese has pointed out, "Church was a place where you showed respect for God, for your brothers and sisters, for yourself."[54] Appropriate clothing, dress clothes or Sunday clothes, comprised instantly visible evidence of that respect.

White observers were simultaneously amused and appalled by the way in which bondpeople attired themselves on Sundays. Frances Kemble, for example, thought that their "Sabbath toilet really presents the most ludicrous combination of incongruities that you can conceive—frills, flounces, ribbons . . . filthy finery, every colour in the rainbow . . . head handkerchiefs . . . beads, bugles, flaring sashes, and above all [a] little fanciful apron." The point, however, is not bondpeople's taste in clothes or their dress sense, but what they could afford and chose to spend on their "Sabbath toilet."[55]

Contrary to the impression many white commentators sought to convey throughout this eighty-year period, the majority of bondmen and bondwomen did not drink or gamble away all their hard-earned income, although, as Charles Ball conceded, some might purchase "an occasional bottle of rum."[56] Baptist and Methodist morality, however, ruled out even the "occasional" use of alcohol and was equally uncompromising on the sin of gambling. In some cases compliance with these requirements would have resulted in changing patterns of expenditure as well as of behavior. Increasingly, both the African and the racially mixed Baptist churches of lowcountry Georgia sought that compliance through the founding of temperance societies. Membership in these societies was not necessarily restricted to the church's congregation.

In 1829 the Second African Church in Savannah reported to the Sunbury association that 138 people had joined its temperance society, a number that had grown to 667 by 1832. The society was based "on the principle of entire abstinence; and with the exception of two or three, [the members] have been true to their engagements."[57] By 1830 a temperance society had also been formed by the racially mixed, but predominantly African, church at Sunbury "of colored people, many of whom are non-professors." This non-Baptist membership, the church leaders averred, was "a severe reflection on rum drinking Christians." Two years later the Ogechee Church recorded that "upwards of three hundred members, blacks," had joined its temperance society, and the North Newport Church asserted that "the use of ardent spirits has become unfashionable, even among the blacks."[58]

Although African-American Baptists joined with their white coreligionists in the definition of Baptist morality, the African churches were solely responsible for ordering their own priorities and ensuring that their members lived up to the spiritual and moral demands being made of them. They and they alone assumed the responsibility for disciplining their members and, if necessary, excommunicating the recalcitrant. That there were men and women who were either unable or unwilling to conform to the standards being set for them by their coreligionists is evident from the fact that between 1794 and 1829 the independent African churches excommunicated at least 382 members, whose gender is not recorded, of whom 207 were subsequently restored to full church membership.[59] What the records do not reveal are the numbers who were disciplined, but who avoided excommunication by mending their ways. Neither is there any indication of the range or comparative frequency of the offenses committed by those who were disciplined, although it may be safely inferred that they almost certainly included drunkenness, gambling, sexual misdemeanors, and, by the 1820s if not earlier, ignoring the strictures on Sunday trading.

Some African-American Baptists, like some of their white coreligionists, found it impossible to live up to the moral expectations and patterns of behavior that church membership demanded of them; several of their compatriots in the quarters saw little virtue in trying to do so. That African-American Protestant Christianity, and more especially the evangelical churches, made great inroads in and around Savannah between the mid-1780s and 1830 is indisputable. That this entailed significant changes in their members' expenditures of time and money is also indisputable. But the enslaved population of lowcountry Georgia continued to include a great many men and women who, for a variety of reasons, rejected Protestant Christianity, regardless of who presented it to them. In 1830 this was true of possibly as many as one-third of Chatham County's African and African-American population. These men and women were coming under increasingly heavy pressure, not least from other bondpeople, and sometimes from those closest to them, to reorder their lives. In the process at least one of their most cherished

rights was also coming under intense threat: not their right to Sunday
but their right to use that day as they wished. By 1830 those bondpeople
who lived in and around Savannah and Darien stood in great danger of being deprived of that right by African-American Baptists and
Methodists acting in concert with their white coreligionists.

Before 1830 most of the bondpeople who lived outside Chatham
County, and in parts of Liberty and McIntosh counties, were virtually
immune to this pressure, a situation that would change dramatically
with the inauguration of the plantation missionary endeavor. During
the next thirty years virtually every bondman and bondwoman in the
lowcountry would be confronted with the same spiritual, moral, social,
and economic choices, if not dilemmas, long familiar to their compatriots in Chatham, McIntosh, and Liberty counties. The battles within
and between the enslaved and free populations of lowcountry Georgia
over the nature, meaning, and function of the informal slave economies did not draw to a close in 1830, but during the next thirty years the
front line was to advance with ever-increasing speed from the towns to
the countryside.

Conclusion

CHATTEL SLAVERY was sanctioned in Georgia in 1750. What was introduced to that colony during the next two decades by the South Carolina planters and their bondpeople who crossed the Savannah River in such large numbers were the imperatives of the formal and the informal slave economies that had evolved in the Carolina lowcountry during the previous three-quarters of a century. The South Carolina migration to Georgia did not prompt a reassessment of, let alone produce any radical changes in, the attitudes and aspirations of either rice planters or their enslaved workers; it did not result in any profound alterations in the characteristics of either the formal or the informal slave economies that these protagonists sought to establish in lowcountry Georgia.

One of the primary, and enduring, attributes of the formal slave economy taken to lowcountry Georgia by South Carolina rice planters was its savagery. Privately and as a matter of public policy these planters and their descendants resorted to physical, psychological, and emotional coercion, often of the most barbarous kind, in order to try to secure their two inextricably related objectives: profits and racial control. Although severely tested by the ideas and events of the American Revolution, the planters' commitment to these goals remained as strong in 1830 as it had been in 1750 when slavery was first permitted in Georgia.

By 1750, as chattel slavery and rice culture were poised to expand across the Savannah River, the bondpeople of lowcountry Carolina had long been engaged in a struggle with their owners to secure for themselves a cluster of interrelated economic rights that stemmed from and in turn reinforced the character of the private lives they were intent on creating for themselves. They waged daily battles, engaged in a constant war of attrition, in order to secure and retain the fundamental right to their own time. The task system that emerged from these struggles was a distinguishing characteristic of the lowcountry's formal slave economy. It was also to be of crucial and continuing significance in the definition of that region's informal slave economies.

Because bondpeople generally refused to work on Sunday without receiving some form of compensation, the right they claimed to that day was usually conceded by owners and tacitly acknowledged in the public laws of slavery. Before the turn of the eighteenth century and the spread of Sabbatarianism both inside and outside the slave quarters of lowcountry Georgia, clashes over bondpeople's right to time and the right to employ that time as they wished focused on weekdays rather than on the Sabbath. The question was clear-cut and critical: how much time would bondpeople be able to wrest from their owners on any given day or in any given week?

By the mid-eighteenth century it was a well-established fact of life on lowcountry plantations that however much time bondpeople managed to snatch from their owners during the course of the week they would not be able to totally avoid the necessity of having to spend at least some of that time working for themselves. Whatever else may have changed in lowcountry Georgia between 1750 and 1830, and much did, this requirement remained intact. The organization of their own time, the balance that was struck between work, religious, and recreational pursuits, comprised one of the main areas of negotiation between bondpeople themselves. Bondmen and bondwomen may have enjoyed a good deal of autonomy in determining how they employed their own time in and around the quarters, but that they were often required to make difficult choices between work, religion, and recreation manifested a requirement that had long been inflicted on them by their owners.

The insistence of planters everywhere in the New World that bondpeople work in their own time to maintain themselves was predicated on their two imperatives of profits and racial control. Productivity, and thereby profits, it was widely held, could be enhanced by coercing bondpeople into working long hours, day in and day out, month in and month out. But, owners believed, profits could also be maximized by trimming production costs to the bare bone. The universal desire to cut costs and the practical problems of securing supervision for enslaved workers on Sundays suggested an obvious solution: oblige bondpeople to work for themselves on that day in order to feed and clothe themselves. Tie them to the plantation, thus lessening the possibility of racial disorder.

Bondpeople were presented with a stark choice that in reality amounted to no choice at all. They could try to survive on, make do with, the meager rations and clothing issued to them by their owners, or they could allocate at least part of their own time to the provision of their material needs and wants. Planters fully appreciated that if bondpeople were to supplement their rations they required something in addition to time: they needed land to cultivate on their own behalf. From the planters' perspective the allocation, which they originally regarded as a gift, of land to be cultivated by their enslaved workers in their own time was considered an excellent investment. Gardens, or patches, were to be the foundation stones on which plantation bondpeople built their informal economies.

Initially, planters somewhat arrogantly assumed that bondpeople would have no greater ambition than to supply their own immediate needs from the cultivation of their gardens or through their hunting, fishing, and trapping activities. The possibility that bondmen and bondwomen might organize themselves, and their time, in ways that would enable them to produce surpluses of a wide range of commodities does not seem to have occurred to the owners, let alone troubled them greatly. What seventeenth-century planters seem originally to have envisaged was that a primitive form of economic self-sufficiency would evolve in the quarters. In each of the plantation colonies, the industry and enterprise displayed by bondpeople rapidly disabused planters of that illusion. Moreover, the rights that bondpeople began to claim concerning the ownership and disposal of their surpluses opened up entirely new areas of negotiation, with each other, and with their owners and other whites.

In keeping with the practice hammered out elsewhere in the Americas between bondpeople and their owners, the rice planters of lowcountry Carolina were forced, during the first half of the eighteenth century, to concede important principles: contrary to the stipulations of the public slavery laws, bondpeople had a legitimate claim to the commodities they produced and the income they generated through the sale of their labor in their own time. As these pragmatic planters understood only too well, the appropriation of the goods produced by their bondpeople without compensation in cash or kind would have provoked a range of assertive responses scarcely conducive to the smooth running of their estates.

By 1750 lowcountry planters had generally conceded the right of ownership that their bondpeople demanded to the fruits of their labor in their own time. What they stubbornly refused to concede, indeed never conceded, was that bondpeople had the unconditional right, which in practice they were asserting, to dispose of their produce and to make purchases as and when they chose. From the standpoint of many planters, the quasi-autonomous economic activities of bondpeople were financially and racially advantageous to owners, and therefore to be tolerated—but only if they took place under close supervision within the confines of the plantation. But as lowcountry Georgia planters increasingly complained, there were two reasons why it proved virtually impossible to contain the informal slave economies: the initiative and enterprise displayed by bondpeople in forging trading links off the plantation and the willingness of many whites to ignore the public laws of slavery and do business with them. Neither brutal physical force, the imposition of curfews, nor the supposed convenience of plantation stores prevented bondpeople from developing a variety of economic links with outsiders.

As lowcountry Georgia's formal slave economy took shape and expanded during the 1750s and 1760s, bondpeople forged relationships with bondmen and bondwomen on neighboring estates. Sometimes those relationships were based on shared West African heritages; increasingly they reflected and reinforced bonds of family and kinship. By the late eighteenth century, as evangelical Protestant Christianity began to take hold in the slave quarters, they also came to be based on shared religious beliefs and membership in the same churches. Whether for religious purposes, economic purposes, or both, the meetings of bondpeople from different plantations involved a degree of mobility, often at night, that horrified many planters. But it was a mobility they were essentially powerless to prevent.

The sometimes casual, and sometimes more regular, relationships that plantation bondpeople developed with the boatmen who plied the rivers and coastal waterways of lowcountry Georgia did not usually require them to leave their plantations. These relationships were significant for many reasons, but principally because they comprised an increasingly significant interface between the informal slave economies of the countryside and the urban economies of Savannah and the smaller lowcountry towns of Darien and Sunbury.

The port of Savannah was the focus, the hub, of lowcountry Georgia's formal slave economy. During the second half of the eighteenth century Savannah came to serve a similar function for the informal slave economies that were evolving in its hinterland. Simultaneously, Savannah's enslaved population, which by the turn of the eighteenth century accounted for roughly 40 percent of the city's inhabitants, was developing its own discreet spheres of informal economic behavior. The formal and the informal slave economies of lowcountry Georgia were juxtaposed and interactive; so too were the urban and rural informal slave economies.

The population growth and economic development of Savannah were crucially important stimuli to the informal slave economies of the countryside. On the one hand, there was an ever-increasing urban demand for a range of fresh foodstuffs that plantation bondpeople were well placed to satisfy. Moreover, an expanding urban economy opened up plentiful opportunities for bondmen and bondwomen, including fugitives, to negotiate terms for the sale of their labor. In addition, Savannah offered its own residents, as well as those bondpeople from the countryside who could reach the city, a wide range of consumer choices and recreational pursuits. Planters continued to complain about the degree of economic autonomy that bondpeople were claiming for themselves in the countryside, but increasingly, and with good reason, white concern came to focus on Savannah.

To some degree, the quasi-autonomous economic activities of bondpeople in the countryside depended on white collaboration, a collaboration that could not be taken for granted or absolutely relied on. The same was true in Savannah, but white complicity there existed on a scale that bore little comparison to the countryside. The motives of urban and rural whites who were willing to conduct business with bondpeople were identical: economic self-interest. Bondpeople turned that self-interest to their own advantage, and in the process they not only exploited but also fostered deepening divisions within the lowcountry's white society. This may have been an unintentional achievement of the lowcountry's informal slave economies; it was no less significant for that.

By the turn of the eighteenth century the economic activities of bondpeople and the white complicity they thrived on, especially but not exclusively in Savannah, were being forced ever higher on the agenda for political debate and political decision making. In part, this heightened interest in the informal slave economies reflected the continuing importance of the essentially pragmatic considerations that had infused white deliberations and informed planter priorities ever since the 1760s. Those pragmatic considerations, especially the fear of serious racial disorder that might stem from the mobility of bondpeople as they went about their personal business, loomed large during and immediately after the American Revolution. They were given an additional impetus by the successful black revolution in Santo Domingo and the Prosser and Vesey rebellions on the mainland. But during the late eighteenth and early nineteenth century, entirely new imperatives began to inform not only white perceptions of the quasi-autonomous economic activities of bondpeople but also the meaning that bondmen and bondwomen themselves attached to these activities. Evangelical Protestant Christianity was to add an entirely new dimension to the meaning, and potentially to the modus operandi, of those economies.

Before 1830 and the formation of the plantation missionary movement, spiritual coercion did not feature as prominently as it would during the antebellum period in either the individual or collective attempts by lowcountry Georgia planters to secure compliance from their bondpeople. Indeed, throughout the eighteenth century Anglican planters had largely spurned the possibility of employing spiritual coercion as a means of instilling the qualities of docility and obedience in their bondpeople. Between the mid-1780s and 1830, however, white commentators began to appreciate how Christianity could be employed as an integral aspect of their self-serving defense of chattel slavery. Increasingly they also came to be persuaded that the Christian bondperson might best serve their racial and economic purposes. But during the half century after the American War of Independence evangelical

Protestant Christianity was not foisted on the bondpeople of lowcountry Georgia.

The spread of evangelical Protestant Christianity, especially the Baptist faith, in the slave quarters of lowcountry Georgia reflected choices made by bondpeople rather than choices forced on them by their owners or other whites. The short- and long-term consequences of this religious reorientation would be many, dramatic, and far-reaching. And the fusion of religious and economic morality that began in the mid-1780s and gathered pace thereafter carried potentially profound implications for the informal slave economies.

African and African-American converts fought long and hard to secure the right to hold their own religious beliefs and to worship as they wished in their own churches. But they joined with their white coreligionists in an effort to secure something else: the imposition of their morality, particularly their Sabbatarianism, on nonbelievers. They sought to overturn a right that bondpeople had battled for decades to obtain: the right to employ their time on Sundays as they wished. Evangelical Protestant Christianity may have created and fostered a new and supportive group identity, a new and supportive sense of community in the slave quarters of lowcountry Georgia, but as bondpeople made different religious choices it also created and fostered tensions and divisions. By 1830 bondpeople, as well as white Georgians, were engaged in a struggle to determine the future meaning that would attach to their informal economies.

By the turn of the eighteenth century most white commentators were in close agreement on one point: in a purely economic sense some whites gained and others lost as a result of the economies bondpeople were forging for themselves, particularly in Savannah. Owners claimed to be universal losers because of the appropriation and sale of their goods by bondpeople and the additional loss of income incurred as a result of self-hire. Savannah's white consumers were also depicted as losers because they were charged exorbitant prices by bondpeople who monopolized the supply and marketing of fresh foodstuffs. Clearly, however, some whites benefited financially from their dealings with bondpeople: Savannah's retailers, landlords who rented accommodations to bondpeople, and whites who illicitly negotiated with bondpeople for the hire of their labor.

It may be suggested that owners greatly inflated the financial cost to themselves of the informal slave economies. Bondpeople, who in the moral economy they devised for themselves made a clear distinction between "theft" and "stealing," did indeed appropriate goods from their owners, but not on a scale that financially embarrassed them, let alone threatened to bankrupt them. Owners probably lost more money through the inability of their bondpeople to work because of the diseases that ravaged them than they ever did through the pilfering of commodities. In most cases pilfering amounted to little more than a financial irritant. The scale of the financial losses incurred by owners from self-hire were variable and in the case of fugitives depended solely on the length of time the bondman or bondwoman could avoid recapture. That, in turn, depended on a great many variables.

Owners complained about their financial losses, but those complaints were closely related to what they regarded as the mounting challenge being posed to their authority by the informal slave economies. Not until the 1820s did some white commentators begin to suggest that in fact the reverse might be true: far from threatening planters' authority, the informal slave economies were actually bolstering that authority and should, therefore, be encouraged. The argument advanced by these commentators was simple. Bondpeople, they asserted, subscribed to the same economic ethos and values as their owners. They would not take flight and abandon their property; neither would they behave in other ways likely to jeopardize their continuing enjoyment of that property. If encouraged, but made subject to continuing scrutiny and regulation, the initiative, enterprise, and energy that characterized the informal slave economies might be channeled in such a way as to further the twin objectives of their owners: profits and racial control. Surely, these commentators concluded, it made more sense to condone the informal slave economies than it did to try to embark on the impossible task of eradicating those economies root and branch.

This line of reasoning prompted a debate that would continue for the remainder of the antebellum period. But the argument was based on the fallacious assumption that the moral economy devised by bondpeople slavishly imitated that of their owners. It signally failed to appreciate that the overriding attachment of bondmen and bondwomen was not to the meager amounts of property they managed to accumulate from their economic activities, but to people, to their families. From first to last, ensuring the welfare of the family was the whole point and purpose of the informal slave economies devised by the bondpeople of lowcountry Georgia.

The bondmen and bondwomen of lowcountry Georgia were realists. They were constantly aware of the awesome power wielded by their owners, of the fact that it would prove virtually impossible for them to overturn Georgia's slave system by their own unaided efforts. Amelioration was a far more viable and realistic strategy than launching a suicidal physical assault on the formal slave economy. Amelioration demanded that bondpeople operate within the constraints imposed on them by the formal slave economy, but that economy also presented them with possibilities. The formal slave economy could be exploited, twisted, and manipulated by bondpeople to serve their own purposes and requirements. Contrary to what some white commentators were arguing by 1830, amelioration and accommodation did not entail an unthinking acceptance and internalization of the economic ethos and morality of the master class; it did not automatically result in groveling collaboration.

Neither did amelioration rule out the possibility that bondpeople might someday, with or without the assistance of an external liberator, be able to engage in an organized armed struggle to secure their liberation. The Revolutionary War had amply demonstrated, and the successful revolution in Santo Domingo confirmed, that amelioration did not extinguish the yearning of bondpeople for their freedom. Amelioration was a pragmatic but not necessarily a permanent strategy. It was, moreover, a strategy that bondpeople individually or collectively would be willing to jettison in exchange for their liberty should the opportunity arise. This much is clear, and ought to have been clear to white Georgians, from the advertisements for fugitive bondmen and bondwomen that filled the pages of their newspapers.

As many white Georgians came to appreciate, what the vast majority of bondpeople were not prepared to jettison in exchange for their liberation from chattel slavery were their loved ones. Bondpeople could and did disagree with one another, and sometimes violently so, over a variety of issues. Disagreements might arise between family members, but they did not seriously dilute the love, loyalty, and mutual respect that were the hallmarks of the African and African-American family. It was the integrity, the well-being of their families that was of paramount importance to the enslaved population of lowcountry Georgia.

The collective welfare of the family, not personal interests or self-advancement, provided the continuing rationale of amelioration and of the informal slave economies. It was in and by the family that quasi-autonomous economic activities were organized, that decisions affecting every member of the family were taken. It was the family that provided the focal point, the essential and creative dynamics of those activities. In every respect, the informal slave economies that evolved in lowcountry Georgia during the second half of the eighteenth century were family economies.

To what extent did those economies actually belong to bondpeople? What were the personal costs to bondpeople in achieving them? And what did bondpeople gain from them?

The bondpeople's ownership of their informal economies was not—could not be—absolute. It never went completely uncontested, and it could never escape the shadow cast by owners' demands. The informal slave economies were apart from, but simultaneously a part of, the formal slave economy. They were autonomous, but also dependent. From the outset the informal slave economies involved much more than work and accumulation simply to ensure the physical survival of the family. They were an essential, an integral part of a continuing struggle for cultural survival waged by the enslaved population of lowcountry Georgia.

Bondpeople may well have recognized that their quasi-autonomous economic activities were never likely to bring about the overthrow of Georgia's slave system or their own personal freedom. They may have realized that their chosen course of amelioration furthered their owners' economic interests. But however costly the strategy of amelioration it helped bondpeople secure whatever degree of quasi-independence they ultimately achieved. The enslaved population of lowcountry Georgia worked long and hard in their own time; they displayed an enormous amount of skill, ingenuity, and courage; they often ran enormous personal risks—all in return for generally pathetic material rewards. Bondpeople did succeed in raising their standard of living above the bare subsistence deemed suitable for them by their owners. And given the demands made on them by the formal slave economy, that was no mean achievement. But the material achievements of bondpeople tell only part of the story, reveal only part of what it was that bondpeople strove for and secured from their informal economies.

Their dress clothes, the few dollars they managed to earn, the rooms and houses they could afford to rent in Savannah were but the outward and visible signs of their labors. A minuscule number could point to the freedom they had scrimped and saved to buy from their owners. But most would not have defined their gains, the benefits they accrued from their informal economic activities, solely in terms of their material possessions and achievements. By 1830, as the nature and meaning of their informal economies were coming under growing scrutiny within and outside the slave quarters, the bondpeople of lowcountry Georgia had secured for themselves a precious, if somewhat precarious, autonomy in the definition and determination of their private lives. That autonomy was not to be taken for granted. It had to be fought for on a daily basis in many different arenas.

By the end of this eighty-year period the vast majority of bondmen and bondwomen in lowcountry Georgia, whose voices have not come down to us, would no doubt have agreed that their greatest gain, their greatest benefit, was something on which it was impossible to put a price. The dignity, pride, and profoundly important sense of self-worth that informed and were expressed by their informal economic activities were qualities deeply rooted in and reinforced by the bonds of family and kinship. They did not make the appalling demands of the formal slave economy acceptable, but they did make them more bearable. This was the ultimate significance of the informal slave economies that took such deep root in lowcountry Georgia in the decades before 1830.

Notes

Introduction

1. For important examples of scholarship on the sugar islands see Sidney W. Mintz and Douglass G. Hall, "The Origins of the Jamaican Internal Marketing System," *Yale University Publications in Anthropology* 57 (1960); Mintz, "The Jamaican Internal Marketing Pattern: Some Notes and Hypotheses," *Social and Economic Studies* 4 (1955): 95–103; Mintz, *Caribbean Transformations* (Chicago, 1974); Mintz, "Caribbean Marketplaces and Caribbean History," *Nova Americana* 1 (1980–81), 333–44; Mintz, "Was the Plantation Slave a Proletarian?" *Review* 2 (1978): 1–20; John H. Parry, "Plantation and Provision Ground: An Historical Sketch of the Introduction of Food Crops in Jamaica," *Revista de Historia de America* 39 (1955): 1–20; Orlando Patterson, *The Sociology of Slavery: An Analysis of the Origins, Development, and Structure of Negro Slave Society in Jamaica* (London, 1967); and Neville Hall, "Slaves' Use of Their 'Free' Time in the Danish Virgin Islands in the Later Eighteenth and Early Nineteenth Century," *Journal of Caribbean History* 13 (1979): 21–43. See also Hilary McD. Beckles, "Slaves and the Internal Market Economy of Barbados: A Perspective on Non-Violent Resistance" and David Barry Gaspar, "Amelioration or Oppression?: The Abolition of the Slaves' Sunday Markets in Antigua (1831)" (papers presented at the twentieth annual Conference of Caribbean Historians, St. Thomas, Virgin Islands, 1988). For the American South before 1830 see Peter H. Wood, *Black Majority: Negroes in Colonial South Carolina from 1670 through the Stono Rebellion* (New York, 1974), 195–217; Philip D. Morgan, "Work and Culture: The Task System and the Work of Lowcountry Blacks, 1700–1800," *William and Mary Quarterly* 3d. ser., 4 (1982): 563–99 (hereafter *WMQ*); Morgan, "Black Society in the Lowcountry, 1700–1810," in Ira Berlin and Ronald Hoffman, eds., *Slavery and Free-*

dom in the Age of the American Revolution (Charlottesville, 1983); Morgan, "Black Life in Eighteenth-Century Charleston," *Perspectives in American History* New Series, 1 (1984): 187–232. For influential studies of the antebellum South, and what, with the exception of Morgan, are usually briefer discussions, see Philip D. Morgan, "The Ownership of Property by Slaves in the Mid-Nineteenth-Century Lowcountry," *Journal of Southern History* 49, no. 3 (1983): 399–420; John W. Blassingame, *The Slave Community: Plantation Life in the Ante-Bellum South* (New York, 1972); Eugene D. Genovese, *Roll, Jordan, Roll: The World the Slaves Made* (London, 1975); Leslie Howard Owens, *This Species of Property: Slave Life and Culture in the Old South* (New York, 1976). For two recent collections that incorporate both the Caribbean and the mainland see Ira Berlin and Philip D. Morgan, eds., *The Slaves' Economy: Independent Production by Slaves in the Americas* (London, 1991), and Morgan and Berlin, eds., *Cultivation and Culture: Labor and the Shaping of Slave Life in the Americas* (Charlottesville, 1993).

2. For a recent, extended, and excellent discussion of these themes see the introduction in Berlin and Morgan, eds., *Slaves' Economy.*

3. See works referred to in note 1 above and John Campbell, "As 'A Kind of Freedom'? Slaves' Market-Related Activities in the South Carolina Upcountry, 1800–1860," in Berlin and Morgan, eds., *Slaves' Economy*, 131–69.

4. For gender divisions in the informal slave economies of the sugar islands see Hilary McD. Beckles, *Natural Rebels: A Social History of Enslaved Black Women in Barbados* (London, 1989); Barbara Bush, *Slave Women in Caribbean Society, 1650–1838* (Kingston, Jamaica, 1990); Marietta Morrissey, *Slave Women in the New World: Gender Stratification in the Caribbean* (Lawrence, Kans., 1989). For the late eighteenth-century South see Jacqueline Jones, "Race, Sex, and Self-Evident Truths: The Status of Slave Women during the Era of the American Revolution," in Ronald Hoffman and Peter J. Albert, eds., *Women in the Age of the American Revolution* (Charlottesville, 1989), 293–337. For the antebellum South see Jacqueline Jones, *Labor of Love, Labor of Sorrow: Black Women, Work, and the Family from Slavery to the Present* (New York, 1985), 29–43; Deborah Gray White, *Ar'n't I a Woman? Female Slaves in the Plantation South* (New York, 1985), 142–60; Elizabeth Fox-Genovese, *Within the Plantation Household: Black and White Women of the Old South* (Chapel Hill, 1988), 146–91.

5. For two short discussions see Betty Wood, " 'White Society' and the 'Informal' Slave Economies of Lowcountry Georgia, c. 1763–1830," *Slavery and Abolition* 11, no. 3 (1990): 313–31; Wood, " 'Never on a Sunday?': Slavery and the Sabbath in Lowcountry Georgia, 1760–1830," in Mary Turner, ed., *From Chattel Slavery to Wage Slavery* (forthcoming).

6. The founding and early history of Georgia have attracted extensive schol-

arly attention. For recent interpretations see Paul S. Taylor, *Georgia Plan* (Berkeley, 1972); B. Phinizy Spalding, *Oglethorpe in America* (Chicago, 1977); Larry E. Ivers, *British Drums on the Southern Frontier* (Chapel Hill, 1974); Harvey H. Jackson and Phinizy Spalding, eds., *Forty Years of Diversity: Essays on Colonial Georgia* (Athens, 1984); Phinizy Spalding and Harvey H. Jackson, eds., *Oglethorpe in Perspective: Georgia's Founder after Two Hundred Years* (Tuscaloosa, 1989). For an extended discussion of the reasons that prompted the trustees to exclude slavery from Georgia and the campaign mounted against them, see Betty Wood, *Slavery in Colonial Georgia, 1733–1775* (Athens, 1984), 1–87.

7. David R. Chesnutt, "South Carolinian Expansion into Colonial Georgia," (Ph.D. diss., University of Georgia, 1971).

8. Wood, *Slavery in Colonial Georgia*, 91–98.

9. For the South Carolina slave code of 1740 see Thomas Cooper and David J. McCord, eds. *The Statutes at Large of South Carolina*, 10 vols. (Columbia, S.C., 1836–41), 7: 397–417. For the Georgia code of 1755 see Allen D. Candler and Lucian L. Knight, eds., *The Colonial Records of the State of Georgia*, 26 vols. (Atlanta, 1904–16), 18: 102–44 (hereafter *Col. Recs.*).

10. *Col. Recs.*, 26: 22; 27, (unpublished) pt. 2: 239; 28, (unpublished) pt. 2: 427.

11. In 1758 Joseph Ottolenghe, who served as an Anglican catechist to Georgia's enslaved population, remarked that "the Negroes of these Parts . . . are mostly African born" (cited in Harold E. Davis, *The Fledgling Province: Social and Cultural Life in Georgia, 1733–1776* [Chapel Hill, 1976], 131).

12. As Robert Glenn, Jr., has observed, Georgia "approximated the pattern of the other southern colonies in that it did not develop a direct slave trade with Africa until its economy was advanced enough to absorb cargoes of 150 to 200 slaves at a time" (Robert S. Glenn, Jr., "Slavery in Georgia, 1733–1793," [senior thesis, Princeton University, 1972], 65).

13. Answers to the Heads of Inquiry Relative to the Present State and Condition of the Province of Georgia, James Wright. 20 December 1773. *Col. Recs.*, 28, pt. 1: 120–21.

14. For South Carolina preferences see Elizabeth Donnan, "The Slave Trade into South Carolina before the Revolution," *American Historical Review* 33 (1928): 816–17; Daniel C. Littlefield, *Rice and Slaves: Ethnicity and the Slave Trade in Colonial South Carolina* (Baton Rouge, 1981). For colonial Georgia see Wood, *Slavery in Colonial Georgia*, 103–4; Julia Floyd Smith, *Slavery and Rice Culture in Low Country Georgia, 1750–1860* (Knoxville, 1985), 93–98; Darold D. Wax, " 'New Negroes Are Always in Demand': The Slave Trade in Eighteenth-Century Georgia," *Georgia Historical Quarterly* 68 (1984): 193–220 (hereafter *GHQ*). See also, Wax, "Preferences for Slaves in Colonial America," *Journal of Negro History* 58 (1973): 371–401.

15. Wood, *Slavery in Colonial Georgia*, 103. Between 1733 and 1807 approximately 20 percent of those shipped directly from West Africa to Georgia and South Carolina probably came from Senegambia and roughly 60 percent from the Angola region. The remaining 20 percent were from a variety of mainly West African locations.

16. Ibid., 103, 108; Ralph Gray and Betty Wood, "The Transition from Indentured to Involuntary Servitude in Colonial Georgia," *Explorations in Economic History* 13 (1976): 363. James C. Bonner has estimated that by 1773 Georgia's sixty premier planters held more than half the colony's enslaved population, which by that date numbered around fifteen thousand (Bonner, *A History of Georgia Agriculture, 1732–1860* [Athens, 1964], 8).

17. Wood, *Slavery in Colonial Georgia*, 108.

18. Wood, *Black Majority*, 153, 160.

19. The Rev. Samuel Frink to the Society for the Propagation of the Gospel, Savannah, 8 July 1771, Society for the Propagation of the Gospel, London Manuscripts, series C, pkg. 7, pt. 3 (microfilm, University of Cambridge Library).

20. This census was taken by an anonymous correspondent to the *Georgia Gazette* (hereafter *Ga. Gaz.*) and published on 6 February 1800. According to this account, Savannah's population totaled 6,226, of whom 3,216 were African or African-American. An informal census taken in 1791, which did not include Europeans under the age of sixteen, indicated that there were 1,104 "Negroes and other slaves of all ages and sexes . . . in Savannah, and the hamlets thereof." Bearing in mind that not all Europeans were enumerated, bondpeople accounted for a maximum of 37.6 percent of the city's population. This census was taken by "OBSERVER" and published in *Ga. Gaz.* on 7 July 1791.

21. For a lengthier extended discussion of this point see Wood, *Slavery in Colonial Georgia*, 24–58, 74–87.

22. Ibid., 89.

23. This phrase is taken from the title of the book published by Davis in 1976. See note 11 above.

24. Wood, *Slavery in Colonial Georgia*, 198–206; Donald Robinson, *Slavery in the Structure of American Politics, 1765–1820* (New York, 1979), 118–20. For an exceptionally fine discussion of British attitudes toward the possible arming of slaves see Sylvia R. Frey, *Water from the Rock: Black Resistance in a Revolutionary Age* (Princeton, 1991), 81–142. For an older but still immensely valuable study, see Benjamin Quarles, *The Negro in the American Revolution* (Chapel Hill, 1961).

25. Kenneth Coleman, *The American Revolution in Georgia, 1763–1789* (Athens, 1958), 145–46, 206–8, 212; as many as seven thousand bondpeople were removed from Georgia by the British or their Loyalist owners. For the

slave trade to Georgia see Wax, "'New Negroes Are Always in Demand'";
Smith, *Slavery and Rice Culture*, 98–103.

26. Census of the District of Georgia in the *Augusta Chronicle*, 5 November 1791.

27. As Sylvia Frey has pointed out, "Whereas in 1775 two-thirds of Georgia's slaves lived within twenty miles of the coast, by 1790 over half of them lived in the backcountry" (Frey, *Water from the Rock*, 214). For a recent analysis of the origins and early history of cotton culture in Georgia see Joyce E. Chaplin, "Creating a Cotton South in Georgia and South Carolina, 1760–1815," *Journal of Southern History* 2 (1991): 171–200.

28. Smith, *Slavery and Rice Culture*, 32.

29. Thomas R. Statom, Jr., "Negro Slavery in Eighteenth-Century Georgia," (Ph.D. diss., University of Alabama, 1982), 176.

30. For rice cultivation in the lowcountry during the Revolutionary and early national periods see Joyce E. Chaplin, "Tidal Rice Cultivation and the Problem of Slavery in South Carolina and Georgia, 1760–1815," *WMQ* 3d ser., 49 (1992): 29–61. For cotton see Chaplin, "Creating a Cotton South."

31. For the number and destination of fugitive bondpeople in the colonial period see Wood, *Slavery in Colonial Georgia*, 169–87.

32. Frey, *Water from the Rock*, 63.

33. Ibid., 81–107.

34. The Spanish, until the end of the Seven Years' War and their defeat by the British, had offered freedom to any bondpeople from British America who could make their way to Florida, and they were willing to enlist those men they had freed into their armed forces. For a discussion of Spanish policy see John J. TePaske, "The Fugitive Slave: Intercolonial Rivalry and Spanish Slave Policy, 1687–1764," in Samuel Proctor, ed., *Eighteenth-Century Florida and Its Borderlands* (Gainesville, Fla., 1975), 1–12. For an account of the settlement at Moosa, near St. Augustine, see "Dispatches of Spanish Officials Bearing on the Free Negro Settlement of Gracia Real de Santa Teresa de Mose, Florida," *Journal of Negro History* 9 (1924) 144–231. The notion that eventually the British might prove to be their liberators persisted even after the evacuation of Savannah. During the War of 1812, when the British fleet was operating off the Georgia coast, African and African-American hopes of freedom were raised by Vice Adm. Sir Alexander Cochrane's proclamation that any bondpeople who were able to reach his forces would be freed and sent to Britain's remaining American colonies (Malcom Bell, Jr., *Major Butler's Legacy: Five Generations of a Slaveholding Family* [Athens, 1987], 170–91).

35. Frey, *Water from the Rock*, 284–325.

Chapter One. The Right to Time in the Countryside

1. See, for example, Mintz and Hall, "Origins of the Jamaican Internal Marketing System"; Neville Hall, "Slaves' Use of Their 'Free' Time"; Beckles, "Slaves and the Internal Market Economy of Barbados"; Morgan, "Work and Culture"; Morgan, "Black Life in Eighteenth-Century Charleston"; Morgan, "Black Society in the Lowcountry"; Morgan, "Task and Gang Systems: The Organization of Labor on New World Plantations," in Stephen Innes, ed., *Work and Labor in Early America* (Chapel Hill, 1988); Wood, *Black Majority*, 195–217.

2. The Anglican clergy who served in the plantation colonies between the late seventeenth and early eighteenth century were appalled by the irreligion of many of the colonists and their failure to proselytize their bondpeople. See, for example, Richard Ligon, *A True and Exact History of the Island of Barbados* (London, 1673); Morgan Godwin, *The Negro's and Indians Advocate, Suing for their Admission into the Church; or, A Persuasive to the Instructing and Baptizing of the Negro's and Indians in our Plantations* (London, 1680); Godwin, *A Supplement to the Negro's & Indians Advocate* (London, 1681); Griffith Hughes, *The Natural History of Barbados* (London, 1750); F. L. Klingberg, ed., *The Carolina Chronicle of Francis Le Jau, 1706–1717* (Berkeley, 1956). For the problems involved in supervising Sunday work of bondpeople in the British sugar islands see Richard S. Dunn, *Sugar and Slaves: The Rise of the Planter Class in the English West Indies, 1624–1713* (London, 1973), 240.

3. For the Barbados slave code of 1661 see Dunn, *Sugar and Slaves*, 239–41; for the South Carolina code of 1712 see A. Leon Higginbotham, Jr., *In the Matter of Color: Race and the American Legal Process: The Colonial Period* (New York, 1978), 167–90. For the part played by Barbadians in the founding and early history of South Carolina see Dunn, *Sugar and Slaves*, 111–16; Wood, *Black Majority*, 13–34.

4. *Col. Recs.* 18: 117. For the South Carolina slave code of 1740 see Cooper and McCord, eds., *Statutes at Large of South Carolina*, 7: 397–417. In 1768 the Georgians stated categorically that their code of 1755 "was framed on the plan of that of So. Carolina" ("Collections of the Georgia Historical Society and Other Documents: Letters to the Georgia Colonial Agent, July 1762 to January 1771," *GHQ* 36 [1952]: 274).

5. See chapters 3 and 6.

6. For an excellent discussion of the possible origins of the task system see Morgan, "Work and Culture," 565–69; Morgan, "Task and Gang Systems," 188–220.

7. Morgan, "Work and Culture," 565–66, 565 n. 7.

8. Wood, *Slavery in Colonial Georgia*, 114.

9. Edwin C. Holland, *A Refutation of the Calumnies Circulated against . . . Slavery* (Charleston, S.C., 1822; reprint, New York, 1969), 52, cited in Morgan, "Work and Culture," 578.

10. For examples of cash payments and holidays see James Habersham to Gov. James Wright, *Letters of the Honorable James Habersham, 1756–1775,* Georgia Historical Society Collections, (Savannah, 1840–19–), 6 (1904): 90–91; *Early Reminiscences of Camden County, Georgia: By an Old St. Mary's Boy in His 82nd Year, 1914–1915* (Southeast Georgians, Kingsland, Ga., n.d.), 8.

11. For the founding and early history of Ebenezer and the Salzburgers' views on chattel slavery, see Wood, *Slavery in Colonial Georgia,* 59–73. For the reports that Bolzius sent to his superiors in Europe see G. F. Jones, trans. and ed., *Detailed Reports of the Salzburger Emigrants Who Settled in America . . . Edited by Samuel Urlsperger,* 15 vols. (Athens, Ga., 1968–).

12. Klaus G. Loewald, Beverly Starika, and Paul S. Taylor, trans. and eds., "Johann Martin Bolzius Answers a Questionnaire on Carolina and Georgia," *WMQ* 3d ser., 14, no. 2 (1957): 259. Bolzius included in his report a lengthier account of the processes associated with rice cultivation. See also, Smith, *Slavery and Rice Culture,* 46–57.

13. Morgan, "Work and Culture," 575.

14. "Georgia: extract of a letter from a gentleman on a tour of business in the Southern Country, to the editors of the National Intelligencer," *Boston Recorder* (1817): 2, cited in William Hampton Adams, ed., *Historical Archaeology of Plantations at Kings Bay, Camden County, Georgia* (Department of Anthropology, University of Florida, Gainesville, 1987), 13.

15. Morgan, "Work and Culture," 576. For a recent analysis of the origins and initial development of cotton culture in Georgia see Chaplin, "Creating a Cotton South."

16. Morgan, "Work and Culture," 571.

17. Loewald, Starika, and Taylor, trans. and eds., "Johann Martin Bolzius Answers a Questionnaire," 257.

18. Everts, (Jeremiah), Diary, 1822, MSS, Georgia Historical Society, Savannah, collection 240, p. 20.

19. Frances Anne Kemble, *Journal of a Residence on a Georgia Plantation in 1838–1839* (London, 1863), 29–30.

20. Loewald, Starika, and Taylor, trans. and eds., "Johann Martin Bolzius Answers a Questionnaire," 257.

21. For Charleston see Michael P. Johnson, "Runaway Slaves and the Slave Communities in South Carolina, 1799 to 1830," *WMQ* 3d ser., 38 (1981): 424.

22. Colerain was purchased in 1817 by John Potter, who had emigrated from Ireland to Charleston in 1784, and was managed by his son James. The work schedule is to be found in James Potter Plantation Journal, Georgia Historical

Society, Savannah, MSS 630, Pinder–Pray Collection, Miscellaneous Papers (hereafter Potter Plantation Journal). The size and efficiency of the plantation are mentioned in the unattributed typescript introduction to the collection.

23. Potter Plantation Journal, 24–26 November 1828.

24. Potter Plantation Journal, 1–22 December 1828.

25. Johnson, "Runaway Slaves and the Slave Communities," 424, 430.

26. Basil Hall, *Travels in North America in the Years 1827 and 1828*, 3 vols. (Edinburgh, 1829), 3: 223.

27. Morgan, "Work and Culture," 578.

28. Charles Ball, *Fifty Years in Chains* (New York, 1837; reprint, New York, 1969), 151.

29. Richard K. Murdoch, ed., "Letters and Papers of Dr. Daniel Turner: A Rhode Islander in South Georgia," *GHQ* 54, no. 1 (1970): 102; Everts, (Jeremiah), Diary, 1822, p. 20; Hall, *Travels in North America*, 3: 223.

30. Kemble, *Journal of a Residence*, 61 (emphasis added). Kemble noted that sometimes the bondpeople who worked on neighboring plantations finished their tasks between 3:00 P.M. and 3:30 P.M. (298, 317, 326, 333, 350).

31. Hall, *Travels in North America*, 3: 223.

32. Murdoch, ed., "Letters and Papers of Dr. Daniel Turner," 102.

33. Frances Kemble remarked that some of her husband's bondpeople had to walk three miles to work (*Journal of a Residence*, 248).

34. Hall, *Travels in North America*, 3: 223.

35. According to Margaret Davis Cate, the length of the Christmas holiday varied from three days to two weeks. She also claimed that "on practically all" plantations in the lowcountry it was the "custom" for bondpeople to be given time off on Good Friday, Easter Monday, the day they finished planting the crop, the day the crop was laid up, and election days (Margaret Davis Cate Collection, Record Group 1, Research Files, Series 1. Subject file, folder 31: Christmas and Other Holidays [St.Simons] [Georgia Historical Society, Savannah, Microfilm Reel 991224], 1–2). On some plantations bondpeople were not required to work on the fourth of July (*Early Reminiscences of Camden County, Georgia*, 8).

36. Anthony Stokes, *A View of the Constitution of the British Colonies in North America and the West Indies: with a Supplementary Index* (London, 1783; reprint, London, 1968), 414–15.

37. Kemble, *Journal of a Residence*, 44.

38. Smith, *Slavery and Rice Culture*, 50.

39. For pertinent examples of this extensive literature see Victor H. Bassett, "Plantation Medicine," *Journal of the Medical Association of Georgia* 20 (1940): 112–22; Felice Swados, "Negro Health on the Ante Bellum Plantations," *Bulletin of the History of Medicine* 10 (1941): 460–72; Weymouth T. Jordan,

"Plantation Medicine in the Old South," *Alabama Review* 3 (1950): 83–107; William D. Postell, *The Health of Slaves on Southern Plantations* (Baton Rouge, 1951); Leslie Howard Owens, *This Species of Property*, 19–49; Peter H. Wood, "People's Medicine in the Early South," *Southern Exposure* (Summer 1978): 50–53; Todd L. Savitt, *Medicine and Slavery: The Diseases and Health Care of Blacks in Antebellum Virginia* (Urbana, Ill., 1978). For the British sugar islands see Kenneth F. Kiple, *The Caribbean Slave: A Biological History* (New York, 1984); Richard B. Sheridan, *Doctors and Slaves: A Medical and Demographic History of Slavery in the British West Indies, 1600–1834* (Cambridge, 1985); B. W. Higman, *Slave Populations of the British Caribbean, 1807–1834* (Baltimore, 1984). For a case study of one of Jamaica's premier sugar plantations see Betty Wood and Roy Clayton, "Slave Birth, Death, and Disease on Golden Grove Plantation, Jamaica, 1765–1810," *Slavery & Abolition* 6 (1985): 99–121. For a South Carolina case study, albeit one that falls outside the period under consideration here, see Ted A. Rathbun, "Health and Disease at a South Carolina Plantation: 1840–1870," *American Journal of Physical Anthropology* 74 (1987): 239–53. For Georgia see Joseph I. Waring, "Colonial Medicine in Georgia and South Carolina," *GHQ* (1975), 141–59; Joseph Krafka, "Notes on Medical Practice in Colonial Georgia," *GHQ* 22 (1939): 351–61; Wood, *Slavery in Colonial Georgia*, 147–54; Gerald L. Cates, "A Medical History of Georgia in the First Hundred Years, 1733–1833," (Ph.D. diss., University of Georgia, 1976).

40. Hall, *Travels in North America* 2: 214.

41. Potter Plantation Journal, 10 March–22 December 1828.

42. Kemble, *Journal of a Residence*, 71.

43. Ibid., 33.

44. In the absence of information from Potter or any other source there is no way to ascertain how many of the bondwomen on Colerain were reported "sick" because of complications that arose during pregnancies that did not run their full term. Frances Kemble made a fleeting reference to "the anguish and bitter disappointment of miscarriages" on the Butler estates and implied a high incidence of gynecological disorders. "A great number of the women," she wrote, "are victims to falling of the womb and weakness in the spine." These conditions, Kemble continued, "are the necessary results of their laborious existence, and do not belong either to climate or constitution" (*Journal of a Residence*, 44–45). The nature of the Colerain evidence also makes it impossible to assess the possible relationship on that estate between women's work, pregnancy, and rates of infant mortality. For a broader discussion of this theme see John Campbell, "Work, Pregnancy, and Infant Mortality among Southern Slaves," *Journal of Interdisciplinary History* 14 (1984): 793–812.

45. Frances Kemble reported that this was the practice on the Butler estates (*Journal of a Residence*, 33).

46. Krafka, "Notes on Medical Practice in Colonial Georgia"; Cates, "Medical History of Georgia"; Waring, "Colonial Medicine"; Wood, *Slavery in Colonial Georgia*, 152–53.

47. William Gibbons, Jr., Papers, 1769–71 file, William R. Perkins Library, Duke University.

48. Bell, *Major Butler's Legacy*, 156 (emphasis in original).

49. Kemble, *Journal of a Residence*, 35, 36.

50. Ibid., 39.

51. For a detailed discussion of the origins and subsequent implementation of what was a metropolitan-inspired attempt to proselytize bondpeople in the British plantation colonies, see the forthcoming study by Sylvia Frey and Betty Wood, provisionally titled *African-American Protestant Christianity in the Plantation South: The Foundation Years, 1700–1830.*

52. Owners were liable to a fine of ten pounds sterling if they failed to send their bondpeople "at some time on the Lords Day for Instruction in the Christian Religion" (*Col. Recs.*, 1: 59).

53. For Ottolenghe's appointment see John C. Van Horne, ed., *Religious Philanthropy and Colonial Slavery: The American Correspondence of the Associates of Dr. Bray, 1717–1777* (Urbana, Ill., 1985), 16–20.

54. Wood, *Slavery in Colonial Georgia*, 89.

55. Joseph Ottolenghe to the Rev. John Waring, Savannah, 19 November 1753, 18 November 1754 in Van Horne, ed., *Religious Philanthropy*, 112, 116.

56. The trustees' regulations were never formally approved by the English Privy Council (Higginbotham, *In the Matter of Color*, 251). For the influx of South Carolinians and their bondpeople into Georgia during the 1750s and 1760s see David R. Chesnutt, "South Carolinian Expansion into Colonial Georgia," (Ph.D. diss., University of Georgia, 1971).

57. *Col. Recs.*, 18: 117.

58. Joseph Ottolenghe to the Rev. John Waring, Savannah, 4 December 1751, 12 July 1758 in Van Horne, ed., *Religious Philanthropy*, 104, 128, 129.

59. For the provisions made by Habersham and Knox for the religious instruction of their bondpeople see *Letters of the Honorable James Habersham*, 190–99. See also, James B. Lawrence, "Religious Education of the Negro in the Colony of Georgia," *GHQ* 14 (1930): 43–57.

60. Records of the Midway Congregational Church, Typescript, Georgia Historical Society, Savannah; James Stacy, ed., *History of Midway Congregational Church: Liberty County, Georgia* (Newnan, Ga., 1903); A. G. Voigt, trans. and ed., *Ebenezer Record Book* (Savannah, 1929); Jones, trans. and ed., *Detailed Reports.*

61. Wood, *Slavery in Colonial Georgia*, 159–65.

62. Walter Rodney, "Upper Guinea and the Significance of the Origins of

Africans Enslaved in the New World," *Journal of Negro History* 54, no. 4 (1967): 327, cited in Bush, *Slave Women in Caribbean Society*, 7.

63. For the nighttime marriages and burials of bondmen and bondwomen see James Barclay, *The Voyages and Travels of James Barclay* (London, 1777), 22, 28; Caroline Gilman, *Recollections of a Southern Matron* (New York, 1839), 81–82; Kemble, *Journal of a Residence*, 139–43. Gilman stated categorically that "plantation slaves prefer to bury their dead at night or before sunrise," (*Recollections*, 81), and, as Lydia Parrish suggested, this was no doubt a carry-over from the practice in parts of West Africa. It was also a common practice in the British sugar islands (Lydia Parrish, *Slave Songs of the Georgia Sea Islands* [New York, 1942], 29).

64. For the origins and development of the informal slave economies of the South Carolina lowcountry through the middle years of the eighteenth century see Morgan, "Work and Culture"; Morgan, "Black Society in the Lowcountry"; Morgan, "Black Life in Eighteenth-Century Charleston"; Morgan, "Task and Gang Systems"; Wood, *Black Majority*, 195–217. For upcountry South Carolina see Campbell, "As 'A Kind of Freeman'?" in Berlin and Morgan, eds., *Slaves' Economy*, and for upcountry Georgia, see Joseph P. Reidy, "Obligation and Right: Patterns of Labor, Subsistence, and Exchange in the Cotton Belt of Georgia, 1790–1860," in Berlin and Morgan, eds., *Cultivation and Culture*.

65. Loewald, Starika, and Taylor, trans. and eds., "Johann Martin Bolzius Answers a Questionnaire," 256.

Chapter Two. Patterns of Production
and Income Generation in the Countryside

1. Gardens comprised varying, but usually relatively small, amounts of land contiguous to the bondpeople's cabins; provision grounds were often some miles from the quarters. Provision grounds were a common feature of the larger islands, notably Jamaica and Cuba, and the sugar-producing regions of the South American mainland, but were not usually to be found on the smaller islands, including Barbados, where land was at a premium. For examples of the extensive secondary literature on gardens and provision grounds in the shaping of the informal slave economies of the British Caribbean see Parry, "Plantation and Provision Ground"; Mintz and Hall, "Origins of the Jamaican Internal Marketing System"; Beckles, "Slaves and the Internal Market Economy of Barbados"; Neville Hall, "Slaves' Use of Their 'Free' Time"; Woodville Marshall, "Provision Ground and Plantation Labour: Competition for Resources," (paper presented at the twentieth annual Conference of Caribbean Historians, St. Thomas, Virgin Islands, 1988).

2. For details of this migration, which was principally from Barbados and to

a lesser extent from Jamaica, see Richard S. Dunn, "The English Sugar Islands and the Founding of South Carolina," in T. H. Breen, ed., *Shaping Southern Society: The Colonial Experience* (New York, 1976), 48–58; Dunn, *Sugar and Slaves*, 110–16.

3. Loewald, Starika, and Taylor, trans. and eds., "Johann Martin Bolzius Answers a Questionnaire," 258, 259.

4. See chapter 3.

5. Ball, *Fifty Years in Chains*, 166, 167; Kemble, *Journal of a Residence*, 249.

6. The formation and character of African and African-American families in the southern United States and Caribbean basin have attracted an enormous amount of scholarly attention and generated an equal amount of controversy. For recent studies that focus primarily on the antebellum South see Blassingame, *The Slave Community*, 77–103; Genovese, *Roll, Jordan, Roll*, 450–535; Herbert G. Gutman, *The Black Family in Slavery and Freedom, 1750–1925* (Oxford, 1976); Owens, *This Species of Property*, 182–213. For works that deal with the period before 1830 see Ira Berlin, "The Slave Trade and the Development of Afro-American Society in English Mainland North America, 1619–1775," *Southern Studies* 20 (1981): 122–36; Berlin, "Time, Space, and the Evolution of Afro-American Society in British Mainland North America," *American Historical Review* 85 (1980): 44–78; Wood, *Black Majority*, 139–41, 159–65, 248–51; Cheryll Ann Cody, "Naming, Kinship, and Estate Dispersal: Notes on Slave Family Life on a South Carolina Plantation, 1786 to 1833," *WMQ* 3d ser., 39 (1982): 192–211; Allan Kulikoff, "The Origins of Afro-American Society in Tidewater Virginia and Maryland, 1700–1790," *WMQ* 3d ser., 35 (1978): 226–59; Kulikoff, "A 'Prolifick' People: Black Population Growth in the Chesapeake Colonies, 1700–1790," *Southern Studies* 16 (1977): 391–444; Kulikoff, "The Beginnings of the Afro-American Family in Maryland," in Aubrey C. Land, Lois Green Carr, and Edward C. Papenfuse, eds., *Law, Society, and Politics in Early Maryland* (Baltimore, 1977); Russell R. Menard, "The Maryland Slave Population, 1658–1730: A Demographic Profile of Blacks in Four Counties," *WMQ* 3d ser., 32 (1975), 29–54. For studies that focus on the roles of women in the enslaved family see White, *Ar'n't I a Woman?*; Jones, "Status of Slave Women"; Jones, *Labor of Love, Labor of Sorrow*; Fox-Genovese, *Within the Plantation Household*. See also, Herbert J. Foster, "African Patterns in the Afro-American Family," *Journal of Black Studies* 24 (1983): 201–31.

7. Bush, *Slave Women in Caribbean Society*, 87, 91.

8. Jones, "Status of Slave Women," 297.

9. There is a voluminous secondary literature that explores this theme. For four highly influential studies see Gutman, *The Black Family*; Genovese, *Roll, Jordan, Roll*; Lawrence Levine, *Black Culture and Black Consciousness: Afro-*

American Folk Thought from Slavery to Freedom (New York, 1977); Charles Joyner, *Down by the Riverside: A South Carolina Slave Community* (Urbana, Ill., 1984).

10. Genovese, *Roll, Jordan, Roll*, 537–38.

11. W. W. Hazzard, "On the General Management of a Plantation," *Southern Agriculturalist and Register of Rural Affairs; Adapted to the Southern Section of the United States*, J. D. Legare, ed., (Charleston, 1828–), July 1831, 352–53.

12. Ball, *Fifty Years in Chains*, 166.

13. ["Scotus Americanus"] *Information Concerning the Province of North Carolina, Addressed to Emigrants from the Highlands and Western Isles of Scotland* (Glasgow, 1773) in William K. Boyd, "Some North Carolina Tracts of the Eighteenth Century," *North Carolina Historical Review* 3 (1926): 616.

14. Hazzard, "On the General Management of a Plantation," 352.

15. Ball, *Fifty Years in Chains*, 166.

16. Fogel and Engerman, who virtually ignored the quasi-independent economic activities of bondmen and bondwomen and the extent to which they contributed to their own standard of living, mistakenly suggest that "gardens" were rewards by owners to their bondpeople (Robert William Fogel and Stanley L. Engerman, *Time on the Cross: The Economics of American Negro Slavery* 2 vols. [Boston, 1974], 1: 148).

17. One owner who did try to determine what was cultivated by his bondpeople was Alexander Telfair. He instructed his overseer: "My Negroes are not allowed to plant cotton for themselves. Everything else they may plant" (Alexander Telfair, "Rules and directions for my Thorn Island Plantation by which my Overseer[s] are to govern themselves in the management of it," [1832], Telfair Family Papers, box 5, folder 51, item 208, Georgia Historical Society, Savannah, Collection 793 [hereafter Telfair Family Papers]). Telfair gave no reason for denying his bondpeople the right to grow cotton. Perhaps he believed they would be likely to supplement their income by augmenting their crop with cotton they appropriated from his fields.

18. Charles Lyell, *A Second Visit to the United States of North America* (New York, 1849), 268. Amelia M. Murray was another traveler who commented on Couper's experiment. See her *Letters from the United States, Cuba, and Canada* (New York, 1856), 22.

19. Kemble, *Journal of a Residence*, 32; Felicity Calhoun, ed., *Pleasure and Pain: Reminiscences of Georgia in the 1840s* (Savannah, 1978), 36–37 (first published as Emily Burke, *Reminiscences of Georgia* [Oberlin, 1850]); *Early Reminiscences of Camden County, Georgia*, 8.

20. Frederick Law Olmstead, *A Journey in the Seaboard Slave States* (New York, 1956), 422.

21. Hazzard, "On the General Management of a Plantation," 352; John Hammond Moore, ed., "Jared Sparks in Georgia–April 1826," *GHQ* 4 (1963): 427 (emphasis added).

22. Owens, *This Species of Property*, 50–69.

23. *Col. Recs.*, 18: 133–34.

24. Loewald, Starika, and Taylor, trans. and eds., "Johann Martin Bolzius Answers a Questionnaire," 235.

25. Ibid., 235–36, 256–57.

26. Stokes, *A View of the Constitution of the British Colonies*, 414.

27. "Georgia: extract of a letter," cited in Adams, ed., *Historical Archaeology*, 12.

28. Everts, (Jeremiah), Diary, 17.

29. Ball, *Fifty Years in Chains*, 188, 268. Basil Hall commented that the owner of one plantation he visited gave his bondpeople "plenty of beef . . . at Christmas" (*Travels in North America*, 3: 224). Jeremiah Everts also commented that "at Christmas . . . all are feasted . . . but generally the fare of the plantation slaves is coarse and scanty" (Everts, Diary, 17).

30. Telfair, "Rules and directions," Telfair Family Papers, box 5, folder 51, item 208.

31. Hall, *Travels in North America*, 3: 224.

32. R. Q. Mallard, *Plantation Life before Emancipation* (Richmond, 1892), 31–32.

33. Loewald, Starika, and Taylor, trans. and eds., "Johann Martin Bolzius Answers a Questionnaire," 259.

34. ["Scotus Americanus"] *Information Concerning the Province of North Carolina*, in Boyd, "Some North Carolina Tracts," 616.

35. Calhoun, ed., *Pleasure and Pain*, 36–37; Ball, *Fifty Years in Chains*, 166; *Early Reminiscences of Camden County, Georgia*, 8.

36. Charles Joyner, int., *Drums and Shadows: Survival Studies among the Georgia Coastal Negroes* (Athens, 1940; reprint, Athens, 1986), 70–71.

37. Ibid., 178.

38. See chapter 3.

39. William Grimes, *Life of William Grimes the Runaway Slave* (New Haven, 1855), 46.

40. Moore, ed., "Jared Sparks in Georgia," 427.

41. Thomas Astley, *A New General Collection of Voyages and Travels*, 4 vols. (London, 1745), 2: 265–66; Thomas Winterbottom, *An Account of the Native Africans in the Neighbourhood of Sierra Leone* (London, 1803; reprint, London, 1969), 75–76.

42. For the chewing of tobacco by bondpeople in the lowcountry see William

Maxwell, Jr.'s, notice in the *Columbia Museum and Savannah Advertiser,* 22 October 1801 (hereafter *CMSA*).

43. Ball, *Fifty Years in Chains,* 190. Ball's account is substantiated by recent archaeological findings. Excavations conducted at Kings Bay, Camden County, in the 1980s revealed long-stemmed white clay pipes "at every site" examined (Adams, ed., *Historical Archaeology,* 206). "Numerous clay pipe fragments" were also discovered in the quarters at Cannon's Point Plantation (John Solomon Otto, *Cannon's Point Plantation, 1794–1860: Living Conditions and Status Patterns in the Old South* [Orlando, 1984], 76).

44. On St. Simons, according to Margaret Davis Cate, owners' Christmas presents to their bondpeople might include "clothing, trinkets, beads, fruits, sweets, handkerchiefs, stockings and tobacco for both men and women . . . to the men alone went whiskey or wine." She also suggests that in return bondmen and bondwomen gave their owners gifts of "a jar of jelly, or preserve, a bottle of 'new' syrup, a chicken, [or] a new laid egg" (Margaret Davis Cate Collection, Georgia Historical Society, Savannah, Record Group 1, Research Files, Series 1, Subject file, folder 31: Christmas and Other Holidays [St. Simons], 3). Georgina Bryan Conrad commented that the bondpeople on her father's rice plantation in McIntosh County were given tobacco "at harvest-time and on holidays" (Conrad, "Reminiscences of a Southern Woman," *Southern Workman* 30, no. 3 (1901): 170). Both Conrad and Frances Kemble reported receiving presents of eggs and chickens from bondpeople (Conrad, "Reminiscences," 79–80; Kemble, *Journal of a Residence,* 64). Leslie Howard Owens has suggested that some planters might have favored tobacco chewing as a method of trying to deter their bondmen and bondwomen from dirt-eating (Owens, *This Species of Property,* 64–65).

45. Ball, *Fifty Years in Chains,* 190–91.

46. Ibid., 190.

47. Loewald, Starika, and Taylor, trans. and eds., "Johann Martin Bolzius Answers a Questionnaire," 259.

48. Mallard, *Plantation Life before Emancipation,* 30.

49. William Smith, *A New Voyage to Guinea* (London, 1744; reprint, London, 1969), 30.

50. For an excellent bibliography of the voluminous contemporary references to music and the manufacture of musical instruments in the slave quarters of the southern mainland and the Caribbean, together with a survey of scholarly works on these themes, see Dena J. Epstein, *Sinful Tunes and Spirituals: Black Folk Music to the Civil War* (Urbana, Ill., 1977).

51. Joyner, int., *Drums and Shadows,* 165, 176, 187, 214.

52. For an example of the type and number of implements that were issued

in the late 1820s to bondpeople on one large estate, Colerain Plantation, see Potter Plantation Journal. In 1828 the workforce, which in that year numbered seventy-six men and women, received thirty-one hoes, nine grubbing hoes, ten axes (issued to men), eight rice hooks, and thirty-seven baskets.

53. Joyner, int., *Drums and Shadows*, 167.

54. Charles Spalding Wylly, *The Seed That Was Grown in the Colony of Georgia* (New York, 1910), 20.

55. C. Oppong, ed., *Female and Male in West Africa* (London, 1983); L. Beneira, ed., *Women and Development: The Sexual Division of Labor in Rural Societies* (New York, 1982).

56. Otto, *Cannon's Point Plantation*, 44.

57. For recent discussions of bondwomen's work within the slave quarters of the American South see Jones, "Status of Slave Women"; Jones, *Labor of Love, Labor of Sorrow*, 29–43; White, *Ar'n't I a Woman?* 142–60; Fox-Genovese, *Within the Plantation Household*, 192–241. For comparisons with the sugar islands see Beckles, *Natural Rebels;* Bush, *Slave Women in Caribbean Society;* Morrissey, *Slave Women in the New World.*

58. Mary Turner, *Slaves and Missionaries: The Disintegration of Jamaican Slave Society, 1787–1834* (Urbana, Ill., 1982), 45.

59. Ball, *Fifty Years in Chains*, 157, 265.

60. Betty Wood, "Some Aspects of Female Resistance to Chattel Slavery in Lowcountry Georgia, 1763–1815," *Historical Journal* 30, no. 3 (1987): 609.

61. Ball, *Fifty Years in Chains*, 108; Mallard, *Plantation Life before Emancipation*, 51.

62. Hogs and poultry were being raised by bondpeople in South Carolina by the 1720s and 1730s, if not earlier (Morgan, "Work and Culture," 572–73; Wood, *Black Majority*, 212–13).

63. Otto, *Cannon's Point Plantation*, 58. The references to poultry and egg production by plantation bondpeople throughout this period are legion. See, for example, Hall, *Travels in North America*, 3: 224; R. King, Jr., "On the Management of the Butler Estate, and the Cultivation of Sugar Cane," in *Southern Agriculturalist and Register of Rural Affairs*, Legare, ed., 525; Conrad, "Reminiscences," 79; Hazzard, "On the General Management of a Plantation," 353. Poultry was included in virtually every state law and Savannah ordinance that itemized the commodities sold by bondpeople.

64. Hazzard, "On the General Management of a Plantation," 353; Kemble, *Journal of a Residence*, 54.

65. Kemble, *Journal of a Residence*, 54.

66. Adams, ed., *Historical Archaeology*, 232.

67. See, for example, Mallard, *Plantation Life before Emancipation*, 18; Olmstead, *A Journey in the Seaboard Slave States*, 422.

68. By the early nineteenth century Chatham County's grand jurors were complaining that bondpeople virtually monopolized the supply of poultry and eggs to Savannah. See, for example, Chatham County, Grand Jury Presentments, 7 January 1811, Chatham County, Superior Court, Civil Minutes, book 9 (1812–18), 161; Presentments of the Chatham County Grand Jury, January Term, 1814, *CMSA* 13 January 1814.

69. Kemble, *Journal of a Residence*, 64.

70. Otto, *Cannon's Point Plantation*, 58–59.

71. R. Q. Mallard suggested that homemade pens were the common practice on plantations in Liberty County (*Plantation Life before Emancipation*, 18).

72. Adams, ed., *Historical Archaeology*, 232; Otto, *Cannon's Point Plantation*, 58.

73. Kemble, *Journal of a Residence*, 56–57.

74. Loewald, Starika, and Taylor, trans. and eds., "Johann Martin Bolzius Answers a Questionnaire," 241; Adams, ed., *Historical Archaeology*, 232.

75. W. W. Hazzard recorded that he gave "to [enslaved] families having six children living, one cow, with the male issue; reserving the heifer calves" ("On the General Management of a Plantation," 353).

76. This list was compiled from items mentioned in Adams, ed., *Historical Archaeology*, 229.

77. *Ga. Gaz.*, 29 August 1765.

78. This right was first established in the slave code of 1755 and reaffirmed in subsequent codes. For the original clause see *Col. Recs.*, 18: 117–19. This right was denied to free African-Americans in 1833 ("An Act concerning free persons of color, their guardians, and colored preachers" [December 1833], in Oliver H. Prince, comp. and ed., *Digest of the Laws of the State of Georgia* [2d ed., Athens, 1837], 808).

79. Ball, *Fifty Years in Chains*, 352. According to William Hampton Adams, "gunflints or lead shot" were discovered at "almost every slave site" excavated in and around Kings Bay (Adams, ed., *Historical Archaeology*, 228).

80. For the range and uses of these trapping devices see Adams, ed., *Historical Archaeology*, 229–30. For an example of the exploitation of these skills by owners see Ball, *Fifty Years in Chains*, 293–98.

81. Adams, ed., *Historical Archaeology*, 229.

82. Ball, *Fifty Years in Chains*, 263.

83. Adams, ed., *Historical Archaeology*, 229.

84. For a detailed discussion of the foodways at Kings Bay, which includes an analysis of the varieties and amounts of wild species in bondpeople's diets, see Adams, ed., *Historical Archaeology*, 225–75.

85. Charles Ball, for instance, remarked that "rackoons [sic], opossums, and rabbits . . . were worth something for their furs." He also recollected that on one

plantation the owner in question did not issue shoes to the bondpeople when they expected them and that the only way he could protect his feet from the frost was by "making mockasins [*sic*] for myself, of the skins of squirrels, that I had caught in my trap" (Ball, *Fifty Years in Chains*, 262, 270). A bondman named Charles, who ran away from David Murray in 1767, was said by his owner to be wearing "an old beaver hat," presumably of home manufacture (*Ga. Gaz.*, 16 September 1767). Will, who absconded in 1818, "had on a round coat and pantaloons, of brown deerskin coating" (*Daily Savannah Republican*, 23 March 1818 [hereafter *DSR*]).

86. Joyner, int., *Drums and Shadows*, 107, 155.

87. Ibid., 148, 187.

88. In the mid-1730s William Glen, a hatter, offered "any person White Man or Negroe that will bring any Fox or Raccoon Skins [to my shop] in Broad-Street . . . 2s 6d for every skin" (*South Carolina Gazette*, 12 October to 19 October 1734 [hereafter *SCG*]). On 25 January 1765 an unnamed trader from New England advertised in the *Ga. Gaz.* offering "cash for deer, otter and raccoon skins." There is no record of how many he bought or who supplied them.

89. Frances Kemble related how two of her husband's enslaved carpenters "had in their leisure time made a boat, which they had disposed of to some neighbouring planter for sixty dollars" (*Journal of a Residence*, 25).

90. Mallard, *Plantation Life before Emancipation*, 30.

91. Kemble, *Journal of a Residence*, 78.

92. Mallard, *Plantation Life before Emancipation*, 30.

93. Blassingame, *The Slave Community*, 92.

94. Mallard, *Plantation Life before Emancipation*, 16, 26.

95. Grimes, *Life of William Grimes*, 46.

96. Kemble, *Journal of a Residence*, 33, 40.

97. Conrad, "Reminiscences," 79.

98. Ibid., 80; Ball, *Fifty Years in Chains*, 191.

99. Joyner, int., *Drums and Shadows*, 101.

100. Adams, ed., *Historical Archaeology*, 14.

101. See, for example, Thomas Winterbottom's description of pottery in Sierra Leone (Winterbottom, *An Account of the Native Africans*, 94). It is by no means clear whether Colonoware was produced by bondmen, bondwomen, or both. However, it is perhaps worth noting that in parts of present-day Sierra Leone and Nigeria pottery is frequently a woman's work. See in Daryll Forde, ed., *Ethnographic Survey of Africa: Western Africa:* part 2, *Peoples of Sierra Leone,* by R. McCulloch (London, 1950), 12–13, part 3, *The Ibo and Ibibo-Speaking Peoples of South-Eastern Nigeria,* by Daryll Forde and G. I. Jones (London, 1967), 14, part 13, *The Benin Kingdom and the Edo-Speaking Peoples of South-Western Nigeria,* by R. E. Bradbury, and *The Itsekiri* by P. C. Lloyd (London, 1964), 176.

102. The Kings Bay excavations revealed only "one Colonoware vessel . . . in the earliest context" (Adams, ed., *Historical Archaeology,* 14). For a recent discussion of the form and function of Colonoware see Leland Ferguson, *Uncommon Ground: Archaeology and Early African America, 1650–1800* (Washington, D.C., 1992). See also William H. Adams and Sarah Boling, "Status and Ceramics for Planters and Slaves on Three Georgia Coast Plantations," *Historical Archaeology* 23, no. 1 (1989): 69–96; Leland G. Ferguson, "Looking for the 'Afro' in Colono-Indian Pottery," *Conference on Historic Site Archaeology Papers,* 12 (1978): 68–86; Ferguson, "Struggling with Pots in Colonial South Carolina," in Randall H. McGuire and Robert Paynter, eds., *The Archaeology of Inequality* (Oxford, 1991), 28–39; Patrick W. Garrow and Thomas R. Wheaton, "Colonoware Ceramics: The Evidence from Yaughan and Curnboo Plantations," in Albert C. Goodyear and Glen T. Hanson, eds., *Studies in South Carolina Archaeology: Essays in Honor of Robert L. Stephenson* (Columbia, S.C., 1989), 175–84; Otto, *Cannon's Point Plantation,* 1984).

103. James Habersham to Gov. James Wright, 16 July 1773, in *Letters of the Honorable James Habersham,* 190–91.

104. Ball, *Fifty Years in Chains,* 187.

105. Henry Laurens to James Theodore Rossel, Charles Town, 8 April 1766 in Philip Hamer, George C. Rogers, and David R. Chesnutt, eds., *The Papers of Henry Laurens,* 9 vols. (Columbia, S.C., 1968–), 5: 99–100. Rossel was the manager of Laurens's Broughton Island plantation.

Chapter Three. Economic Transactions in the Countryside

1. For an extended discussion of this point see chapter 7.

2. AN ACT for establishing a Watch in the Town of Savannah, July 1757; AN ACT for regulating the Watch in the town of Savannah [1759], *Col. Recs.,* 18: 212–17, 290–95.

3. See, for example, G. F. Jones, ed., *Detailed Reports,* 1: 56–106 and the notices placed in the *Ga. Gaz.* by Patrick Mackay on 16 October 1763 and by John Stevens on 27 June 1765.

4. See chapter 7.

5. James Houstoun's notice appeared in the *Ga. Gaz.* on 22 October 1766.

6. Loewald, Starika, and Taylor, trans. and eds., "Johann Martin Bolzius Answers a Questionnaire," 259.

7. AN OVERSEER, "On the Conduct and Management of Overseers, Driver, and Slave," *Southern Agriculturalist and Register of Rural Affairs,* J. D. Legare, ed., 230.

8. Calhoun, ed., *Pleasure and Pain,* 36–37, 89.

9. Everts, (Jeremiah), Diary, 20.

10. *Ga. Gaz.,* 6 October 1763, 27 June 1765.

11. Pastor Bolzius reported that the bondpeople sent from South Carolina in 1734 to help with the construction of Ebenezer collected honey (Jones, ed., *Detailed Reports*, 1: 56–106); passim. Honey also appeared on the list of commodities sold to Henry Ravenel by his bondpeople in the mid-1760s (Thomas R. Wheaton, Amy Friedlander, and Patrick H. Garrow, *Yaughan and Curnboo Plantations: Studies in Afro-American Archaeology* [Marietta, Ga., 1983], 308). Wild fruits were referred to less frequently as an item sold to owners, but James Gunnell reported to his employers that a bondwoman named Phillis was sending them, presumably for sale rather than as a gift, "a gord [*sic*] with some huckel burys [*sic*] in it" (James Gunnell to the misses Telfair, Mills Plantation, Burke County, 21 June 1833, Telfair Family Papers, box 5, folder 45, item 158).

12. Calhoun, ed., *Pleasure and Pain*, 36–37.

13. See, for example, Mallard, *Plantation Life before Emancipation*, 30. For recent archaeological discoveries of skillets and cooking pots of one kind or another in the quarters of lowcountry plantations see Adams, ed., *Historical Archaeology*, 118, 197–98. See also, John Solomon Otto, *Cannon's Point Plantation*.

14. Loewald, Starika, and Taylor, trans. and eds., "Johann Martin Bolzius Answers a Questionnaire," 236.

15. Ibid., 235–36.

16. Ibid., 256.

17. Ibid., 235, 236.

18. *Ga. Gaz.*, 16 September 1767, 25 September 1783; *CMSA* 25 February 1805.

19. *Ga. Gaz.*, 21 February 1793; *Republican and Savannah Evening Ledger*, 21 March 1809 (hereafter *RSEL*); *Savannah Republican*, 3 September 1816, 26 June 1817 (hereafter *Sav. Rep.*).

20. *Ga. Gaz.*, 16 April 1789; *RSEL*, 19 June 1810; *Darien Gazette*, 23 November 1818.

21. Notice placed in the *Ga. Gaz.*, 20 March 1800 by W. Stephens advertising for the return of his bondman Smart. Stephens noted that Smart had "carried off, with other clothes, a brown jacket with a yellow collar, and mixed colored Negro cloth under waistcoat, and overalls with his dress clothes, consisting of a green linen suit, with yellow cuffs and collars."

22. *Ga. Gaz.*, 11 June 1793; *Sav. Rep.*, 4 October 1817; *CMSA*, 12 July 1799.

23. For examples of earrings see *CMSA*, 12 July 1799, 18 July 1800, 22 June 1803; *Ga. Gaz.*, 20 March 1800. For examples of distinctive hairstyles, which usually involved plaiting or braiding the hair, see *CMSA*, 25 October 1796, 24 December 1802; *Ga. Gaz.*, 20 March 1800. As in "virtually every slave cabin excavated in the South," faceted beads were discovered in the quarters at Cannon's Point Plantation (Otto, *Cannon's Point Plantation*, 73).

24. Genovese, *Roll, Jordan, Roll*, 557–58.

25. Hall, *Travels in North America*, 3: 254–55.

26. Henry Laurens to Frederick Wiggin, Charles Town, 30 November 1765, in Hamer, Rogers, and Chesnutt, eds., *Papers of Henry Laurens*, 4: 41.

27. Calhoun, ed., *Pleasure and Pain*, 89.

28. For the accounts kept by the Ravenels see Henry Ravenel's Daybook, 1756–74, "Money due to me from the Negroes for articles [furnished]," "Memorandum" notebook, Thomas P. Ravenel Collection, South Carolina Historical Society, Ref. 12/313/9.

29. Henry Laurens to Abraham Schad, Charles Town, 30 April 1765 in Hamer, Rogers, and Chesnutt, eds., *Papers of Henry Laurens*, 4: 616.

30. Calhoun, ed., *Pleasure and Pain*, 89.

31. James Gunnell to the misses Telfair, Mills Plantation, Burke County, 27 June 1833 in Telfair Family Papers, box 5, folder 45, item 158.

32. Ravenel, "Money due to me," "Memorandum" notebook, Thomas Ravenel Collection.

33. Wheaton, Friedlander, and Garrow, eds., *Yaughan and Curnboo Plantations*, 306, 308.

34. Henry Laurens to Abraham Schad, Charles Town, 7 October 1765, 31 March 1766, and Laurens to John Smith, Charles Town, 29 January 1766 in Hamer, Rogers, and Chesnutt, eds., *Papers of Henry Laurens*, 5: 19–20, 41, 57.

35. Laurens to Schad, 19–20.

36. Ibid., 93.

37. The mean value of the transactions conducted on the plantation during the mid-1760s was £1.6.0 (Wheaton, Friedlander, and Garrow, eds., *Yaughan and Curnboo Plantations*, 386).

38. Ravenel, "Money due to me," Thomas Ravenel Collection.

39. Calhoun, ed., *Pleasure and Pain*, 89.

40. Henry Laurens to Abraham Schad, Charles Town, 30 April 1765 in Hamer, Rogers, and Chesnutt, eds., *Papers of Henry Laurens*, 4: 616.

41. Loewald, Starika, and Taylor, trans. and eds., "Johann Martin Bolzius Answers a Questionnaire," 257.

42. Boats carrying ten tons of cargo could travel the 250 miles or so downstream from Augusta to Savannah in four or five days. The journey upstream took roughly three times as long. This was still much quicker, and for bulky goods a cheaper proposition, than the overland route of some 130 miles between the two towns (Davis, *Fledgling Province*, 45).

43. Ibid., 118.

44. Luke Dean, of Briar Creek, was cited by the grand jury in 1767 "for keeping a disorderly house . . . and harbouring and entertaining slaves." Peter Johnson was presented eight years later for "keeping a most disorderly and

riotous house, [and] for dealing with Negroes and loose people at all hours of the day and night." The grand jury recommended that his liquor license "be revoked, and no license be granted to him in the future" (Presentments of the Georgia Grand Jury, 9 June 1767, 14 June 1774 in *Ga. Gaz.*, 22 July 1767, 22 June 1774).

45. Ball, *Fifty Years in Chains*, 191.

46. Ibid.

47. Ibid.

48. Kemble, *Journal of a Residence*, 299.

49. Virginia Steele Wood and Ralph Van Wood, eds., "The Reuben King Journal, 1800–1806," *GHQ* 50, no. 2 (1966): 202. King (1779–1867) was a tanner by trade who moved from Connecticut to Georgia after the Revolutionary War. His elder brother, Roswell (1765–1844), was employed as an overseer by Pierce Butler. For a discussion of the latter's work in that capacity see Bell, *Major Butler's Legacy*, 137–53, 159–69, 173–88, 212–28, 234–68.

50. Wood and Wood, eds., "Reuben King Journal," *GHQ* 50, no. 4 (1966): 424.

51. John Newton Diary, 1781–1790, Hargrett Rare Book and Manuscript Library, University of Georgia. MSS 2022, 5 October 1782, 8 November 1782.

52. *Gazette of the State of Georgia*, 9 October 1788; *Ga. Gaz.*, 30 December 1790.

53. Piraguas were flat-bottomed boats that could carry "from twenty to thirty-five tonnes" of freight and "operate in coastal waters as well as on rivers and creeks." They usually had sails and "all were equipped with oars." Droghers, or droggers, were "slow and clumsy coastal vessels" (Davis, *Fledgling Province*, 44).

54. Henry Laurens to Timothy Creamer, Charles Town, 26 June 1764, and to John Smith, Charles Town, 4 June 1765 in Hamer, Rogers, and Chesnutt, eds., *Papers of Henry Laurens*, 5: 319, 633.

55. Henry Laurens to John Smith, Charles Town, 4 June 1765, 1 October 1765, and to Abraham Schad, Charles Town, 30 April 1765, in Hamer, Rogers, and Chesnutt, eds., *Papers of Henry Laurens*, 5: 11, 4: 319, 633.

56. According to Charles Ball, river boats "never moved at night" (Ball, *Fifty Years in Chains*, 300).

57. Ibid., 301–2.

58. Ibid., 302, 305.

59. An Act To regulate the navigation of the Savannah river, between the cities of Savannah and Augusta, so far as it respects the patroons of boats [1806], *Acts of the General Assembly of the State of Georgia* (Louisville, 1806), 49–50. Free African-Americans caught captaining river boats were liable to the same fine.

60. AN ACT For the better regulation of Boats and Boats' Crews navigating the Savannah River, from the city of Augusta to the head waters of said river [1815], Lucius Q. C. Lamar, ed., *A Compilation of the Laws of the State of Georgia: Passed by the Legislature Since the Year 1810 to the Present Year 1819, inclusive* (Augusta, 1821), 112–13.

61. AN ACT TO alter and extend an act, entitled AN ACT TO prevent Boat owners or Patroons from permitting Boathands, or other negroes, from trafficking in corn or other produce, or from carrying the same to market on board of the boats accustomed to navigate the river Savannah, between Augusta and Savannah [1817], Lamar, ed., *Compilation of Laws*, 114–15.

62. AN Act to amend, explain, and cause to be enforced, the several acts of the general Assembly of the State of Georgia, assented to the 4th of December, 1815, and that of the 13th of December 1816, and an Act amendatory of the last specified Act, assented to the 10th day of December, 1817 [1836], Thomas R. R. Cobb, *A Digest of the Statute Laws of the State of Georgia, IN Force Prior TO The Session Of The General Assembly of 1851* (Athens, 1851), 16.

Chapter Four. Marketing in Savannah

1. To the Right Honourable the Lords Commissioners for Trade and Plantations, the Memorial of the Trustees for Establishing the Colony of Georgia in America, 19 June 1752, [signed] Benjamin Martyn, *Col. Recs.* (unpublished), 33: 565–66.

2. In 1756 Gov. John Reynolds informed the Board of Trade that "the best account [he could] get" suggested that there were 4,500 Europeans and 1,855 "Negroes" in Georgia (Governor Reynolds to the Board of Trade, *Col. Recs.* (unpublished), 27: 239.

3. AN ACT FOR Establishing a Market in the Town of Savannah and to prevent Forestalling Ingrossing and unjust Exactions in the said Town and Market [March 1755], *Col. Recs.*, 18: 80.

4. Ibid., 80–82. The first five commissioners were William Rusell, James Campbell, Robert Bolton, Isaac Yonge, and Thomas Rasberry.

5. For Charleston see Morgan, "Black Life in Eighteenth-Century Charleston"; for Britain's sugar islands see Mintz and Hall, "Origins of the Jamaican Internal Marketing System"; H. McD. Beckles and Karl Watson, "Social Protest and Labour Bargaining: The Changing Nature of Slaves' Responses to Plantation Life in Eighteenth-Century Barbados," *Slavery & Abolition* 8 (1987); Beckles, *Natural Rebels*.

6. This census was taken by an anonymous correspondent to the *Ga. Gaz.* and published on 6 February 1800. In 1821, when the decision was made to build a public market in Ellis Square, it was estimated that for eight months

of the year (autumn, winter, and spring) Savannah's white population totaled 6,000, but that during the four summer months it dropped to half that number as those who could afford to left the city in search of healthier climes. The African-American population was said to remain constant throughout the year at "probably 3,500" (Letter to the Editor of the *Georgian*, [signed] "AN INHABITANT OF ANSON WARD," 26 February 1821).

7. B. W. Hodder and U. I. Ukwu, *Markets in West Africa: Studies of Markets and Trade among the Yoruba and Ibo* (Ibadan, Nigeria, 1969); Leonard Barrett, "African Religion in the Americas: The 'Islands in Between,'" in Newell S. Booth, Jr., ed., *African Religions* (New York, 1977), 210.

8. Paul Bohannon and George Dalton, eds., *Markets in Africa* (Evanston, Ill., 1962), 15–18.

9. AN ACT For the better Ordering and Governing Negroes and other Slaves in this Province [1755], *Col. Recs.*, 18: 102–44. In 1768 the Georgians stated categorically that they had framed their code "on the plan of that of So. Carolina" ("Collections of the Georgia Historical Society and Other Documents: Letters to the Georgia Colonial Agent, July 1762 to January 1771," *GHQ* 36 [1952]: 274). For the South Carolina slave code of 1740 see Cooper and McCord, eds., *The Statutes at Large of South Carolina*, 7: 397–417.

10. Presentments of the [Georgia] Grand Jurors, 21 June 1764, 10 December 1766 in *Ga. Gaz.*, 28 June 1764, 24 December 1766.

11. For the Georgia slave codes of 1765 and 1770 see AN ACT For the better Ordering and Governing Negroes and other Slaves in this Province and to prevent the inveighling or carrying away Slaves from their Masters or Employers [1765], *Col. Recs.*, 18: 649–88; An Act for ordering and governing slaves within this province, and for establishing a jurisdiction for the trial of offences committed by slaves, and other persons therein mentioned, and to prevent the inveighling, and carrying away slaves from their masters, owners, or employers [1770], *Col. Recs.*, 19, pt. 1, 209–49).

12. An Act To Empower certain Commissioners herein appointed to regulate the hire of Porters and Labour of Slaves in the Town of Savannah [12 March 1774], *Col. Recs.*, pt. 2, 27. Owners who failed to secure the requisite badge for their bondpeople were liable to a fine of "ten shillings for every day such slave shall be so let out on hire" (*Ga. Gaz.*, 15 June 1774). For the legislation in force in colonial South Carolina see Wood, *Black Majority*, 210–11.

13. The act of 1774 was reconfirmed by the state government in 1783 under the title of AN ACT, To empower certain Commissioners herein Appointed to regulate the hire of Porters, and labour of Slaves in the Town of Savannah, and for other purposes therein mentioned [31 July 1783] (*Col. Recs.*, 19, pt. 2, 256–62). In 1790 and 1792 the Savannah City Council enacted ordinances providing for annually renewable badges that had to be "suspended and exposed to

publick view on [the bondperson's] breast." The cost of badges for those who worked as hawkers, peddlers, and vendors of small wares was set at ten shillings in 1790. Two years later the cost for those "who shall be employed as a hawker or pedlar, for selling any goods, wares or merchandise" was increased to sixty shillings. That for vendors of small wares remained at ten shillings. A decade later the fee was fixed at $7.50 (An Ordinance, Regulating the Hire of Drays, Carts, and Waggons; as also the Hire of Negro and other Slaves; and for the better Ordering Free Negroes, Mulattoes, or Mestizoes, within the City of Savannah [28 September 1790], *Ga. Gaz.*, 7 October 1790; An Ordinance, For Regulating the Hire of Drays, Carts and Waggons, as also the Hire of Negroes and other Slaves; and for the better ordering Free Negroes, Mulattoes, or Mestizoes, within the City of Savannah [15 October 1792], *Ga. Gaz.*, 8 November 1792; *Georgia Republican and State Intelligencer*, 3 January 1803 [hereafter *GRSI*]).

14. See below, pp. 182–88.

15. The exact site of Savannah's first public market is unknown, but in 1763 it was in Ellis Square. That market was destroyed by the fire of 1820 and, as a temporary measure, operations were moved to a site "at the intersection of South Broad and Barnard Street." The market returned to Ellis Square in 1821 (An Act to empower the Commissioners appointed in and by an act of the general assembly of this province, entitled "an act for repairing of Christ Church in Savannah," to lay out a spot of ground for erecting a parish church thereon, and to remove the present market, and lay out a spot of ground for erecting the same [April 1763], in Robert Watkins and George Watkins, comps., *A Digest of the Laws of the State of Georgia* [Savannah, 1800], 87–88); An Ordinance to authorize the erection of a Public Market in South-Broad Street [1820], *Daily Georgian*, 26 January 1820 [hereafter *DG*]; Martha Gallaudet Waring, ed., "Charles Seton Henry Hardee's Recollections of Old Savannah," pt. 1, *GHQ* 12, no. 4 [1928]: 357).

16. For recent discussions of the organization, regulation, and operation of provincial urban markets in early modern England see Alan Everitt, "The Marketing of Agricultural Produce," in Joan Thirsk, ed., *The Agrarian History of England and Wales, 1540–1640* (Cambridge, 1967), 4: 581–86; John Chartres, "The Marketing of Agricultural Produce," in Thirsk, ed., *Agrarian History*, vol. 5, chap. 17 (Cambridge, 1985); John Chartres, "Markets and Marketing in Metropolitan Western England in the Late Seventeenth and Eighteenth Centuries," in Michael Havinden, ed., *Husbandry and Marketing in the South-West* (Exeter, 1973), 63–74; Peter Bosay, *The English Urban Renaissance: Culture and Society in the Provincial Town, 1660–1770* (Oxford, 1989), 107–8. I am grateful to Dr. Steve Hindle for drawing my attention to this literature.

17. Rosemary Arnold, "Separation of Trade and Market: Great Market of

Wydah," in Eugene Genovese, ed., *The Slave Economies*, vol. 1, *Historical and Theoretical Perspectives* (New York, 1973), 123.

18. For the rental of market stalls by the corporations of provincial towns in early modern England see Alice Clark, *Working Life of Women in the Seventeenth Century* (London, 1919; reprint, London, 1968), 202.

19. Arnold, "Separation of Trade and Market," 128; Astley, *A New General Collection of Voyages and Travels*, 3: 11.

20. Waring, ed., "Charles Seton Henry Hardee's Recollections," 358.

21. Astley, ed., *A New General Collection of Voyages and Travels*, 3: 11; 2: 651.

22. Clark, *Working Life of Women*, 51.

23. Morgan, "Black Life in Eighteenth-Century Charleston." For a detailed description of the Charleston market in the 1820s, and one that mentions the preponderance of female vendors, see Warren S. Tryon, comp. and ed., *A Mirror for Americans: Life and Manners in the United States 1790–1870 as Recorded by American Travellers*, 3 vols. (Chicago, 1952), 2: 285–87. This account was penned by a Mrs. Royall who visited the southern states between 1818 and 1822.

24. Bush, *Slave Women in Caribbean Society*, 49.

25. For more recent discussions of the marketing activities of West African women see Bohannon and Dalton, eds., *Markets in Africa*; E. Boserup, *Women's Role in Economic Development* (London, 1970); Claude Meillassoux, ed., *The Development of Indigenous Trade and Markets in West Africa* (Oxford, 1971); Meillassoux, *Maidens, Meal, and Money: Capitalism and the Domestic Economy* (Cambridge, 1981); and Hodder and Ukwu, *Markets in West Africa*.

26. Astley, ed., *A New General Collection of Voyages and Travels*, 2: 597; 3: 11; R. Lander and J. Lander, *Journal of an Expedition to Explore the Course and Termination of the Niger*, 3 vols. (London, 1832), 1: 108, cited in Hodder and Ukwu, *Markets in West Africa*, 24.

27. Astley, ed., *A New General Collection of Voyages and Travels*, 3: 11.

28. Cited in Arnold, "Separation of Trade and Market," 123.

29. Astley, ed., *A New General Collection of Voyages and Travels*, 3: 11.

30. Hodder and Ukwu, *Markets in West Africa*, 24.

31. Sir Anthony Herbert, *Book of Husbandry* (1555) cited in Clark, *Working Life of Women*, 49.

32. Clark, *Working Life of Women*, 210.

33. Astley, *A New General Collection of Voyages and Travels*, 3: 15; 2: 267, 639–40, 643. In view of these European references to beer and bread, it is perhaps worth noting Alice Clark's comment that a "large proportion of the bread and beer consumed [in seventeenth-century England] was produced by women in domestic industry" (*Working Life of Women*, 210).

34. K. Y. Daaku, "Trade and Trading Patterns of the Akan in the Seventeenth

and Eighteenth Centuries," in Meillassoux, ed., *Development of Indigenous Trade and Markets*, 177.

35. *Sav. Rep.*, 16 August 1817. "Cake Wenches" was the label used by an author who styled himself "ANTI-MULATTO." Georgina Bryan Conrad recalled that "the very best cake maker and baker [in Savannah] was [a] Negro woman, whose fruit cakes had such a reputation that they were sent for from many places, England included" ("Reminiscences," 255).

36. For examples see Savannah City Council Minutes, 2 April 1793, 3 March 1825, 9 June 1825.

37. *Sav. Rep.*, 25 May 1822; City Council Minutes, 1822–24, 41. See also the letter signed "JUSTICE" in *Sav. Rep.*, 13 June 1818.

38. For examples of butchers who were fined by the Savannah City Council for this offense see Savannah City Council Minutes, 17 February 1825.

39. In 1817 six free African-American women, but no men, who lived in Savannah reported their occupation as being a "vendor of small wares." Their number increased to eleven in 1823 and to sixteen in 1824 and 1825. It is possible that the four women in 1823, and the two in 1824 and 1825, who described themselves as "shopkeepers" secured the capital necessary to begin their businesses by vending in the public market (Savannah, Clerk of Council, Register of Free Persons of Color, 1817–29, Georgia Historical Society, Savannah, Ref. 32-G-2A).

40. *Ga. Gaz.*, 16 August 1787, 13 September 1787; Savannah City Council Minutes, 10 August 1790, 8 January 1793; *GRSI*, 27 June 1802; *RSEL*, 31 August 1813. The accounts of the city treasury were published periodically in Savannah's newspapers and the examples cited here regarding the manufacture and sale of badges are typical of those for the years around the turn of the eighteenth century.

41. A distinction drawn in Bohannon and Dalton, eds., *Markets in Africa*, xi.

42. See chapter 3.

43. King, "On the Management of the Butler Estate," 524.

44. See, for example, the notice to this effect published in *Sav. Rep.* on 26 December 1818.

45. *Early Reminiscences of Camden County, Georgia*, 8.

46. Murdoch, coll. and ed., "Letters and Papers of Dr. Daniel Turner," 477. The prices cited are those being asked in 1805.

47. Mallard, *Plantation Life before Emancipation*, 51.

48. Waring, ed., "Charles Seton Henry Hardee's Recollections," 358.

49. Mrs. Royall commented that "market is held on Sunday morning in Savannah, all the Negroes (who reap the benefit) for many miles round come in, and the market is numerously attended" (Tryon, comp. and ed., *A Mirror for*

Americans 2: 292). Twenty years later Emily Burke claimed that "people travel a great distance for the purpose of buying and selling in the market" and that she had "known women to come one hundred miles to sell the products of their own industry" (Calhoun, ed., *Pleasure and Pain*, 10).

50. Astley, ed., *A New General Collection of Voyages and Travels*, 2: 651–52.

51. Woodville K. Marshall, ed., *The Colthurst Journal* (New York, 1977), 53.

52. Conrad, "Reminiscences," 80; Kemble, *Journal of a Residence*, 48, 60, 272.

53. See especially, Morgan, "Black Life in Eighteenth-Century Charleston." For recent discussions of vending by enslaved women in the public markets of the British sugar islands see Beckles, *Natural Rebels*, 72–89; Bush, *Slave Women in Caribbean Society*, 48–50. For the dominant role of bondwomen and free Creole women in the markets of the French Caribbean islands see Arlette Gautier, "Les Esclaves femmes aux Antilles francaises, 1635–1848," *Reflexions Historiques* 10, no. 3 (1983): 409–35.

54. F. G. Bailey, "Gifts and Poison," in Bailey, ed., *Gifts and Poison: The Politics of Reputation* (Oxford, 1971), 2.

55. There is an extensive anthropological literature on the functions of gossip. See, for example, Bailey, "Gifts and Poisons"; Max Gluckman, "Gossip and Scandal," *Current Anthropology* 4 (1963): 307–16; Don Handelman, "Gossip in Encounters: The Transmission of Information in a Bonded Social Setting," *Man* n.s., 8 (1973): 210–27.

56. The "STRANGER," *SCG*, 24 September 1772 cited in Morgan, "Black Life in Charleston," 203.

57. For white allegations of overcharging by market traders see chapter 7.

58. In 1734 the South Carolina grand jury complained that in Charleston "Hucksters of Corn, Pease, Fowls etc. . . . watch Night and Day on the several Wharfes [*sic*], and put up many Articles necessary for the Support of the Inhabitants, and make them pay an exorbitant Price for the same" (*SCG*, 23–30 March 1734).

59. By the late 1730s the grand jurors of Charleston were complaining about "Negroes going in Boats and Canoes up the Country trading with Negroes in a clandestine Manner." In 1744 they again complained that bondpeople were "allowed to go from Town into the Country, under Pretence of picking Myrtle berries etc. and who at the same time carry Rum and other goods to trade with Negroes in the Country, by which they are debauched and encouraged to steal and robb [*sic*] their Masters of their Corn, Poultry and other Provisions" (*SCG*, 29 October–5 November 1737, 5 November 1744).

60. An Act to prevent itinerant or unauthorized persons from locating themselves on or near the river Savannah, under the pretence of fishing, and to prevent obstructions to the passage of fish up the said river, and farther to pro-

hibit trading with slaves, and to extend the powers of civil officers and patrols [26 December 1831] (Cobb, *A Digest of the Statute Laws of the State of Georgia*, 910–11). Whites who moored their craft within twenty miles of Savannah were liable to a minimum fine of four hundred dollars "and imprisonment of not less than three years." Bondpeople and free African-Americans might" expect to receive at least thirty-nine lashes.

61. See chapter 6.

62. Waring, ed., "Charles Seton Henry Hardee's Recollections," 358.

63. Tryon, comp. and ed., *A Mirror for Americans*, 2: 292. The visitor was Mrs. Royall.

64. *Ga. Gaz.*, 18 October 1775.

65. Savannah, Minutes of the City Council, 1791–96, 8 July–17 October 1791.

66. Ibid., 1805–12, 26 August 1805.

67. For examples of the naming of convicted whites in the press see *GRSI*, 25 April 1803, 5 May 1803, 9 September 1803.

68. AN ACT To alter and amend an act, entitled "AN ACT to prohibit Slaves from selling certain commodities therein mentioned" passed the 18th December 1816 [December 1818], Lamar, ed., *A Compilation of the Laws of the State of Georgia*, 809.

69. Ibid., 810.

70. See chapter 5 for a discussion of fugitives negotiating for the sale of their labor.

71. *CMSA*, 11 July 1814.

72. *Ga. Gaz.*, 27 July 1774, 20 August 1789, 25 October 1792, 7 June 1769.

73. *Ga. Gaz.*, 25 October 1792.

74. *The Savannah Daily Republican*, 19 February 1820 (hereafter *SDR*).

75. *Sav. Rep.*, 19 November 1820, letter signed "HUMANITAS."

76. Savannah City Council Minutes, 10 February 1806.

77. Ibid., 22 December 1806.

78. Elizabeth Cosson to the Countess of Huntington, Bethesda [Orphanage], 3 February 1773, Countess of Huntingdon Papers, Cheshunt Foundation, Westminster College, Cambridge, Ref. A3/3/26–A3/4/12.

79. Calhoun, ed., *Pleasure and Pain*, 52.

80. Loewald, Starika, and Taylor, trans. and eds., "Johann Martin Bolzius Answers a Questionnaire," 233.

81. For a superlative analysis of the religious dimensions of this ideology of paternalism see Frey, *Water from the Rock*, 243–83. For two studies that locate the roots of this impulse in the first Great Awakening see Allan Gallay, *The Formation of a Planter Elite: Jonathan Bryan and the Southern Colonial Frontier* (Athens, 1989); Gallay, "The Origins of Slaveholders' paternalism: George Whitefield, the Bryan Family, and the Great Awakening in the South," *Jour-*

nal of Southern History 53 (1987): 369–94. See also Harvey H. Jackson, "Hugh Bryan and the Evangelical Movement in Colonial South Carolina," *WMQ* 3d ser., 43 (1986): 594–614.

82. These examples are taken from issues of the *Georgia Republican* published between 28 April 1808 and 14 January 1817 (hereafter *GR*). Other items said to be in the possession of bondpeople included "a bundle of Worsted stockings" (*GR*, 29 October 1810); "a pair of silver mounted spectacles" (*GR*, 25 August 1812); "a bladder of Putty" (*GR*, 27 September 1814); "three Silver Spoons" (*GR*, 21 August 1815); "a parcel of rice" (*GR*, 12 December 1815); "a bale of upland cotton" (*GR*, 14 January 1817).

83. The tryal of certain Negroes the property of Charles C. Pinckney on complaint of Wm. Savage esq. 2 July 1804, Bryan County, Inferior Court Minutes, 1794–1811. Two of the bondmen were sentenced to seventy-five lashes; two others to seventy-five lashes "& to be crop'd by cutting off one ear"; and Fanny, the bondwoman, to fifty lashes.

84. Proceedings of the Trial of Frank & Abram Two Negro Fellows for a Burglary committed on the Dwelling house of William Mowbray in the Town of Saint Mary's [17 January 1797], Telamon Cuyler Collection, Hargrett Library, University of Georgia, Box 71, File: Georgia-Slavery, Folder: Georgia, Slavery, Trials. For an extended discussion of the judicial treatment of bondpeople see Wood, "'Until He Shall Be Dead, Dead, Dead': The Judicial Treatment of Slaves in Lowcountry Georgia, 1760–1815," *GHP* 71 (1987), 377–98.

85. The items recorded as having been turned in by bondpeople were as follows: "a Gold Watch" (*GR*, 13 June 1809); "two Bills of One Hundred Dollars each" (*GR*, 15 June 1809); "a sum of money in Bank Notes" (*GR*, 5 December 1809); "a Silver Spoon" (*GR*, 11 January 1810); "a bag of Greenseed Cotton" (*GR*, 12 May 1810); "a Patent Buckle or Latchet" (*GR*, 11 September 1810); "a piece of cotton bagging" (*GR*, 5 February 1811); "a small silver watch" (*GR*, 19 March 1811); "a Golden Watch Key" (*GR*, 2 April 1811); "a man's saddle" (*GR*, 18 June 1812); "a Snuff box" (*GR*, 17 October 1812); "a Surtout Coat" (*GR*, 10 November 1812); "a double cased Silver Watch" (*GR*, 16 January 1813); "a Watch and a Breast Pin" (*GR*, 20 February 1813); "a Silk Handkerchief" (*GR*, 20 February 1813).

86. For extended discussions of a distinction that came to be widely drawn in the American South see Genovese, *Roll, Jordan, Roll*, 599–609; Alex Lichtenstein, "'That Disposition to Theft, with Which They Have Been Branded': Moral Economy, Slave Management, and the Law," *Journal of Social History* 21 (1989): 413–30.

87. John Brown, *Slave Life in Georgia: a narrative of the life, sufferings, and escape of John Brown, a fugitive slave*, edited by F. N. Boney (Savannah, 1972), 83.

Chapter Five. Self-hire in Savannah

1. See chapter 2.

2. For the comparative profitability of enslaved Africans and indentured Europeans in early Georgia see Ralph Gray and Betty Wood, "The Transition from Indentured to Involuntary Servitude in Colonial Georgia," *Explorations in Economic History* 13 (1976): 353–70.

3. Wood, *Slavery in Colonial Georgia*, 1–23, 44–58, 74–87.

4. Ibid., 116–19.

5. Ibid., 131–32, 234 n. 1.

6. Ibid., 132–33.

7. Ibid., 132.

8. See chapter 7.

9. Venus Green, "A Preliminary Investigation of Black Construction Artisans in Savannah from 1820 to 1860," (master's thesis, Columbia University, 1982), 46.

10. See, for example, *Ga. Gaz.*, 24 December 1766, notice placed by John Eppinger; *Ga. Gaz.*, 26 February 1789, notice placed by Gabriel Leaver; *Ga. Gaz.*, 1 January 1789, notice placed by Samuel Iversen; *CMSA*, 28 April 1804, notice placed by Michael Crosby.

11. See, for example, *GR*, 27 January 1807, notice placed by Edward Stebbins; *RSEL*, 24 May 1810, notice placed by William Parker; *RSEL*, 11 January 1810, notice placed by William Smith; *Ga. Gaz.*, 19 July 1792, notice placed anonymously seeking to hire a bondwoman "who understands all kinds of needlework." For examples of those seeking and those hiring out bondwomen as wet nurses see *Ga. Gaz.*, 18 March 1790, 16 June 1791, and 13 February 1794. Those placing these and similar advertisements seldom if ever gave their names. It was the usual practice to request that replies be directed to "the Printer," or editor, of the newspaper.

12. For gender and occupations in the sugar islands see Bush, *Slave Women in Caribbean Society*, 33–50; Morrissey, *Slave Women in the New World*, 62–90; Beckles, *Natural Rebels*, 24–71. For the American South see Jones, "Status of Slave Women," 302–24; Jones, *Labor of Love, Labor of Sorrow*, 11–29; White, *Ar'n't I a Woman?* 112–30.

13. Wood, "Some Aspects of Female Resistance to Chattel Slavery," 603–23.

14. By the mid-1730s South Carolina's grand jurors complained that "it is a common practice by several persons in Charles-Town to suffer their Negroes to work out by the week, and oblige them to bring in a certain Hire" (*SCG*, 23–30 March 1734).

15. Jones, ed., *Detailed Reports*, 1: 116–17.

16. An Act To Empower certain Commissioners herein appointed to regulate

the hire of Porters and Labour of Slaves in the Town of Savannah [1774] (*Col. Recs.*, 19, pt. 2, 23–30).

17. Ibid., 25.

18. For the essentially minor amendments to the act of 1774 in 1783, 1787, 1790, and 1792, which retained the same categories of employment, see AN ACT, To empower certain Commissioners herein Appointed to regulate the hire of Porters, and labour of Slaves in the Town of Savannah, and for other purposes therein Mentioned [1783] (*Col. Recs.*, 19, pt. 2, 256–62); An Ordinance, For Regulating the Hire of Porters, and daily labour of slaves, and Drays, Carts and Waggons in the Town of Savannah [1787] (*Ga. Gaz.*, 26 June 1787); An Ordinance, Regulating the Hire of Drays, Carts, and Waggons; as also the Hire of Negro and other Slaves; and for the better ordering Free Negroes, Mulattoes, or Mestizoes, with the City of Savannah [1790] (*Ga. Gaz.*, 7 October 1790); An Ordinance, For Regulating the Hire of Drays, Carts and Waggons, as also the Hire of Negroes and other slaves; and for the better ordering Free Negroes, Mulattoes or Mestizoes, within the City of Savannah [1792] (*Ga. Gaz.*, 8 November 1792).

19. AN ACT, To empower certain Commissioners [1774] (*Col. Recs.*, 19, pt. 2, 25); An Ordinance, For Regulating the Hire of Porters [1787] (*Ga. Gaz.*, 26 June 1787); An Ordinance, Regulating the Hire of Drays [1790] (*Ga. Gaz.*, 7 October 1790); An Ordinance, For regulating the Hire of Drays [1792] (*Ga. Gaz.*, 8 November 1792).

20. AN ACT, To empower certain Commissioners [1783] (*Col. Recs.*, 19, pt. 2, 257).

21. According to Richard Wade, in 1820 the City of Savannah secured an income of $1,311 from the sale of badges for bondpeople who were hired out by their owners (Wade, *Slavery in the Cities: The South, 1820–1860* [London, 1964], 41).

22. The Rev. Samuel Frink to the Rev. John Burton, Savannah, 8 July 1771, Society for the Propagation of the Gospel, London Manuscripts, letter series C, pkg.7, pt. 3.

23. For patterns of flight elsewhere in the mainland during the years covered by this study see Gerald W. Mullin's early and influential study, *Flight and Rebellion: Slave Resistance in Eighteenth-Century Virginia* (1972); Wood, *Black Majority,* 239–68; Daniel E. Meaders, "South Carolina Fugitives as Viewed through Local Colonial Newspapers with Emphasis on Runaway Notices," *Journal of Negro History* 60 (1975): 288–319; Philip D. Morgan, "Colonial South Carolina Runaways: Their Significance for Slave Culture," *Slavery & Abolition* 6 (1985): 57–78; Johnson, "Runaway Slaves and the Slave Communities in South Carolina." For Georgia see Wood, *Slavery in Colonial Georgia,* 169–87; Wood, "Some Aspects of Female Resistance to Chattel Slavery"; Wood, "Pris-

ons, Workhouses, and the Control of Slave Labour in Lowcountry Georgia, 1763–1815," *Slavery & Abolition* 8 (1987), 267–71.

24. Wood, *Black Majority*, 241.

25. For an extended discussion of this point see Wood, "Some Aspects Of Female Resistance to Chattel Slavery," 609–10, 612–17. See also, Darlene C. Hine and Kate Wittenstein, "Female Slave Resistance: The Economics of Sex," in Filomina Chioma Steady, ed., *Black Women Cross-Culturally* (Cambridge, Mass., 1981), 289–99.

26. *Ga. Gaz.*, 5 January 1785.

27. *DSR*, 29 April 1820.

28. Notice placed in the *Darien Gazette*, 26 July 1819, by Simon Ellington of Laurens County.

29. *CMSA*, 6 January 1797.

30. Brown, *Slave Life in Georgia*, 72.

31. *GR*, 27 January 1807; *RSEL*, 23 May 1807.

32. *Ga. Gaz.*, 22 April 1784. For other examples see notices placed in *Ga. Gaz.*, 7 June 1769, Philip Dell; *Ga. Gaz.*, 11 December 1783, John Channing; *Ga. Gaz.*, 24 October 1793, Godin Guerard.

33. For an extended and excellent discussion of this point, see Frey, *Water from the Rock*, especially chaps. 3, 7, 8, and 9.

34. Frey, *Water from the Rock*, 223–42. See also Wood, "Prisons, Workhouses, and the Control of Slave Labour." For a broader discussion of the impact of Santo Domingo see Alfred N. Hunt, *Haiti's Influence on Antebellum America: Slumbering Volcano in the Caribbean* (Baton Rouge, 1988).

35. Johnson, "Runaway Slaves and the Slave Communities in South Carolina," 432–33; Genovese, *Roll, Jordan, Roll*, 647.

36. Johnston's advertisement, which was for the return of three bondmen and three bondwomen, appeared in *Ga. Gaz.*, 27 May 1784. Tufts's advertisement was published in *RSEL*, 6 May 1813.

37. Savannah City Council Minutes [1791–96], 13 September 1791–17 December 1793.

38. For examples of these occupational skills, see *Ga. Gaz.*, 18 December 1783, James Houstoun; *Ga. Gaz.*, 22 January 1784, Thomas Carter; *Ga. Gaz.*, 8 July 1784, James Gunn; *Ga. Gaz.*, 26 February 1789, Gabriel Leaver; *CMSA*, 21 October 1796, Elizabeth Course; *CMSA*, 21 March 1797, Worthington Gale; *CMSA*, 26 June 1800, Ann Elon; *DSR*, 26 December 1818, Jonathan Thomas; *Darien Gazette*, 21 December 1818, Jonathan Thomas; *Darien Gazette*, 18 July 1819, Seaborn Jones; *Darien Gazette*, 9 January 1823, P. L. Chartier. The names are those of the owners who advertised for the return of their fugitive artisans.

39. For typical examples of the many owners who knew or believed their bondmen were working as boat hands or on the wharves in Savannah, see

Ga. Gaz., 14 February 1793, B. Putnam; *Ga. Gaz.*, 8 August 1799, Elizabeth Smith; *Ga. Gaz.*, 3 August 1803, John King; *Darien Gazette,* 21 December 1818, Jonathan Thomas; *DSR*, 13 March 1821, Alex Smets.

40. *DSR*, 17 September 1815. There is no record of whether Warren initiated legal proceedings against Jordan for the illicit hire of his bondman. Neither is there any evidence of Jordan being charged by the state or local authorities with the offense of harboring a runaway.

41. *CMSA*, 26 June 1800.

42. For a detailed analysis of these records, which do not distinguish between vending and work-for-hire, see Wood, "Prisons, Workhouses, and the Control of Slave Labour."

43. Savannah City Council Minutes [1822–25], 15 May 1823, 12 June 1823; Savannah City Council Minutes [1825–28], 17 February 1825, 10 May 1827.

44. By the 1780s and 1790s a great many advertisements were being placed in the Savannah newspapers by those who wished to hire out their domestic bondpeople and those who hoped to employ them. The vast majority of these advertisements referred to bondwomen rather than to bondmen.

45. "ANTI-MULATTO"'s critique of Savannah's market women appeared in a series of articles published in *Sav. Rep.*, 16, 19, 26 August 1817, 6, 20, 27 September 1817, 17 January 1818.

46. Grimes, *Life of William Grimes,* 51–52.

47. Ball, *Fifty Years in Chains,* 368.

Chapter Six. Patterns of Expenditure in Savannah

1. In view of the part he played in the organization of the First African Church in Savannah, perhaps the most famous example of a bondman who purchased his manumission for a nominal sum was Andrew Bryan. He bought his freedom from his owner and coreligionist, Jonathan Bryan, in the early 1790s. There is no record of the sum he was asked to pay. Leaving aside theological considerations, the practical support Jonathan Bryan offered to African and African-American Baptists makes it somewhat surprising that he demanded any payment from Andrew before manumitting him (James M. Simms, *The First Colored Baptist Church in North America* [Philadelphia, 1888; reprint, New York, 1969], 30). For a more extended discussion of the financial considerations involved in the founding and early history of the independent African churches in lowcountry Georgia see chapter 8.

2. Georgia, Miscellaneous Bonds, Book J, 2–3, 3 June 1775.

3. Georgia, Miscellaneous Bonds, Book R, 489–90, 3 July 1771.

4. Cases cited by William A. Byrne, "The Burden and Heat of the Day:

Slavery and Servitude in Savannah, 1733–1865," (Ph.D. diss., Florida State University, 1979), 99–100.

5. Keith Read Collection, Hargrett Library, University of Georgia, MSS 921, Box 19, Negroes, Folder 19:32, Manumission, 1792.

6. Case cited by Byrne, "The Burden and Heat of the Day," 99–100.

7. Will of Hermon Hertson, [signed] 24 June 1801, Probate Court of Chatham County, Estate Accounts, Microfilm Reel N–1, File nos. 1–166 (1783–96) HI (hereafter Chatham Co. Probate Court).

8. Will of David Johnston, Chatham County, Planter, [signed] 29 August 1812, Chatham Co. Probate Court, IJ.

9. Will of Francis Henry Harris, Parish of Christ Church, [signed] 27 April 1777, Chatham Co. Probate Court, HI.

10. Will of Moses Nunes, of Savannah, 1790, Chatham Co. Probate Court, N1. For other examples of owners who manumitted and made financial provision for at least some of their bondpeople see Chatham Co. Probate Court: Will of John Deville, Savannah, [signed] 9 December 1798, D1; Will of John Currie of Savannah, 27 September 1799, C1; Will of Joseph Hill, Ogechee, Chatham County, [signed] 11 October 1808, H1.

11. Frey, *Water from the Rock*, 81–107.

12. On the maroon community, which established itself after the Revolutionary War in the swamps not too distant from Savannah, the military action taken against it in 1787, and the subsequent trial and execution of one of its leaders see Wood, " 'Until He Shall Be Dead, Dead, Dead'," 390–92.

13. According to a census taken in 1798 there were 219 "French Negroes," of whom 20 were free, above the age of fifteen in Savannah (Census of "all the people of color above the age of Fifteen in the city of Savannah, 28 May 1798, Negro History Files, File 2: 1773–1800 folder, Georgia State Department of Archives and History, Atlanta).

14. An Act prescribing the mode of manumitting Slaves in this State [5 December 1801], Cobb, *A Digest of the Statute Laws of the State of Georgia*, 983.

15. Savannah, Clerk of Council, Register of Free Persons of Color 1817–29, Georgia Historical Society, Ref. 32–G–2A. The comparable figures for 1823, 1824, and 1825 were 205, 186, and 140, respectively.

16. *Sav. Rep.*, 4 October 1817.

17. *Darien Gazette*, 3 April 1819. Eighteen of those listed were children under the age of ten years.

18. Smith, *Slavery and Rice Culture*, 217.

19. Precisely the same was true of other southern towns. See Wade, *Slavery in the Cities*, 62–75.

20. Presentments of the Georgia Grand Jury, *Ga. Gaz.*, 6 July 1768.

21. Presentments of the Georgia Grand Jury, December 1771 in Helen T. Catterall, ed., *Judicial Cases Concerning American Slavery and the Negro*, 5 vols., (Washington, D.C., 1926; reprint, Shannon, 1968), 2: 6.

22. *Royal Georgia Gazette*, 19 April 1781.

23. Savannah City Council Minutes, 1791–96, 27 October 1791.

24. Savannah City Council Minutes, 1791–96, 24 June 1794.

25. AN ORDINANCE For preventing Slaves hiring Houses, and for other purposes herein mentioned [1800], *CMSA*, 11 July 1800.

26. Society for the Propagation of the Gospel, Manuscripts, letter series B, 18, item 147, and letter series C, pkg. 7, pt. 3.

27. Ralph B. Flanders, *Plantation Slavery in Georgia* (Chapel Hill, 1933), 52; Smith, *Slavery and Rice Culture*, 217.

28. Rev. Samuel Frink to the Rev. John Burton, 8 July 1771 in Society for the Propagation of the Gospel, letter series C, pkg. 7, pt. 3; *Ga. Gaz.*, 7 July 1791; *Ga. Gaz.*, 6 February 1800. A census of "all the people of color above the age of Fifteen in the city of Savannah" dated 28 May 1798 indicated that 1,280 bondpersons, of whom 636 were women, fell into this category (Negro History Files, File 2: 1773–1800 folder, Georgia State Department of Archives and History, Atlanta). The estimate for 1821 is to be found in a letter signed "AN INHABITANT OF ANSON WARD" published in the *Georgian* on 26 February 1821. According to the 1820 census Savannah's total population stood at 7,523 (Wade, *Slavery in the Cities*, 9).

29. Savannah's first city directory was not published until the 1840s. This estimate is based on a survey of advertisements in Savannah newspapers. An informal census taken by an anonymous white Georgian in 1798 claimed that there were "618 dwelling houses, 415 kitchens, [and] 288 out houses, stores and shops" in the city ("From a correspondent, an accurate statement of the number of houses and inhabitants in the City of Savannah, taken from the 1st to the 12th day of November 1798," *Ga. Gaz.*, 6 February 1800).

30. Wood, *Black Majority*, 211.

31. For early nineteenth-century Charleston see Wade, *Slavery in the Cities*, 153–55.

32. *GRSI*, 24 November 1802.

33. *GR*, 28 February 1815, 16 July 1816.

34. *Ga. Gaz.*, 18 October 1775. For the comments of the South Carolina grand jury in 1744 see *SCG*, 5 November 1744. See also, Morgan, "Black Life in Charleston," 211.

35. One visitor to Georgia, in 1840, who did comment on the standard of the clothing worn by bondpeople in Savannah was Emily Burke. She noted that "as a general thing the slaves in [Savannah] wear good clothing & many dress

extravagantly and decorate their persons with a great deal of costly jewelry." Burke claimed to "have seen colored men with no less than six or eight rings upon one finger" (Calhoun, ed., *Pleasure and Pain*, 24).

36. Charleston Grand Jury, Presentment, October 1822 cited in Wade, *Slavery in the Cities*, 129–30.

37. Grimes, *Life of William Grimes*, 27.

38. For one of the earliest recorded horse races in Sunbury see *Ga. Gaz.*, 20 October 1763. For early examples of horse racing in Savannah see Davis, *Fledgling Province*, 174–75.

39. Chatham County, Grand Jury Presentments, 4 June 1818, Chatham County, Superior Court, Civil Minutes, book 9, 540.

40. AN ACT For the better regulation of Tavern and Shop-Keepers, and more effectually to prevent their trading with Slaves [1808], *Acts of the General Assembly of the State of Georgia, 1805–1808* (Milledgeville, 1809), 33–35. The maximum fine for those caught breaking this law was set at thirty dollars and the offender would be bound over for the sum of two hundred dollars as a guarantee of his or her good behavior for a year.

41. *CMSA*, 3 June 1800.

42. In 1802 the Savannah City Council enacted an ordinance that required every person licensed to retail "spirituous liquors in less quantity than a quart" to "have plainly painted, in letters not less than two inches in length, on some conspicuous place over the door, on the outside of the shop or house, fronting the street . . . the name of such person, together with the words 'Licensed Retailer of Spirituous Liquors.'" The maximum fine for not displaying such a sign was set at fifty dollars (*CMSA*, 13 August 1802).

43. Savannah City Council Minutes, 4 April 1822–22 December 1825.

44. Precisely the same was true of many other southern towns and cities. For an extended discussion of this point see Wade, *Slavery in the Cities*, 85–87, 149–51, 152–55.

45. Chatham County, Grand Jury Presentments, 15 September 1811, 7 June 1816, Chatham County, Superior Court, Civil Minutes, book 9, 6, 345.

46. Wood, "Prisons, Workhouses, and the Control of Slave Labour," 262.

47. Hazzard, "On the General Management of a Plantation," 352.

48. Ball, *Fifty Years in Chains*, 190–91.

49. Chatham County, Grand Jury Presentments, 22 January 1817, Chatham County, Superior Court, Civil Minutes, book 9, 394. For other examples of grand jury complaints and demands for action on the part of the city council see Chatham County, Superior Court, Civil Minutes, book 7, 49 [2 February 1805]; ibid., 253 [28 April 1806]; ibid., book 9, 345 [7 June 1816]; ibid., book 7, 195 [7 June 1820], and the *Daily Georgian*, 10 February 1821.

Chapter Seven. White Critiques of the Informal
Slave Economies, 1785–1830

1. The demands for moral and social reform that informed and stemmed from the Second Great Awakening have received fairly extensive scholarly attention. For recent studies that bear directly on the early national South see Bertram Wyatt-Brown, "Prelude to Abolitionism: Sabbatarian Politics and the Rise of the Second Party System," *Journal of American History* 63 (September 1971): 316–41; Anne C. Loveland, *Southern Evangelicals and the Social Order, 1800–1860* (Baton Rouge, 1980); John B. Boles, *The Great Revival, 1787–1805: The Origins of the Southern Evangelical Mind* (Lexington, 1972); Fred J. Hood, *Reformed America: The Middle and Southern States, 1783–1837* (University of Alabama, 1980); Donald G. Mathews, *Religion in the Old South* (Chicago, 1977). See also, Mathews, "The Second Great Awakening as an Organizing Process, 1780–1830," *American Quarterly* 21 (1969): 23–43; Clifford S. Griffin, *Their Brother's Keepers: Moral Stewardship in the United States, 1800–1865* (New Brunswick, N.J., 1960); Louis W. Banner, "Religious Benevolence as Social Control: A Critique of an Interpretation," *Journal of American History* 55 (1973): 23–41.

2. Frey, *Water from the Rock*, 284–325.

3. Henry Holcombe, *The First Fruits: In A Series of Letters* (Philadelphia, 1812), 62. For a recent study of Holcombe see John B. Boles, "Henry Holcombe, A Southern Baptist Reformer in the Age of Jefferson," *GHQ* 54 (Fall 1970): 381–407.

4. AN ACT For the better regulation of Tavern and Shop-Keepers, and more effectually to prevent their trading with Slaves [1808], *Acts of the General Assembly of the State of Georgia, 1805–1808* (Milledgeville, 1809), 33–35.

5. An Ordinance, To prohibit negro slaves or free people of color from gambling, or playing at any game, and for other purposes, *Sav. Rep.*, 29 September 1818.

6. An Ordinance to Amend and repeal certain parts of an Ordinance entitled "An ordinance . . . [passed 15 October 1792]," *Ga. Gaz.*, 5 February 1795.

7. Savannah City Council Minutes, 3 July 1812 in *RSEL*, 9 July 1812.

8. An Ordinance regulating the Public Markets in the City of Savannah [passed 17 September 1818], *Sav. Rep.*, 22 September 1818. This ordinance sought to prohibit the sale of, or "promise" to buy, various commodities intended for sale in the public market before the official opening of the market. It also stipulated that bondmen and bondwomen who sold goods in the market that were not enumerated precisely in a ticket provided by their owners were liable to have the same confiscated by "any white person."

9. *Sav. Rep.*, 16 August 1817, article entitled "Hucksters and Cake-Wenches" by "ANTI-MULATTO."

10. *Sav. Rep.*, 13 June 1818, letter signed "JUSTICE."

11. A bill entitled "An Ordinance to prohibit free persons of Color from purchasing stalls on the Market, and exposing meats for sale therein. And to prevent slaves from butchering and selling meats on Market on their own account and for their [own] benefit" was discussed by the city council on 25 May and 8 August 1822. The council postponed further discussion until 21 February 1823, when it appears that no action was taken (Savannah City Council Minutes, 25 May 1822, 8 August 1822, City Council Minutes, 1822–24, 41, 48–49).

12. In 1854 the Savannah City Council passed an ordinance that stipulated that "no slave shall act as a butcher unless in the presence of . . . a white person" (cited in Claudia Dale Goldin, *Urban Slavery in the American South, 1821–1860* [Chicago, 1976], 29).

13. *Sav. Rep.*, 16, 19, 26 August; *Sav. Rep.*, 6, 20, 27 September 1817; *Sav. Rep.*, 17 January 1818.

14. See, for example, Savannah City Council Minutes, 21 September 1812.

15. *Sav. Rep.*, 16 August 1817.

16. *Sav. Rep.*, 26 August 1817.

17. For "ANTI-MULATTO"'s lengthy elaboration of this theme see *Sav. Rep.*, 19 August 1817, 6, 20, 27 September 1817.

18. *Sav. Rep.*, 16 August 1817, 20, 27 September 1817.

19. For a case study that invites comparison with the evangelical drive to effect the social and moral reform of Savannahans see Paul E. Johnson, *A Shopkeeper's Millenium: Society and Revivals in Rochester, New York, 1815–1837* (New York, 1978).

20. AN ACT for preventing and punishing Vice, Profaneness, and Immorality, and for keeping holy the Lords day, commonly called Sunday [4 March 1762] (*Col. Recs.*, 18: 508–15). The legislation permitted "works of necessity or charity" on Sundays and allowed individuals to travel to and from church or to visit the sick. It was not an offense to buy or sell milk and fish before nine o'clock in the morning or milk after four o'clock in the afternoon. The "Publick Sports, or pastimes" enumerated in the Act included "bearbating, bullbating, Foot Ball, Playing Horseracing, Shooting, Hunting, ffishing [sic], Interludes or common Plays."

21. *Ga. Gaz.*, 28 January 1767.

22. Proclamation of Gov. Archibald Bulloch, 9 April 1776, State of Georgia, Proclamations Book H, 1754–94, 209.

23. Presentments of the Chatham County Grand Jury, 20 January 1802, Chatham County, Superior Court, Civil Minutes, book 5, 226.

24. Presentments of the Chatham County Grand Jury, 2 February 1805, ibid., book 7, 49.

25. Presentments of the Chatham County Grand Jury, 2 February 1805, ibid.

26. Presentments of the Chatham County Grand Jury, 29 April 1808, ibid., 495.

27. Presentments of the Chatham County Grand Jury, 22 January 1817, ibid., book 9, 394. For examples of similar complaints see the grand jury presentments for 7 June 1820 and 1 February 1821; ibid., Book 10, 195; *Daily Georgian*, 10 February 1821.

28. *Minutes of the Georgia Association*, 1815 (n.p., n.d.), 10–11.

29. In 1824, for example, the *Minutes of the Sunbury Association* (Savannah, 1824) included a circular letter on the importance of observing the Sabbath, which was reprinted in the *Darien Gazette* on 18 January 1825.

30. AN ORDINANCE, To permit MARKET on Sundays, and for other purposes, *Sav. Rep.*, 13 June 1820.

31. *Sav. Rep.*, 5 September 1820. For examples of other elections and election returns see *Sav. Rep.*, 8 September 1818, 8 September 1819. In these two city elections twenty-one and twenty candidates, respectively, presented themselves to the electorate.

32. In 1820, for example, when "the old board [was] Re-elected by a handsome majority" (*Sav. Rep.*, 5 September 1820), the city council included at least four lawyers, two doctors, and three merchants. Nine of the aldermen were Episcopalians, three were members of the Baptist church, and two were Jewish.

33. Unfortunately there appears to be no extant copy of the edition of the *Georgian* in which "HONESTUS" published his letter. The reply by "HUMANITAS" appeared in *Sav. Rep.*, 29 November 1820.

34. *Sav. Rep.*, 29 November 1820.

35. King, "On the Management of the Butler Estate," 525; Bell, *Major Butler's Legacy*, 170–91.

36. The ordinance, which raised the cost of a license to "retail spirituous liquors less than a quart" to seventy-five dollars and "a quart upwards" to forty-five dollars, was published in the *Savannah Daily Georgian* on 8 July 1826.

37. As Richard Wade pointed out many years ago, during the early 1820s Charleston's grocers also found themselves coming under increasingly heavy pressure to cease their dealings with bondpeople (Wade, *Slavery in the Cities*, 254–55).

38. *Savannah Daily Georgian*, 17 August 1826, 5 September 1826. The fourteen nominees were Charles Harris (Episcopalian, lawyer), Joseph W. Jackson (Episcopalian, lawyer), James Morrison (Episcopalian, lawyer), John Shellman (Episcopalian, custom house officer), J. P. Scriven (Episcopalian, planter), Charles Gilden (Episcopalian, storekeeper), Moses Sheftall (Jewish, doctor), Michael Brown (Baptist, ?), James Roberts (Baptist, ?), Edward Harden (Episcopalian, merchant), Thomas Clark (Baptist, ?), A. J. C. Shaw (Episcopalian, ?), W. C. Wayne (Episcopalian, ?), and George Shick (Baptist, grocer). Two hun-

dred ninety-three votes were cast in the election, and only James Roberts failed to get elected.

39. For this ordinance, which was amended by the city council on 12 October 1826, see *Sav. Rep.*, 7 November 1826.

40. Minutes of City Council Meeting, 10 May 1827, 11 May 1827.

41. The seven aldermen who voted in favor of the report were Shellman (Episcopalian), Goodman (?), Scriven (Episcopalian), Sheftall (Jewish), Shaw (Episcopalian), Porter (Presbyterian), and Williams (Episcopalian). Those who voted against were Brown (Baptist), Philbrick (?), Gilden (Episcopalian), and Clark (Baptist). City Council Meeting, 24 May 1827, Savannah City Council Minutes, 1822–28, 266.

42. This comparison with other cities may have reflected a growing sensitivity to mounting northern critiques of the manners and morality of southern society. For a discussion of this point see Wyatt-Brown, "Prelude to Abolitionism, 316–41.

43. City Council Meeting, 24 May 1827, Savannah City Council Minutes, 1822–28, 263–66.

44. City Council Meeting, 22 May 1828, the *Argus* (Savannah), 30 May 1828. There is no record of whether Mrs. Donager was able to pay her fine.

45. REPORT of the Committee on the Memorial of the Citizens of Savannah, the *Argus*, 9 July 1829. The committee claimed that local planters had given "their written agreement" to permit their bondpeople to market in this way, but it has proved impossible to locate a copy of the document in question.

46. *Argus*, 9 July 1829.

47. City Council Meeting, 28 July 1829, *Argus*, 29 July 1829.

48. *Argus*, 29 July 1829.

49. *Argus*, 23 July 1829 (emphasis in original).

50. *Argus*, 20 August 1829. Those standing for office on this ticket were W. T. Williams (Episcopalian, bookseller), H. Lord [?Baptist/?Presbyterian, ?), Thomas Clarke (Baptist, ?), George A. Ash (Baptist, ?), G. W. Anderson (Presbyterian, president of Planters Bank), F. H. Welman (Episcopalian, merchant), W. R. Waring (Episcopalian, doctor), R. R. Cuyler (Episcopalian, lawyer), Jacob Shaffer (Baptist, saddler), Levi S. D'Lyon (Jewish, lawyer), M. Brown (Baptist, ?), Charles Gilden (Episcopalian, storekeeper), R. Wayne (Episcopalian, doctor), and George W. Owens (Episcopalian, ?).

51. *Argus*, 27 August 1829 (emphasis in original).

52. Ibid. (emphasis in original).

53. *Sav. Rep.*, 5 September 1827 (emphasis in original).

54. *Argus*, 20 August 1829, 3, 10 September 1829; *Sav. Rep.*, 5 September 1829.

55. For the election results see *Sav. Rep.*, 8 September 1829. Those elected

from the Peoples Ticket were W. T. Williams (Episcopalian, bookseller) 280 votes, Wm. R. Waring (Episcopalian, doctor) 280 votes, George W. Owens (Episcopalian, ?) 262 votes, Michael Brown (Baptist, ?) 254 votes, George W. Anderson (Presbyterian, president of Planters Bank) 220 votes, R. R. Cuyler (Episcopalian, lawyer) 206 votes, F. H. Welman (Episcopalian, merchant) 190 votes, Jacob Shaffer (Baptist, saddler) 187 votes, Thomas Clarke (Baptist, ?) 181 votes, and Charles Gilden (Episcopalian, storekeeper) 166 votes.

56. *Sav. Rep.*, 8 September 1829.

57. Charles S. Henry, comp., *A Digest of All the Ordinances of the City of Savannah: Which Were of Force on the 1st July 1854* (Savannah, 1854), 310–13.

58. For an extended discussion of the fierce and, during local elections, often violent political divisions caused by the issue of Sunday trading see R. M. Haunton, "Savannah in the 1850s," (Ph.D. diss., Emory University, 1968).

Chapter Eight. African-American Christianity and the Informal Slave Economies, 1785–1830

1. See especially Frey, *Water from the Rock*, 284–385; Frey, " 'Shaking the Dry Bones': The Dialectic of Conversion," in Ted Ownby, ed., *The Interaction of Cultures in the Antebellum South* (Oxford, Miss., 1993); Frey, " 'The Year of Jubilee is Come': Afro-American Christianity in the Plantation South in Post-Revolutionary America," forthcoming in the United States Capitol History Society Symposia Publication Series, University Press of Virginia. See also, Albert J. Raboteau, *The "Invisible Institution" in the Antebellum South* (New York, 1978).

2. Frey, " 'The Year of Jubilee is Come'," 15; Frey, " 'Shaking the Dry Bones'," 1; Frey, *Water from the Rock*, 241–325.

3. I am grateful to Mary Turner for this observation.

4. For examples of the attendance of African-American pastors and deacons at association meetings, see the minutes itemized in notes 6 and 9 below.

5. This is a theme elaborated by Frey in the works listed in note 1 above.

6. *Minutes of the Sunbury Baptist Association* (hereafter *Sunbury Minutes*) 1818 (n.p., n.d.); *Sunbury Minutes* 1820 (Savannah, 1820); *Sunbury Minutes* 1821 (Savannah, 1821); *Sunbury Minutes* 1823 (Savannah, 1823); *Sunbury Minutes* 1824 (Savannah, 1824); *Sunbury Minutes* 1825 (Savannah, 1825); *Sunbury Minutes* 1827 (Savannah, 1827); *Sunbury Minutes* 1829 (Savannah, 1829); *Sunbury Minutes* 1830 (Savannah, 1830).

7. Simms, *The First Colored Baptist Church*, 1–36; Frey, " 'The Year of Jubilee is Come'," 9–10; Frey, *Water from the Rock*, 287–89.

8. Frey, " 'The Year of Jubilee is Come'," 10.

9. *Sunbury Minutes; Minutes of the Georgia [Baptist] Association 1788* (here-

after *Georgia Minutes*) (Augusta, n.d.); *Georgia Minutes* 1814 (n.p., n.d.); *Georgia Minutes* 1830 (Charleston, 1830). *Minutes of the Savannah River Baptist Association* 1812 (hereafter *Savannah Minutes*) (n.p., n.d.); *Savannah Minutes* 1814 (n.p., n.d.); *Savannah Minutes* 1830 (Charleston, 1831).

10. [Henry Holcombe], *The Georgia Analytical Repository* (Savannah, 1802–), 1, no. 4, 187–88.

11. David Benedict, *A General History of the Baptist Denomination in America, And Other Parts of the World*, 2 vols. (Boston, 1813), 2: 192.

12. Mallard reported that in Liberty County during the 1830s some bondpeople made their way to church "in Jersey wagons" (*Plantation Life before Emancipation*, 83); Simms, *The First Colored Baptist Church*, 19.

13. The bondpeople who worshiped at the Congregational church at Midway, in Liberty County, spent the hour's "intermission" between the "communion service" and the "second sermon" at "the edge of the forest" where an enslaved preacher named Toney Stevens would lead them in prayer and singing (Mallard, *Plantation Life before Emancipation*, 88–89).

14. "Account of the Negro Church at Savannah, and of two Negro Ministers, by Jonathan Clarke," Savannah, 22 December 1792 in John Rippon, ed., *The Baptist Annual Register for 1790, 1791, 1792 and Part of 1793* (London, n.d.), 540–41.

15. Ibid., 63. The relevant law was An Act to protect Religious Societies in the exercise of their Religious Duties [13 December 1792], Cobb, ed., *A Digest of the Statute Laws of the State of Georgia*, 920–21.

16. Presentments of the Chatham County Grand Jury, City of Savannah, City Council Minutes, 1791–94 [4 March 1794].

17. Resolution adopted by a special meeting of the Savannah City Council, *GRSI*, 13 December 1804.

18. Smith, *Slavery and Rice Culture*, 217.

19. In Charleston, for instance, there were just under 2,800 African and African-American members (including at least 170 free African-Americans) listed on the roll of the Trinity Methodist Episcopal Church in 1821–22 (Trinity Methodist Episcopal Church, Charleston, South Carolina Historical Society, Collection 11/579, Folder 3, book C: Roll of Colored Members, 1821–26). Between 1817 and 1830 the African-American membership of the Methodist Church in Georgetown, South Carolina, did not fall below 1,200 (Georgetown Methodist Church Records, 1811–79, White and Colored Members, Microfiche, South Carolina Historical Society). The original manuscript is as follows: "Georgetown Methodist Church records in the Collections of the Historical Society of the South Carolina Conference, Wofford College, Spartanburg." I am grateful to the Historical Society of the South Carolina Conference of the United Methodist Church for giving me permission to cite these records.

20. *Minutes of the Annual Conferences of the Methodist Episcopal Church for the Years 1773–1828* (New York, 1840), cited in Christopher H. Owen, "By Design: The Social Meaning of Methodist Church Architecture in Nineteenth-Century Georgia," *GHQ* 65, no. 2 (1991): 227.

21. Extract (pp. 215–16) from *Life of William Capers* in Joseph F. Waring Papers, Box 22, folder 306: Churches–Methodist, Georgia Historical Society, Savannah, MSS 1275.

22. Frances Kemble noted that in and around Darien "almost all" of the bondmen and bondwomen who professed Christianity were Baptists (*Journal of a Residence*, 67).

23. Smith, *Slavery and Rice Culture*, 217.

24. Ibid., 158.

25. Rippon, *Baptist Annual Register*, 541.

26. Restricting religious gatherings was one of the rules drawn up by Alexander Telfair in 1832 for the bondpeople on his Thorn Island plantation ("Rules and directions," Telfair Family Papers, Box 5, folder 51, item 208).

Georgina Bryan Conrad recollected that as a child she had been invited by those participating to attend "the servants' meetings" which "generally took place in the afternoon of Sunday, and Saturday and Sunday nights" ("Reminiscences," 167).

27. King, "On the Management of the Butler Estate," 524.

28. Kemble, *Journal of a Residence*, 67.

29. Gilman, *Recollections*, 271–72; Kemble, *Journal of a Residence*, 139–43.

30. Gilman, *Recollections*, 81; Parrish, *Slave Songs*, 29.

31. Barclay, *Voyages and Travels*, 22.

32. Gilman, *Recollections*, 81.

33. *Georgia Minutes* 1815 (n.p., n.d.), 10–11; *Sunbury Minutes* 1824 (Savannah, 1824), 10–14; *Darien Gazette*, 18 January 1825.

34. See chapter 7.

35. Simms, *The First Colored Baptist Church*, 18–19.

36. Ibid., 16.

37. Ibid., 23.

38. Ibid., 29–32.

39. Ibid., 31.

40. Ibid.; Rippon, *Baptist Annual Register*, 541.

41. Rippon, *Baptist Annual Register*, 540.

42. Simms, *The First Colored Baptist Church*, 34. There is no detailed information about the financing and building of the Second African Church in Savannah, which when completed was a "comfortable house" measuring "62 feet by 30" (Benedict, *A General History of the Baptist Denomination*, 2: 193).

43. The plate in question is still at the First African Church.

44. As Jacqueline Jones points out, some bondwomen, especially elderly ones, "often gained informal influence [in the slave quarters] by virtue of their knowledge of herbal medicine, poisons, conjuring, and midwifery" ("Status of Slave Women," 320). The theme of women's influence inside the evangelical Protestant churches of the early national South is addressed at length in Frey and Wood, *African-American Protestant Christianity* (forthcoming).

45. *Memoirs of the Late Rev. Abraham Marshall; Containing a Journal of the Most Interesting Parts of His Life* (Mount Zion, Ga., 1824), 129–30.

46. Simms, *The First Colored Baptist Church*, 30, 75. Simms clearly derived his information from "Account of the Negro Church at Savannah, and of two Negro Ministers," Jonathan Clarke, Savannah, 22 December 1792, in Rippon, *Baptist Annual Register*, 540, 541. Henry Holcombe claimed that Bryan's estate "is worth upwards of five thousand dollars" (*The Georgia Analytical Repository*, 1, no. 4, 185). David Benedict, on the other hand, recorded a figure of three thousand dollars (*A General History of the Baptist Denomination*, 2: 192).

47. Simms, *The First Colored Baptist Church*, 76.

48. Clerk of Council, Savannah, Register of Free Persons of Color, 1817–29. In unpaginated entries for 1817 he described himself as a waggoner, for 1823 as a pastor, for 1824 as a preacher, and for 1825 as a minister.

49. Ibid., 1823, 1824.

50. *Sunbury Minutes* 1822 (Savannah, 1822), 7.

51. *Sunbury Minutes* 1824 (Savannah, 1824). Each of the two Savannah churches subscribed $2.00, those at White Bluff $1.00, and those at Ogechee $5.00. The largest donation, of $12.50, came from Savannah's white Baptist church. The remaining money came from the churches at Sunbury ($5.40) and Newport ($10).

52. *Sunbury Minutes* 1825 (n.p., n.d.). The churches at Sunbury and Newport contributed $15 and $20, respectively. Smaller donations were made by the congregations at Salem ($5), Power's ($4), and Little Cahouchee ($1).

53. Simms, *The First Colored Baptist Church*, 35.

54. Mallard, *Plantation Life before Emancipation*, 83 (exclamation point in original); Genovese, *Roll, Jordan, Roll*, 556.

55. Kemble, *Journal of a Residence*, 68–69.

56. Ball, *Fifty Years in Chains*, 190–91.

57. *Sunbury Minutes* 1830 (Savannah, 1830), 7; *Sunbury Minutes* 1832 (Savannah, 1833), 8.

58. *Sunbury Minutes* 1830 (Savannah, 1830), 7; *Sunbury Minutes* 1832 (Savannah, 1833), 9–10.

59. These figures are derived from the *Sunbury Minutes* (1818–30), the *Georgia Minutes* (1788–1830), and the *Savannah Minutes* (1812–30).

Index

Abercorn, 163, 164, 172, 173
Abraham (bondman), 75
Abram (bondman), 98
Adam (bondman), 75
Adam (bondman), 96
Adams, William Hampton, 46, 205
  (n. 79)
Africa. *See* West Africa
African-American Baptists, 161,
  162–76. *See also* Churches
African-American Methodists, 162,
  165, 231 (n. 19). *See also* Churches
"A FRIEND TO LIBERAL
  PRINCIPLES . . ." 157–58
Agricultural implements, 40, 204
  (n. 52)
Alcohol, 57, 64; licenses to sell, 70,
  152, 225 (n. 42), 228 (n. 36); sale of
  in Savannah, 148, 152, 156; fines
  for selling to bondpeople, 141, 137,
  138; temperance societies, 174–75.
  See also Bondpeople, Dram shops,
  Taverns
Aleck (bondman), 60
American Revolution, 4, 7, 8–9, 28,
  29, 32, 54, 55, 57, 77, 81, 97, 110

Amos (bondman), 75
Anderson, G. W., 229 (n. 50), 230
  (n. 55)
Andrew (bondman), 63
Anglicans. *See* Churches
Angola. *See* West Africa
"ANTI-MULATTO," 118, 144–45
Aprons. *See* Clothing
Argus, 157
Artisans: white, 102–5, 106, 123;
  enslaved, 22, 47, 48, 66, 103, 105,
  106, 109, 116, 117, 166, 170, 221
  (n. 38); free African-American,
  105, 170. *See also* Fugitives,
  Savannah
Ash, George A., 229 (n. 50)
Associates of Dr. Bray, 27
August (bondman), 66
Augusta, 70, 77, 103, 116, 209 (n. 42)

Backcountry, 8, 9, 70, 77, 111
Bacon, 37, 44, 76
Badges: for enslaved vendors, 82–83,
  87, 212–13 (n. 13); for hiring out
  enslaved workers, 103, 108–11, 112,
  212 (n. 13), 220 (n. 21)